Subject to Delusions

AGM STUDIES

AVANT-GARDE & MODERNISM

Subject to Delusions

Narcissism, Modernism, Gender

CAROLINE RUPPRECHT

Northwestern

University Press

Evanston

Illinois

Northwestern University Press
www.nupress.northwestern.edu

Printed in the United States of America

10 9 8 7 6 5 4 3 2 1

ISBN 0-8101-2234-0 (cloth)
ISBN 0-8101-2235-9 (paper)

Library of Congress Cataloging-in-Publication Data

Rupprecht, Caroline.
Subject to delusions : narcissism, modernism, gender / Caroline Rupprecht.
p. cm.—(Avant-garde & modernism studies)
Includes bibliographical references and index.
ISBN 0-8101-2234-0 (alk. paper)—ISBN 0-8101-2235-9 (pbk. : alk. paper)
1. Narcissism in literature. 2. Psychoanalysis and literature. 3. American literature—20th century—History and criticism. 4. German literature—20th century—History and criticism. 5. Hardenberg, Henriette—Criticism and interpretation. 6. Barnes, Djuna. Nightwood. 7. Zürn, Unica—Criticism and interpretation. 8. Freud, Sigmund, 1856–1939. Zur Einführung des Narzissmus. I. Title. II. Avant-garde and modernism studies.
PS228.P74R87 2005
810.93530904—dc22

2005031822

∞ The paper used in this publication meets the minimum requirements of the American National Standard for Information Sciences—Permanence of Paper for Printed Library Materials, ANSI Z39.48-1992.

For Gregg

Contents

Illustrations

Acknowledgments

Completion of this project was made possible through a grant from the PSC-CUNY Research Foundation, which enabled me to conduct research at the Staatsbibliothek zu Berlin, Preußischer Kulturbesitz, and at the Wertheim Study of the New York Public Library. My thanks go to Ali Jimale Ahmed, Hilary Beattie, Erich Brinkmann, Clare Carroll, Almuth Carstens, Vincent Crapanzano, Tamara Evans, Lilli Gast, Anja Grothe, Ruth Henry, Carola Hilmes, Ingeborg Hoesterey, Andreas Huyssen, David Kleinbard, Damon Krukowski, Louise Lasson, Ruth Löffelholz, Gloria McLean, Dorothea von Mücke, Philip Rupprecht, John Shostrom, Cathy Shuman, Susan Suleiman, Joshua Wilner, and Katrin Ziemke. I would especially like to thank Rainer Rumold for accepting this study into this series and the three anonymous readers for providing me with insightful comments. Last but not least, I would like to thank my students and colleagues at Queens College; the Columbia Psychoanalysis and Literature Study Group; and all my friends and family.

Early versions of chapters 3, 4, and 5 have appeared in *Die Magie der Unterbrechung*, edited by Carola Hilmes and Dietrich Mathy (Bielefeld: Aisthesis, 1999); *Women in German Yearbook* 17, edited by Patricia Herminghouse and Susanne Zantop (Lincoln: University of Nebraska Press, 2001); and *Studies in 20th Century Literature* 27, no. 2 (2003), edited by Jordan Stump.

I would also like to thank the copyright holders for permission to reproduce the artwork in this book. The painting *Glassy Day* by Erich Heckel on page 82 is reprinted with permission from the Bayerische Staatsgemäldesammlungen, Collection of Modern Art at the Pinakothek der Moderne, Munich, which owns the work, and the Artists Rights Society on behalf of the Heckel Estate; copyright © 2004 Artists Rights Society (ARS), New York/VG Bild-Kunst, Bonn. The drawings by Unica Zürn on pages 142 and 143, *Begegnung* and *Berührung*, are copyright © Verlag Brinkmann & Bose, Berlin.

Subject to Delusions

Part One : **Paradigms of Narcissism**

It was the smile of Narcissus leaning over the mirroring water, that deep, beguiled, unresisting smile that comes as he extends his arm toward the reflection of his own beauty—a very slightly distorted smile, distorted by the hopelessness of his desire to kiss the lovely lips of his shadow.

—Thomas Mann, *Death in Venice*

1. Historical Overview

Narcissus's Paradox

The fatal attraction of Narcissus to his reflection in the pool involves a paradox: on the one hand, he is encapsulated within his own private universe, unable to relate to anyone besides himself; on the other hand, he is profoundly engaged with an "other." To Narcissus, the image is real: it is the object of his desire, and he is enamored by it as any lover would be. Hence the fiction functions as an "object," yet it fails to be one in reality. Unable to reach into the pool and embrace his lover (who disappears as soon as the surface of the water ripples), Narcissus suffers from the mere "shadow of a reflected form" (Ovid 1967, 9), while at the same time experiencing actual physical pain. The intensity of his desire makes him wish for death—"Oh, that I might be parted from my own body!" (10)—yet it is also what brings him to life: only after he has fallen in love with his own image is he able to love at all. Clearly, Narcissus is doomed by what is described as a form of self-knowledge: "When asked whether this child would live to reach well-ripened age, the seer replied: 'If he never knows himself' " (8). While not knowing oneself may guarantee a longer life, the profound passion experienced by Narcissus seems infinitely more attractive, as it is connected to delusions of grandeur, independence, and omnipotence. The promise of being able to return to some kind of primal unity, of mending what has been divided (and thereby doubling oneself), involves a peculiar kind of pleasure: the pleasure of fantasy.

What came to be called "narcissism" at the end of the nineteenth century is in fact a transgression, a forbidden knowledge that seems, nonetheless, essential to the way in which human subjectivity represents itself. The figure of Narcissus—torn between intimacy and distance, attraction and alienation, insight and delusion—is a figure of reflexivity, which suggests the possibility of dialectics. Perpetually oscillating between seeing and not seeing the truth about himself, Narcissus's vantage point is both internal and external, his position at once static and dynamic. It is an impossible position to be in, yet he derives great pleasure from it. Suspended between "I" and "not-I," he remains still while, at the same time, continuing to be in motion. Thus the myth is connected to "narc-otics": it tells the history of a flower whose name, according to Havelock Ellis's citation of an 1856 definition by Wieseler, "indicates the effects of frost, terror, syncope, death, these effects being attributed to the action of the plant" (1897a, 347). The son of Cephissus, a river god, and Liriope, a water nymph, Narcissus dies from seeing what he is not supposed to see—himself—and is transformed into a flower. According to Frankfurt School philosopher Herbert Marcuse, Narcissus represents "silence, sleep, night, paradise—the Nirvana principle" (1966, 164), in opposition to Prometheus, "the culture-hero of toil, productivity, and progress" (162). Refusing to participate in the economy of social relations, Narcissus symbolizes what Marcuse has called "the Great Refusal . . . the negation of *all* order" (171).

From a psychoanalytic point of view, however, Narcissus is not the heroic figure he may believe himself to be. Narcissistic personalities, according to Otto Kernberg, suffer from "a remarkable absence of interest in and empathy for others in spite of the fact that they are so very eager to obtain admiration and approval from other people" (1986, 214). As William Meissner explains,

> these patients . . . have considerable difficulty in maintaining meaningful or mutually gratifying relationships. . . . At more pathological levels . . . the narcissism becomes even more needy, clinging and demanding. The need to be given to, supported and taken care of, which reflects a sense of peremptory and uncompromising entitlement, is heightened. . . . Consequently, these patients are constantly exposed to the threat of disappointment and frustration, feeling deprived and often desperate. In such states they can become sullen and pouting, even whining and complaining, in their attempts to wheedle the necessary response from the important other. (1986, 411–12)

Compared to the tragic image of madness suggested by the myth, there is something truly pathetic about this description, for it suggests that narcissists are in fact needier than others, that their apparent self-sufficiency is simply a show to hide their desperation over being unable to connect with other people. Again, there is the paradox: narcissism can be construed as a form of heroic refusal, a state of independence, yet it can also seem pathological. In this sense, it becomes merely a question of degree: it can be a "contribution . . . to health, adaptation and achievement," as Heinz Kohut has argued (1986, 61), or it can involve symptoms of bipolar disorder, schizophrenia, and paranoia, which include fantasies of omnipotence and severe withdrawal from others.[1] However, since narcissism tends to be equated with self-esteem, the relationship between it and antisocial behavior might as well appear in reverse: as clinical data have proven, "individuals with high self-esteem are precisely those most able to be more interested in others, while those with low self-esteem are most likely to concentrate upon themselves" (Pulver 1986, 105).

My own interest in narcissism is based on the fascination with the uncertain epistemological status of the "object." Narcissus is deluded, yet he knows that the "other" he sees is himself (in Ovid [1967], he cries out: "Oh, I am he!"). The "other" is both real and unreal, like a visual or verbal text transporting the reader-viewer into the world of make-believe. To me, narcissism is about the fictions we create about ourselves and others, the uncertainty over what is "real" and what is imaginary. Consequently, the texts in which I am interested are radically experimental, as they attempt not only to transgress the norms of realism but also to construct "subjectivity" through language. The authors examined in this book are all part of the avant-garde: the German expressionist poet Henriette Hardenberg (1894–1993) focuses on capturing physical movement as a way of escaping a fixed body image; the American writer Djuna Barnes (1892–1982), in her 1936 novel *Nightwood*, portrays the love story of two women in terms of poetic images that gradually arrest the narrative; and the surrealist Unica Zürn (1916–70) connects madness and art through a hallucinatory figure who forces the protagonist to write in the autobiographical text *Der Mann im Jasmin* (1977, later translated as *The Man of Jasmine* [1994]). Central to my inquiry about the relationship between narcissism and representation is Sigmund Freud's foundational essay "Zur Einführung des Narzißmus" (1914), later translated as "On Narcissism: An Introduction" (see Morrison 1986). Each of the three texts by Hardenberg, Barnes, and Zürn corresponds to one of the aspects of narcissism Freud describes in his essay ("primary narcissism," object relations, and the ego ideal) so that literature and psychoanalysis may enter into a kind of interdisciplinary dialogue.

With a particular focus on gender that is connected to narcissism itself, each of these female authors is introduced within the context of her particular "movement": expressionism, with its fascination with madness and nostalgia for the primitive; Anglo-American modernism, with its emphasis on formal innovation and radical commitment to art as truth; and surrealism, with its program to eliminate all barriers between life and art. As women, Hardenberg, Barnes, and Zürn are doubly "other": situated on the margins of modernism, their work particularly appears in opposition to the nonverbal image of female narcissism on which Freud's essay is based. And, while modern art is often accused of being solipsistic and escapist, supposedly alienated from real social concerns due to its emphasis on formal experimentation, all three authors show that "identity" (gender, race, and class) is itself constructed through language, which means it can be *rewritten*. Just as the "object" of his reflection is real to Narcissus, the texts created by these writers are performative in that they transport the reader into a new kind of reality, where things could be different from what they seem to be. On the other hand, as the following section will show, there is the objective "truth" of science—a language which conceives of itself in opposition to the "subjective" truth of poetry (and yet may be no less subjective).

Narcissism and Homosexuality

While there is an abundance of artistic and literary representations of Narcissus throughout the history of Western culture,[2] the history of the term "narcissism" does not begin until the late nineteenth century, when it was defined by the practitioners of sexual science interested in labeling various "perversions," chief among which were masturbation[3] and "sexual inversion," that is, homosexuality.[4] According to Ulrike May-Tolzmann (whose findings I can only summarize and paraphrase here), "narcissism" in its most basic version denoted masturbating in front of a mirror but became connected to homosexuality because it was the "perversion" most widely discussed (she cites more than one thousand publications on "inversion" between 1898 and 1908 alone; May-Tolzmann 1991). In fact, as we now know from Michel Foucault's *History of Sexuality,* the concept of "homosexuality" did not actually come into existence until 1870, when it was first introduced by Carl Westphal as "contrary sexual sensations" (*konträre*

Sexualempfindung). As Foucault has shown, "the nineteenth century homosexual became . . . a species" (1978, 43) placed under surveillance by sexologists, such as Richard von Krafft-Ebing, whose widely used catalog of sexual perversions, *Psychopathia Sexualis,* was published in 1886 and continued to be in print through 1924.[5] The connection between "narcissism" and "inversion," which continued into early psychoanalysis, was based on the notion of the mirror, whereby the homosexual was, supposedly, unable to recognize sexual difference. As Michael Warner has shown, narcissism was used in conjunction with homosexuality as a symbol for "sameness," that is, the supposed inability or unwillingness to recognize and enter into a reproductive relationship with the "opposite" sex. Clearly, this notion is absurd—as Warner asks: "When another man, this 'other who is also the same' becomes the object of desire, has the male subject failed to distinguish self and other?" (1990, 191). However, unfortunately, while psychoanalysis eventually moved away from the connection between narcissism and homosexuality, conservative critics continue "to conflate homosexuality with egoism and selfishness, with self-delusion and excessive introspection" (Bruhm 2001, 2).

Freud, who was trained as a neuropathologist to study "the nervous system" through the use of hypnosis (which he studied with Jean Martin Charcot in France), did not directly concern himself with "perversion" until the late 1890s, when his studies of female hysterics with Josef Breuer led him to the notion of sexual repression. In 1905, he published his groundbreaking *Three Essays on the Theory of Sexuality,* which emphasizes the basic bisexuality of human beings[6] along with the impossibility of truly distinguishing "perverse" from "normal" sexual behaviors. At the same time, however, his psychoanalytic method was perceived as a new way of "curing" homosexuality by many of his contemporaries—just like the earlier method of hypnosis, which had been employed with the express intent to "cure" homosexuals by practitioners such as Freiherr von Schrenck-Notzing. Consequently, there came to be an opposition between many early psychoanalysts, who thought in terms of the "unconscious" (established by Freud's publication of *The Interpretation of Dreams* in 1900) and a second, more tolerant, generation of sexologists, some of whom—such as Magnus Hirschfeld—actively fought for gay rights.[7] Hirschfeld, who was a member of the Berlin Psychoanalytic Society from 1908 to 1911, developed a theory of homosexuality that was to be grounded in biology, based upon the notion of "intermediary sexual stages" (*sexuelle Zwischenstufen*).[8] Contrary to many psychoanalysts, who had come out of the medical establishment and were concerned with establishing their new discipline, gay-rights activists were motivated by pressing political reasons: homosexuals were persecuted and declared to be "criminal" according to the law.[9] Consequently, it appears that, within the process of the two movements gradually distancing themselves from one another (while continuing, however, to publish within the same journals), homosexuality also became disconnected from the concept of "narcissism" as used by psychoanalysis.

Still, if one looks at documents from the first decade of the twentieth century, there is a confusing degree of overlap between sexology, psychoanalysis, homosexuality, and narcissism. Freud himself associated the latter two until 1911 (the Schreber case) and did not "liberate" narcissism from its connotation as a "perversion" until 1914 (as will be discussed in the next chapter). Another example of an early psychoanalyst who connected narcissism and homosexuality is Otto Rank, who published essays on homosexuality in 1911 and on mirroring in 1914 ("The Double," in which he uses as an example Oscar Wilde's *The Picture of Dorian Gray*, a novel whose author had been placed on trial for sodomy in 1895). Another, lesser known sexologist and early psychoanalyst was Isidor Sadger, whose views on narcissism and homosexuality, as May-Tolzmann has shown, had a definite influence on Freud.[10] Apparently, it was Sadger who "discovered" the connection between narcissism and the supposed overidentification of homosexuals with their mothers in 1908, a notion which was then developed further by Freud. Sadger based his observations on narcissism on his finding that homosexual men were overly attached to their mothers, prompting them to love other men in the same way their mother had loved them. What Sadger failed to explain, however, was why the mother would eventually be rejected by those men—it was Freud who, subsequently, explained it with the concept of "castration anxiety."[11] However, what was significant, according to May-Tolzmann, was not the assumption that gay men loved "themselves" in one another, which had been well established, but rather Sadger's finding that another element (the mother) was involved: in Freud's new constellation, human beings had not one but two "objects" to be attached to, their mothers *and* themselves, a notion to be discussed in more detail in the next chapter.

Further discussion on the historic connections between narcissism and homosexuality would exceed the scope of this chapter, yet it should have become obvious that the relationship between the histories of homosexuality and psychoanalysis are fraught with tension. On the one hand, psychoanalysis can rightfully be accused of deep-seated homophobia; on the other hand, as Tim Dean and Christopher Lane, the editors of the recent volume *Homosexuality and Psychoanalysis,* point out: "the resistance of the unconscious to all norms [can be] very helpful to queer theorists" and "psychoanalysis can be [useful] for antinormative politics and alternative ways of thinking about sexuality" (2001, 7). In this sense, there seem to be two ways of approaching the topic of "narcissism": it may be used strategically, for what Foucault has called "the formation of a 'reverse' discourse: homosexuality began to speak in its own behalf, to demand that its legitimacy or 'naturality' be acknowledged, often in the same vocabulary, using the same categories by which it was medically disqualified" (1978, 101)[12]; and, there can be a more serious, interdisciplinary form of engagement with psychoanalysis, as it may offer the possibility of dismantling the whole concept of "normalcy." It is this latter promise that has attracted me to the discipline in spite of its many obvious shortcomings.

Narcissism and Gender

Since the literary texts under discussion were all written by women, let me now connect narcissism more specifically to the issue of gender, which appears in conjunction with that other narcissistic "perversion," masturbation. The first official use of the term "narcissism" was by Paul Näcke[13] in an 1899 definition that became the point of reference for Freud: "the attitude of a person who treats his own body in the same way in which the body of a sexual object is ordinarily treated—who looks at it, that is to say, strokes it and fondles it" (Näcke 1899, 17). Although not directly mentioned by Näcke, the notion of the mirror comes into play here, insofar as masturbation involves, by definition, an *as if.* In fact, Näcke came up with the term only after reading an 1898 essay on "auto-erotism" by the well-known English sexologist Havelock Ellis, which mentions a "Narcissus-like tendency" in conjunction with numerous examples about mirroring, such as the case recorded by another famous sexologist, Albert Moll, "of a man of 43, . . . sexually attached to both men and women, who found much pleasure in gazing at his own image naked in a mirror, and who would compare his shape with that of other men he knew" (Ellis 1897a, 354).[14] Here, as in many other versions that connect narcissism and masturbation, the mirror is a central prop without which this particular "perversion" would not have its name. The existence of the mirror represents the moment of mediation, which is what defines narcissism. A particularly striking comment in this respect can be found in a 1908 essay by a certain Theodor Petermann (published in Hirschfeld's *Zeitschrift für Sexualwissenschaft*) which makes reference to the myth of Narcissus as part of an effort to introduce a whole new perversion, the "love of demons and phantoms": Petermann cites the case of a fifteen-year-old male caught "in the act of standing and looking, with his shirt pulled up, at his genitals in the mirror" and arrives at the following conclusion: "Why did said young man take the detour of using the mirror when, in fact, he could have looked at that which he found important more easily and comfortably *in natura*? Because he wanted to have an ideational partner!" (Petermann 1908, 295; my translation). This "ideational partner," evidently, involves both fantasy and the need for an actual reflection, that is, the physical representation of an "object."

The emphasis on the mirror helps explain why narcissism has been associated not only with male homosexuality but also, to a great extent, with women. Ellis himself bases his views on the notion of narcissism as excessive vanity—which he attributes primarily to women and only "in minor degree in some feminine-minded men" (1897a, 355). Freud, too, came to explain aspects of narcissism in connection to "femininity" (which resonates with the unfortunate stereotype of gay men as "effeminate"), yet his version of female narcissism is devoid of sexual content because it is based on the notion of an earlier, pregenital stage of development. Usually narcissism was defined in terms of the subject's overinvestment in a particular body part: the male member. Jenö Hàrnik, in the *International Journal of Psychoanalysis* in 1924, was the only one, apparently, who attempted to explain female narcissism in relation to this definition:

> Once more I made use of the formula that the narcissism of the adolescent female which originally centred on the genital organs undergoes a secondary displacement to the whole of the rest of the body. I then endeavoured to connect up this idea with Radò's[15] hypothesis that the "narcissistic" foetal state is characterized by a special erotogenicity of the surface of the skin. This leads in the first instance to the conjecture that in post-natal development the narcissistic libido migrates . . . from the surface of the skin to the genitals . . . the narcissism of women in its mature form reproduces once again the "narcissistic" distribution of libido which was characteristic of the prenatal period. (Hàrnik 1924, 78)

Here female narcissism is transferred back into the womb, yet the emphasis on the phallus is circumvented. Subsequently feminists have dismantled such phallocentric psychoanalytic concepts as "penis envy" on the basis of a similar line of argument.[16] For example, Teresa de Lauretis states that "in lesbian subjectivity the ultimate meaning of castration as narcissistic wound is not the lack of a penis but the loss of the female body" (1994, 275); and Carolyn Allen offers a perceptive reading of Djuna Barnes's novel *Nightwood* (the subject of chapter 4) as a representation of lesbian desire, which is connected to narcissism as a form of "objectless desire."

A similar emphasis on "the body" in its entirety is suggested by Freud himself, as he mentions the notion of a "skin ego" in *The Ego and the Id* (*Das Ich und das Es;* 1923). This concept was further explored in 1970 by Didier Anzieu, who argued that "the surface of the body is the missing piece" (27) in the predominant school of post-Freudian psychoanalysis, "object relations theory," which he criticized as focusing too much on genitalia;[17] and it is central to the issue of the "body image," which is theorized by feminist philosopher Elizabeth Grosz (and will be discussed in conjunction with the poetry of Henriette Hardenberg, the subject of chapter 3).

The most important issue about narcissism and gender is raised by Lilli Gast, whose overall thesis is that the history of psychoanalysis is a history of "desexualization," which she says is evident from the changes to the concept of "narcissism." According to Gast, psychoanalytic theories of narcissism—including those by feminists, such as Julia Kristeva—no longer represent an engagement with questions of sexuality and gender but rather focus, conveniently, on the pre-Oedipal, pregenital mother-child relationship. I would agree with Gast that

> this not only negates the bisexuality of human beings but also subjectivity, which necessarily expresses itself through the recognition of sexual difference. . . . This is like negating the subject itself, for it is above all gender which marks the subject's place in culture and identifies it as something that has "become," something to be "constituted." (Gast 1992; my translation)

This is not to promote the emphasis on "sexual difference" in its stereotypical form but rather to acknowledge that the assumption of "sameness" is erroneous because it posits a universal norm to which "difference" can then be declared inferior. As Shoshana Felman asked in 1975: "How can the woman be thought about outside of the Masculine/Feminine framework, *other* than as opposed to man, without being subordinated to a primordial masculine model? . . . How can difference as such be thought out as *non-subordinate* to identity?" (4). In this sense, my project here is not about demonstrating that women's writing is essentially different from that of men but rather to question preconceived notions of identity—female or otherwise—by acknowledging the "subjectivity" conveyed through experimental writing. It seems that narcissism's transgressive potential is particularly useful when it comes to question notions of normalcy, universality, and coherence. At least from the point of view of gender studies, narcissism seems central—not because it has been tied, historically, to concepts of homosexuality and "femininity" but because the figure of Narcissus itself is about a *difference* which cannot be thought of in hierarchical terms. Furthermore, narcissism raises the question of representation (the text) in relation to the (gendered) subject. Texts that focus on narcissism—issues of physical appearance, sexual desire, fantasies, and so on—not only deconstruct gender stereotypes but also attempt to redefine "subjectivity" on the author's own, that is, "different" terms from the established norm.

If psychoanalysis has disconnected narcissism from gender and sexuality, as Gast has convincingly argued, there must be a reason.[18] Perhaps Leo Bersani is correct in his assessment that earlier versions of narcissism do not fit the tenets of object relations theory, which holds that narcissism is antithetical to developing "object relations" (relationships to others):

> The history of Freud's thought—and, to a large extent, of psychoanalysis itself—is the history of the repression of the psychoanalytic definition of the sexual. . . . Fearful of what might be called an intrinsic indifference to others in human sexuality, Freud managed to reinterpret his theory of primary narcissism as he formulated it so that narcissistic pleasure itself would appear as a derivative of object relations. . . . Freud's most original speculative move was to deconstruct the sexual as a category of intersubjectivity, and to propose a definition of sexual excitement as both a turning away from others and a dying to the self. The appeal of that dying—the desire to be shattered out of coherence—is perhaps what psychoanalysis has sought most urgently to repress. (1990, 45)

Whether or not the sexual is indeed based on "an intrinsic indifference to others," narcissism certainly involves "a turning away from others and a dying to the self" that may not be fully explained in terms of pathology. Insofar as narcissism proposes that the relationship between self and other is complex, involving questions of differentiation and mediation, my rationale for returning to Freud's essay is based in part on the need to recover the engagement with questions of how gender and sexuality are "constituted" through language.[19] As Ann Pellegrini states, "whether psychoanalysis is 'true' in any descriptive sense is not the issue . . . psychoanalysis is a powerful cultural narrative, providing patterns of order and interpretation for telling, retelling, and making sense of life experiences, and this is no less the case when the story told emerges in reaction against psychoanalysis" (1997, 3). Consequently, the literary texts I will be discussing here are both "with" and "against" psychoanalysis: they reflect similarities in regard to narcissism while at the same time challenging the ways in which psychoanalytic theory has formulated this concept.

"Primary Narcissism" and Early Psychoanalysis

Before turning to Freud's essay (which is discussed in detail in the next chapter), let me briefly contextualize the three writers in relation to psychoanalytic theory by some of the people around Freud. The analyst Freud credited in the twenty-fifth of his *Introductory Lectures on Psycho-Analysis* ("Die Libidotheorie und der Narzißmus" 1916–17) for identifying the process associated with narcissism[20]—the withdrawal of cathexis from the object and its turning back on to the subject—was one of his former students, Karl Abraham (1877–1925). Often called "the first psychoanalyst in Germany," Abraham, who practiced psychoanalysis in Berlin and was the head of the regional group of the International Psychoanalytic Association for fifteen years, gave a paper in 1908, entitled "The Psycho-Sexual Differences between Hysteria and Dementia Praecox." In it, he described the symptoms of schizophrenia (dementia praecox) in terms of the patient's complete withdrawal:

> He is standing in a corner of a room or running about restlessly. He stares vacantly before him, hallucinates, whispers a couple of words, and gesticulates in a strange manner. He speaks to nobody and avoids everyone. He has no desire to occupy himself, neglects his appearance, eats noisily, is dirty, smears himself with excrement and masturbates openly without shame. It is as though his surroundings did not exist for him. (K. Abraham 1908/1953, 68)

Abraham likened the symptoms of this condition to "auto-erotism," or autoeroticism, a term Freud had adapted from Ellis to define early infantile sexuality in his *Three Essays*. Autoeroticism denotes a lack of boundaries between the self and the rest of the world, when infants are not yet able to distinguish between themselves and the nourishing breast. According to Abraham, the schizophrenic's inability to relate to his or her surroundings marks "the return of the patient to auto-erotism" (1908/1953, 73) because "the mental patient transfers on to himself alone as his only sexual object the whole of the libido which the healthy person turns upon all living and inanimate objects in his environment. . . . The origin of megalomania in dementia praecox is thus a reflected or auto-erotic sexual over-estimation—an over-estimation which is turned back on to the ego" (75). The notion of reflecting or reverting back the libido onto the ego (*reflexive Rückwendung*) instead of attaching it to an external object, with the result that the self becomes the "object," was Abraham's contribution to the study of psychoses, that is, narcissistic disorders. It corresponds with Freud's expansion of the libido theory in 1915 (based on "On Narcissism") which holds that

> when [the object-libido] is withdrawn from objects, it is held in suspense in peculiar conditions of tension and is finally drawn back into the ego, so that it becomes ego-libido once again. In contrast to object-libido, we also describe ego-libido as "narcissistic" libido [which] seems to be the great reservoir from which the object-cathexes are sent out. . . . The narcissistic libidinal cathexis of the ego is the original state of things, realized in earliest childhood. (Freud 1905/1962, 84)

Using the metaphor of a body of water—"the great reservoir"—Freud's thinking on narcissism is based on an originally undifferentiated state. Abraham's work, on the other hand, developed along the lines of what was later to become object relations theory. Although it was the Hungarian analyst Sàndor Ferenczi (1873–1933), Freud's closest disciple, who in 1909 first used the term "introjection," it was Abraham who came up with a detailed theory about the way in which the subject introjects and incorporates the "object" in fantasy. In Abraham's description of melancholia, in "A short study of the development of the libido," the loss of an object precipitates the desire to incorporate and continue to keep it alive in fantasy, which involves "the regression of the libido to the cannibalistic level" (K. Abraham, 1924/1965, 420). Abraham drew elaborate distinctions among the various levels of development, ranging from the early oral stage (sucking) to the stage in which complete object love becomes possible. And, where Freud conceived of a latent narcissism that would continue into adulthood,

Abraham saw narcissism as an intermediate stage that needed to be overcome. He connected narcissism to "ambivalence" (including the conflict between feelings of love and hate, as well as ambivalence in regard to sexual orientation) and concluded that "it is only the normal person . . . who is in the main without ambivalence. His libido has . . . achieved a full capacity for adapting itself to the external world" (1924/1965, 452). Since Abraham considered object love "the touchstone of real mental health" (1924/1965, 477), his thinking appears to be in opposition to narcissism, yet the fact that objects take on an imaginary quality when they are introjected (or projected, as in paranoia) means that they are "real" only to the subject. Abraham's student Melanie Klein characterizes them as "imagos, which are a phantastically distorted picture of the real objects upon which they are based" (Klein 1986, 40). Since, according to her theory, "from the beginning the ego introjects objects 'good' and 'bad,' for both of which its mother's breast is the stereotype," one can compare the primitive state of the infant to that of adult psychotics, except that in the latter, the mechanisms of introjection and projection are restricted, leading to a "*denial of psychic reality* [which results] in the denial of external reality" (Klein 1986, 40).

While the symptoms of schizophrenia—withdrawal and megalomania—may only appear to be truly "narcissistic" (they may be in actuality based on distorted object relations), they include another element of how narcissism was theorized by early psychoanalysis. Freud himself conceived of "primary narcissism" as a primitive state of undifferentiation, in which the subject is no longer autoerotic but still believes himself or herself to be the center of the universe. As an example, Freud, in "On Narcissism," uses "the mental life of children and primitive peoples," whom he believes to have "an over-estimation of the power of their wishes and mental acts" (1905/1962, 19). The dangers of such thinking are obvious, especially if one considers the hierarchy established among those who are seen as more "primitive" (which, in Freud, includes women) on account of their supposed inability to perceive the boundaries between themselves and the external world, and those who grow up to repress their "primary narcissism" in favor of object relations. And yet, this initial state of undifferentiation suggested by Freud—ironically, in opposition to the Swiss psychologist Carl Gustav Jung, whom Freud accused of not differentiating between sexual and ego libido in the same essay—was of great interest to Ferenczi, whose theory subsequently led to a break of the friendship with Freud (which had lasted for twenty-five years).

In *Thalassa: A Theory of Genitality* (1924/1968), Ferenczi proposed a vision of his understanding of the human psyche as biologically shaped by the desire to return to the womb. Unlike Jung's mythical "collective unconscious," Ferenczi's theory was based on biology, yet it resembled that of Jung insofar as it promoted a vision of something vast and undifferentiated at the origin of all things. Instead of working with the notion of tension and conflicting drives within the individual and in relation to culture, these simplified views of the human psyche contain the notion of a lost paradise (a tendency of this notion exists in Freud as well, yet his thinking developed away from it).

Where narcissism appeared to be connected to pathology in Abraham, Ferenczi described it as a reality of the subject in the womb, followed by the brutal disappointment of the trauma of birth.[21] In 1913, in "Stages in the Development of the Sense of Reality," Ferenczi wrote: "If . . . the human being possesses a mental life when in the womb, although only an unconscious one . . . he must get from his existence the impression that he is in fact omnipotent. For what is omnipotence? The feeling that one has all that one wants, and that one has nothing left to wish for" (1913, 186). He concluded that "the first great repression is made necessary by the process of birth. . . . The foetus would much rather remain undisturbed longer in the womb, but it is cruelly turned out into the world" (200). The vision here is nostalgic, that is, everyone is damaged already from the experience of having been born. Consequently Ferenczi's controversial work *Thalassa*, named after the Greek word for "ocean," argues that all of human development is an attempt at restitution (recovery).[22] Even the act of coitus is "an imitation of the act of birth" (1924/1968, 34), where "the partner forces himself onto the other in order to *merge* again" (33) with the mother's body, all of which is presented in biological terms:

> The motive which could have actuated the amphibians and the reptiles to provide themselves with a penis . . . may well be the striving to restore the lost mode of life in a moist *milieu* . . . in other words, to bring about *the reestablishment of the aquatic mode of life in the form of an existence within the moist and nourishing interior of the mother's body* . . . the mother would, properly, be the symbol of a partial substitute for the sea. (1924/1968, 54)

Ferenczi, whose emphasis on the male genital is consistent with his contemporaries' view that it is the organ most invested with narcissism—at some point, he even states that the male member is nothing but "a miniature version of the self"[23]—does not make direct reference to "primary narcissism," yet the two concepts seem closely connected. Whereas Freud eventually discarded "primary narcissism," Ferenczi held on to the idea that human beings are essentially in need of being cared for—this is apparent from his disagreement with Freud over psychoanalytic technique (which led to the breakup of their friendship): unlike Freud, who believed in remaining neutral toward the patient, Ferenczi began to pamper his patients, including hugging and kissing them, because he believed that they had been fundamentally hurt and needed the analyst's support in order to recover.

Fantasies of regression into a primitive, preverbal paradise—the mother's womb or some other, more "natural" existence—were also featured in the works of many expressionists. Henriette Hardenberg, the first of the three writers I will examine, depicts a similar condition of wanting to merge with one's environment in her poetry, yet she does not idealize this condition as harmonious and free of tension. Since differentiation is inherent to the very act of verbalizing, the narcissism described in the discourse of psychoanalysis as a condition beyond language now raises the question of the relationship between the subject (body) and language (representation).

Although Hardenberg may not have been directly familiar with the psychoanalytic discourse of her period, there is an overall emphasis on regression and the primitive among both psychoanalysts and expressionists. The latter had been prompted to react against the "art for art's sake" aesthetics of the turn of the century, by which they had been, however, informed. One might well say that narcissism continued to be "in the air" if one considers that the motif of Narcissus was the subject of numerous visual and verbal texts, among them Wilde's *The Picture of Dorian Gray* (1891), Mann's *Death in Venice* (1912), André Gide's *Le Traité du Narcisse* (1892), and the impressionist paintings of Monet, in which the viewer's gaze is confronted with surfaces of large, placid bodies of water.[24] Narcissus appeared in symbolist and Pre-Raphaelite art, as well as in sculpture (especially fountains), and poets such as Paul Valéry and Rainer Maria Rilke (with whom Hardenberg maintained a close friendship) were fascinated by his image.

Expressionism, in comparison, was a self-declared political and spiritual avant-garde movement that saw itself in opposition to decadence and aestheticism, yet placed a similar emphasis on the power of art. Expressionists believed that art could change the world, or as Kasimir Edschmid stated in 1917, "reality must be created by us." His contemporary, Paul Hatvani, explains the difference between impressionism and expressionism as follows: "Impressionism created a harmony between internal and external worlds, whereas *in Expressionism, the 'I' floods the world.* There is no longer any outside."[25] All of this is evident in Hardenberg's poetry, which is clearly expressionist, yet can also be connected to the aesthetics of narcissism.

The discourse of psychoanalysis, in turn, often drew from art and literature, so that a similar concern with "narcissism" during this period can be identified in relation to cultural production. For example, Freud's version of narcissism was influenced by his student Lou Andreas-Salomé, who had been close to Friedrich Nietzsche (as well as to Rilke) and developed her own "feminist" theory of narcissism, published in the 1921 essay, "Narzißmus als Doppelrichtung."[26] Although Hardenberg may not have been directly familiar with psychoanalytic theories of narcissism, her own artistic production may have been indirectly influenced by this connection, which is indicative of the intellectual climate of her time.

In Hardenberg's poetry, the body of the speaker becomes a kind of internal landscape in which the "I" has difficulty locating herself or himself. The "natural" environment merges with the human body, which then becomes the text itself, so that the medium of language appears to act as a kind of virtual "body." Evocative of Ferenczi's concept of *thalassale Regression,* Hardenberg also features human bodies immersed in bodies of water, yet she draws attention to their constructedness—as well as to potential problems for the individual who might suffer from this loss of boundaries. Her writing can be read in relation to the concept of a "body image," discussed by feminist philosopher Elizabeth Grosz: as my later chapter will demonstrate, Hardenberg's shifting representations of the "body" attempt to escape the confines of gender by making the construction of such an image impossible.

Object Relations and Lacanian Psychoanalysis

Whereas Hardenberg's writing appears related to "primary narcissism," the other authors in my study, Djuna Barnes and Unica Zürn, can be understood in terms of "secondary" (adult) narcissism, which involves, according to Freud, both "object relations" and the "ego ideal." Barnes's novel *Nightwood,* which takes up chapter 4, raises the question of narcissism in opposition to biologically determinist ways of thinking. Although published later, in 1936, *Nightwood* harks back to the discourse of sexology by referring to the paradigm of "the third sex"—the soul of a woman in the body of a man—which had been promoted by Germany's first gay-rights activist, Karl Heinrich Ulrichs, in the mid-nineteenth century.[27] Later adopted by a number of sexologists, the concept of homosexuals as a "third sex," thought to be biologically different and unique, supported the idea that homosexuality was "inborn" and hence could not be "cured." Since homosexuals were persecuted as "criminals," the emphasis on biological determinism was (and continues to be) politically important.[28]

In this sense, it is understandable that one of the three homosexual characters in *Nightwood,* the transvestite Doctor Matthew O'Connor, consistently defines his identity in strictly biological terms, yet his continued references to another biologically determinist discourse, namely, that of "race," are highly problematic.[29] In contrast, Barnes recounts the love story between the two female protagonists, Nora Flood and Robin Vote, in strictly nonbiological terms, that is, as narcissism. Although one might argue to what extent there is a real opposition between the two concepts (especially considering that narcissism *was* a stereotype of homosexuality), the formal structure of the novel shows the doctor's biological narrative to be undermined by the narcissistic encounters between the two women. Their narcissism appears as true love, whereas the doctor's version reduces all relationships to the biological body.

Barnes, an American journalist and playwright, was a contemporary of Gertrude Stein, who also lived as an expatriate in Paris during the 1920s. Her nine-year relationship with the artist Thelma Wood served as a model for the relationship between the two women depicted in the novel (hence *Night-Wood*), yet Barnes's style is all but realistic. Her language is highly experimental, so that critics have been divided over how to read, for example, the various disturbing references to "blood," "heredity," and "degeneracy." While some see *Nightwood* as a parody which is therefore antifascist (Burke 1968; Marcus 1991), Erin Carlston (1998) has argued that *Nightwood* "flirts" with fascism. My own sense is that this discrepancy is precipitated by the structure of the novel itself, which not only lends itself to reflect back whatever a given critic may wish to read into it but also sets up an opposition between "referential" and "performative" ways of reading, by way of juxtaposing the two competing paradigms—that is, a correlation to the figure of narcissism itself.

Like Hardenberg, Barnes raises the question of the body and how it is constituted in regard to representation (discourse). *Nightwood* opposes the extratextual, biological body ("the third sex") to which the doctor refers, to the imaginary bodies of the lovers which appear to be governed, in terms of object relations theory, by experiences of introjection, incorporation, and loss. For example, Nora's comparison of Robin's absence with the feeling of "an amputated hand" (1995, 53) resonates with the following passage by Abraham from "A Short Study of the Development of the Libido":

> The ambivalence of the subject's feelings . . . is manifested in his identification of a person with a part of his own body. To compare another person with a part of one's body which is the object of a specially high narcissistic estimation is without doubt a proof of exceptional love. In German we often call a loved person "my heart" (*mein Herz*); and we say of a mother that she loves her child as the "apple of her eye." (K. Abraham 1924/1965; 493)

The discourse of object relations seems pertinent to interpretations of *Nightwood*—such as Carolyn Allen's reading of the novel as a representation of "objectless desire" (1993)—insofar as *Nightwood* invokes the notion of loss. Much of the text focuses on the process of Nora's mourning the breakup of the relationship, and this process seems linked to "primary narcissism," which entails a similar emphasis on loss. Only here, the loss refers to the actual absence of another person, not the nostalgia for a primal unity with one's own self. Since Robin may or may not be a reflection of Nora's own self, *Nightwood* raises the question of narcissism as related to but also distinct from object relations. Read in conjunction with the middle section of Freud's essay, it suggests a conflict between emphasizing representation and perceiving it as secondary to a supposed "reality" outside the text, which in turn highlights the discrepancy between Lacanian and object relations theory that is the hidden undercurrent of my project. Michael Rustin compares these two psychoanalytic schools of thought as follows:

> There is an emphasis in the Lacanian tradition on the necessarily "negative" and "antagonistic" aspects of psychoanalytic and other "critical" forms of social thought. . . . By contrast, the object relations and Kleinian traditions postulate a "positive" core of ideas about human nature and its more benign form of development. . . . The first tradition is above all adapted to the unending investigation of the inauthentic, idealized and self-regarding aspects of human consciousness. The second tradition regards psychoanalytic investigation . . . as a

source of "grounded" understanding of "authentic" states of feeling. (1995, 226)

The question whether feelings can be "authentic" and object relations immediate or whether representation is always already involved can be asked even more forcefully in relation to the texts written by the third author in my study, Unica Zürn. They can be understood as a kind of antithesis to Barnes, especially when it comes to the difference between these two psychoanalytic approaches. For example, object relations theorist W. R. D. Fairbairn reduces narcissism to just another form of object relations, "an attitude arising out of identification with the object. Indeed primary narcissism may be simply defined as just such a state of identification with the object, secondary narcissism being a state of identification with the object which is internalized" (1986, 91). While this approach might work for a reading of Barnes, Zürn's *The Man of Jasmine* refuses to present the reader with an external "object," thereby lending itself much more easily to a Lacanian reading. As the final chapter of my study shows, her writing can be connected to the final part of Freud's essay about the "ego ideal":[30] Zürn's protagonist, a writer and artist who diagnoses herself as schizophrenic, depends on an image that emerges from within her own self and hence does not seem to have any external point of origin. This image, the hallucinatory figure of the Man of Jasmine, is an all-powerful dictator who compels her to write and thus drives her deeper and deeper into madness, yet as I argue, "he" is also a projection of her own desire to write.

Informed by surrealism and its emphasis on the origins of the work of art (as well as on the connection between madness and art),[31] Zürn's seemingly autobiographical "she" is determined by her relationship to representation, not by a real "other" (object). Although one could argue that Nora's lover in *Nightwood*, Robin, is also more of a self-reflection than a real character, Zürn's text truly forces the reader to participate in madness by raising constant doubts over which of the experiences narrated are or are not "real." Although *The Man of Jasmine* appears to be the spontaneous outpourings of a "madwoman," it could not have been written by a person who was truly in the condition "she" is said to be in. Zürn's text creates the effect of a split consciousness by using the present tense, as if the narrator were recording the events experienced by the protagonist simultaneously as they occur. Grammatically, through the third person, Zürn's text establishes a difference between author, narrator, and protagonist that undermines the generic conventions of autobiography: the reader may be tempted to read the "she" as an "I" (Weigel 1987a, 211); yet Zürn's text must be understood as not simply representing but rather reenacting "madness" in textual terms.[32]

The problem with Zürn is that it becomes nearly impossible to distinguish her "art" from her "life." For example, one might interpret the Man of Jasmine as Zürn's real-life companion, the artist Hans Bellmer (1902–75) whose sculptural oeuvre continues to cause controversy.[33] However, Zürn insisted on the fact that her imaginary figure was modeled after Henri Michaux, an artist and writer whom she admired (and who might be considered in terms of an opposition to or escape from Bellmer). Zürn, like her nameless protagonist, was repeatedly confined to mental institutions during the last decade of her life, which she decided to end through suicide. According to Bellmer, she had "written herself into madness" (which had been the sole subject of her writings), yet it is ironic that there may not be, in fact, a correlation between her madness and her writing other than the one she herself produced.[34]

Significantly, one of Zürn's manuscripts was dedicated to Lacan. Of the three writers I am discussing, her work seems most closely related to Lacanian theory, which places a similar priority on the imaginary and the symbolic as mediating functions. Whereas object relations theory assumes an immediate relationship between subject and object, Lacan argues—with reference to Freud—that all relationships are determined by an image that arises during the so-called mirror stage:

> The *mirror stage* is a drama . . . which manufactures for the subject, caught up in the lure of spatial identification, the succession of phantasies that extends from a fragmented body image to a form of its totality that I shall call orthopaedic—and, lastly, to the assumption of the armour of an alienating identity, which will mark with its rigid structure the subject's entire mental development. (1977, 4)

Like Zürn, Lacan shows the subject to be dependent, first and foremost, on the ability to maintain physical integrity by way of relating to an image—with the only difference that in Zürn, the image appears "real" to the subject, who experiences it as external in the form of a hallucination. Compared to Hardenberg, whose textual subject also refuses to take on the "armour" of a (gendered) identity and is threatened with the potential dissolution of subject-object boundaries (another potential form of psychosis),

Zürn's "she" is severely disembodied. Whereas Hardenberg's subject merges with the landscape, Zürn's "she" watches herself dance on a stage as if she were watching a movie, all the while remaining seated (i.e., physically immobile) on the bed of her hotel room. Fully aware that she is hallucinating, "she" is addicted to these out-of-body experiences, like Narcissus to his reflection.

In 1961, Zürn was treated at the Hôpital de Sainte Anne by, among others, the Lacanian psychoanalyst Guy Rosolato, who in 1975 published an essay, "The Narcissistic Axis of Depression," in which he reminds us that it was Abraham "who pointed out that 'in melancholia the whole psychological process centres *in the main* around the mother'" (1980, 281). This observation is consistent with the fact that *The Man of Jasmine* begins with a flashback to the protagonist's childhood, including the disavowal of her mother, which sets up the relationship between her and the Man of Jasmine (which lasts throughout the remainder of the text). According to Rosolato, "the sense of lack and the dependent relation to the mother are what give rise to the narcissistic pattern and particularly to projective doubling" (1980, 288). Rosolato, who refers to Rank's notion of the "double," observes that

> the first clear image of this double can be found in the child . . . in the rise and fall of *imaginary companions* [who] contradict the loss of the object. They are but projected shadows of the object. One can see therein a major narcissistic image, something we all mentally construct, which preserves the memory not only of what we were but of what we would like to have been, ideally, in some glorified past, like paradise or the promised land of all our dreams. (1980, 288)

In this sense, the image is primary, and the Man of Jasmine can be read as an imaginary companion whose presence fills the void left by the "object," the absent mother. For Zürn, madness becomes "the promised land" for which there can be no "cure" because it is the source of creativity itself. *The Man of Jasmine* affirms its author's radical belief in art, along the lines of Foucault's dictum that "madness is contemporary with the work of art, since it inaugurates the time of its truth" (1965, 288). Perhaps Zürn's work may be understood against the background of R. D. Laing and the antipsychiatry movement of the sixties in France, where she continues to be a cult figure (Zürn, a "second-generation" surrealist, had come to France from Germany in 1953 to follow Bellmer).[35] Clearly, Zürn's interest in the relationship between madness and textuality is related to Lacanian theory with its anti–object relations stance, yet her text continues to raise questions about the materiality of "the body" that may not be answered by any preexisting psychoanalytic theory. Zürn's writing suggests that it may be possible to "construct" one's identity through writing—but also that the subject is determined by discourses (such as psychoanalysis) in a Foucauldian sense. Like Barnes and Hardenberg, Zürn draws attention to textuality yet raises the question of the connection between representation (art) and the "real" more forcefully. Merging the "body" of the text with that of herself, the author, she shows her subject to suffer from the limitations of corporeality and, at the same time, to live in the realm of "fiction." Like Narcissus, Zürn is neither inside nor outside her own text.

One of the questions that seems particularly relevant to my project has recently been asked by Charles Sheperdson: "How can we say that Narcissus is responsible for his failure to respond to the other . . . when there is no subject there before he arrives at the pool, where he sees himself for the first time?" (2000, 103).[36] In other words, how can we apply theories that presuppose a "self" already in existence, if the subject must first constitute himself or herself vis-à-vis the imaginary object, his or her own reflection? As I will demonstrate in the remainder of this book, texts about narcissism derive their significance from precisely the fact that they do not presuppose anything, that they question all notions of objectivity, and that they are, so to speak, mad in their desire to escape "reality." That may be, after all, why Thomas Mann's Narcissus is smiling in spite of his hopelessness.

2. Reading Freud's "On Narcissism"

Definitions

The question I have posed in terms of the history of psychoanalysis and narcissism is that of the discrepancy between different schools of thought: object relations theory and Lacanian psychoanalysis. Narcissism, with its unclear definition of what constitutes an "object," raises the question to what extent the subject is, as in Lacan, a function of the imaginary and, therefore, the symbolic, that is, language—where relationships to others are by definition, mediated; or whether there is an immediate (direct) relationship between subject and object, as in the more biologically oriented object relations theory (where the subject takes as his or her first object the mother's breast). In this chapter, I conduct a close reading of Sigmund Freud's 1914 essay, "On Narcissism: An Introduction" (*Zur Einführung des Narzißmus*), which continues to represent the foundation for most contemporary psychoanalytic discourses on narcissism—although much of psychoanalytic theory conceives of itself as having developed away from Freud, it will become apparent, over the course of this chapter, that the various contradictions and possibilities of his essay continue to inform our thinking about narcissism. This chapter, in turn, should function as the theoretical groundwork for the reader to approach the following chapters, on the experimental writings by Henriette Hardenberg, Djuna Barnes, and Unica Zürn, each of which corresponds to a major concept in Freud's essay (primary narcissism, object relations, and the ego ideal). I hope that there can emerge a dialogue between these two generically different texts—literature and psychoanalytic theory—on the issues of language, representation, and the body, as they are central to any discussion of narcissism. In this sense, my method differs from that of psychoanalytic criticism, where one might read the literary texts through a Freudian lens—as I attempt to show instead, it is the voices of the women writers that challenge and revise at least some of the preconceptions about narcissism that have been established by psychoanalytic theory.

Freud's essay "On Narcissism: An Introduction" is notoriously difficult, and this difficulty begins with its very title: since Freud had been using the term "narcissism" for four years, starting in 1910 with *Leonardo da Vinci,* it is not actually an "introduction." What differs in 1914, however, is that he now conceives of narcissism no longer in conjunction with homosexuality, but rather as part of the "regular course of human sexual development" (Freud 1914/1986, 17). In *Leonardo,* he had used the term "narcissism" with reference to homosexual object choice as a form of mirroring, that is, choosing a love object that resembles the image of one's own self; now he officially "introduces" the concept of narcissism into psychoanalytic discourse by stating that it is *not* a "perversion" but rather a "natural" condition, common to all human beings and animals, regardless of sexual orientation: narcissism is "the libidinal complement to the egoism of the instinct of self-preservation, a measure of which may justifiably be attributed to every living creature" (18). However, with this emphasis on libidinal instincts, Freud also continues his earlier thinking about sexuality, his so-called libido theory, which the essay "On Narcissism" is, in fact, designed to defend against his colleague, Carl Gustav Jung. Jung had attacked the libido theory for its differentiation between two kinds of libido, which he thought to be unnecessary. Freud, instead of positing a single, undifferentiated psychic and sexual energy at the heart of everything, had thought of a new kind of libido, which would attach itself to one's self rather than to others (objects), and he had called this libido "narcissistic."

Freud had proposed this libido theory as early as 1905, in *Three Essays on the Theory of Sexuality,* to which he then added a footnote in 1910, for the second edition, published the same year as *Leonardo.* It is this footnote (cited in Strachey's newly edited 1962 reprint) I would take as the actual beginning of the central thesis of "On Narcissism," which holds that the choice of a love object is not always the first object one encounters—one's mother—but rather can be the "object" that is one's self:

> Future inverts, in the earliest years of their childhood, pass through a phase of very intense but short-lived fixation to a woman (usually their mother), and . . . after leaving this behind, they identify themselves with a woman and take *themselves* as their sexual object. That is to say, they proceed from a narcissistic basis, and look for a young man who resembles themselves and whom *they* may love as their mother loved *them.* (11)

Freud here still holds on to the connection between narcissism and homosexuality that had been established by sexology, yet he opens up the possibility for a conception of bisexuality that was also espoused by gay-rights activists, such as Magnus Hirschfeld, around the same period of time. In "On Narcissism," Freud states that "a human being has originally two sexual objects—himself and the woman who nurses him—and in doing so we are postulating a primary narcissism in everyone, which may in some cases manifest itself in a dominating fashion in his object choice" (1914/1986, 31). What exactly determines this "choice" is not discussed in "On Narcissism," whose main line of argument departs from any theory of homosexuality. Nevertheless, I believe it is important to keep in mind that the supposed departure from homosexuality is, in fact, grounded in Freud's very own thinking about that "perversion"—so that in spite of the fact that "On Narcissism" "straightens out" the connection between narcissism and homosexuality (now, everyone can be a narcissist), the basis of this "introduction" is largely derived from these previous conceptions.

Another issue that precedes "On Narcissism" is the connection between narcissism and mental illness, to which Freud makes immediate and overt reference at the very beginning of his essay, where he claims that narcissism is "normal." This claim may come as a surprise to the reader, who might wonder why one would take the example of a schizophrenic patient to make a case for "primary and normal narcissism," yet it is consistent with Freud's method, which he himself defines as "understanding . . . normal phenomena [through] the field of pathology with its distortions and exaggerations" (1914/1986, 25). In fact, it is particularly necessary in the case of narcissism because, as Freud acknowledges, there are "certain special difficulties . . . in the way of a direct study."

"Primary narcissism," as a concept, is purely hypothetical and, by definition, escapes empirical proof. In "On Narcissism," it functions as the basis for the much more important concept of the "ego ideal" (later: superego), said to arise from primary narcissism's repression and hence cannot be simply discarded. However, it seems to me that the real conceptual difficulty arises from the way in which the self can or cannot be defined as an "object." Freud himself admits that it is not really possible to distinguish between the two types of libido by way of empirical observation. The main component of his original libido theory, in *Three Essays,* is the concept of a "great reservoir" from which libido is sent out to attach itself to objects, so that it is really "narcissistic" (ego) libido to begin with and only turns into "object libido" later on. Freud relates this concept to the notion of an "original state of things," which also informs his essay "On Narcissism," especially in regard to "primary narcissism." As I mentioned in chapter 1, Freud was influenced by Karl Abraham's 1908 concept of *reflexive Rückwendung,* which solidifies this idea of withdrawal from attachment to objects and a subsequent reverting back (*Rückwendung*) to the self. Abraham provided empirical proof for this concept in the form of his observations of schizophrenics, whom he saw as self-absorbed and unable to form attachments to others. Freud, in "On Narcissism," also cites observations of schizophrenics, by Emil Kraepelin (1889) and Eugen Bleuler (1911), so as to support his case against Jung (whose main field of interest was schizophrenia) and to argue that there really were *no objects* involved when it came to "primary narcissism." In contrast to what most object relations theorists would now assume (namely, that there is always an object involved, either in reality or in fantasy), Freud describes primary narcissism as an objectless state, where the patient "seems to really have withdrawn his libido from people and things in the external world, *without* replacing them by others in phantasy" (1914/1986, 18; my emphasis). It is here that the otherwise antiquated, scientifically untenable supposition of "primary narcissism" becomes interesting to my project, at least in theoretical terms, as it posits a stage existing prior to object relations.

To return to the question of mental illness, which is bound up with the question of narcissism, it seems to have been essential for Freud to posit a developmental model, in which narcissism could appear normal and natural at one point while becoming pathological at another (this idea is echoed by the "Kernberg-Kohut debate," as mentioned in chapter 1, where narcissism appears on a continuum from health to illness, the difference being in quantity, not kind).

The notion of "regression" is central to Freud's conception of both mental illness and narcissism, which goes back to the Schreber case of 1911 (*Über einen autobiographisch beschriebenen Fall von Paranoia*). Here Freud introduced narcissism as an "intermediary stage" between autoeroticism and object relations, a definition subsequently adopted by others, such as Abraham (in "A Short Study of the Development of the Libido"; 1924/1965). The concept of "auto-erotism" had been defined in the *Three Essays* in 1905 as the hypothesis of the earliest developmental stage, in which the nursling (and/or fetus) is unable to perceive any boundaries between its body and the rest of the world. Narcissism subsequently involves some kind of rudimentary differentiation between "I" and "not-I" on the part of the infant, which is eventually replaced by a full appreciation of others as "objects." In Freud as in Abraham, narcissism and object relations are pitted against one another; since especially Abraham claims that the aim of normal, healthy development is to get away from narcissism, to focus one's attention on others. Narcissistic behavior, at that point still associated with homosexuality, was seen as a regression, and that is how it appears in Freud's description of Judge Schreber, who he observes "did not exhibit symptoms of homosexuality during periods of mental health" (1914/1986, 296)—the implication being that the homosexual behavior associated with narcissism is a sign of Schreber's regression into an earlier, more primitive stage. In other words, the same behavior that may seem "natural" at an earlier stage becomes "pathological" if it appears later on. A similar paradigm is used for the conceptualization of narcissism as a "female" characteristic, as will be shown in the following section.

Female Cats; or, Primary Narcissism

Freud's designation of women as the subjects of primary narcissism differs from the earlier view of homosexuals as narcissistic because it is no longer based on object choice. When Freud described the schizophrenics at the beginning of his essay, he did so with reference to delusions of grandeur and megalomania—both of which continue to be considered "narcissistic disturbances" as part of psychotic illnesses—and proceeds to call these states "a magnification and plainer manifestation of a condition which had already existed previously [that is] primary narcissism" (1914/1986, 19). Women, unlike the mentally ill, are said to be more narcissistic by nature. They are situated at a developmentally earlier stage than men, as Freud compares their narcissism to the apparent self-absorption of children, animals, and "primitive people." In doing so, he resorts to the ancient stereotype that women are somehow closer to nature, which is precisely what makes up their attraction. As outlined earlier, Freud's newly "introduced" narcissism posits a continuum between a state of nature and its later, pathological manifestations, yet it draws a definite distinction between the sexes.

To begin with, it has to be clarified that the main theoretical contribution of "On Narcissism" is the introduction of the ego ideal, a secondary form of narcissism which, in effect, arises from the *repression* of primary narcissism. This ego ideal, which later becomes the "superego," is what enables subjects to develop object relations while at the same time maintaining the illusion of their original narcissism, so as to protect the ego from injury. I will discuss this ego ideal in more detail later on, but for the moment it should be noted that Freud's women, because of their "arrested development," are not in as favorable a position as men to take on an ego ideal, so that their ability to relate to others in society appears to be severely hampered. Nevertheless, their narcissistic self-absorption is construed as attractive by Freud, whose entire way of thinking rests on this nature/culture opposition. For example, the emergence of the ego ideal is described by Freud in the last third of "On Narcissism" within the context of the "psychology of repression," according to which "libidinal instinctual impulses" are bound to come into conflict with "the subject's cultural and ethical ideas" (1914/1986, 35). In that sense, the position of the women seems more desirable than that of the men, for they are said to be less repressed by culture, to which, however, they also do not have access.

Unlike the ego ideal, which is connected to society, primary narcissism appears as a manifestation of biology: "With the onset of puberty the maturing of the female sexual organs, which up till then have been in a condition of latency, seems to bring about an intensification of the original narcissism, and this is unfavorable to the development of a true object choice" (1914/1986, 31). According to this line of thinking, women are destined biologically to be incapable of loving others—with the exception of motherhood, when they are forced to renounce their narcissism to love the "part of their own body [that now] confronts them as an extraneous object" (32). Before I proceed to discuss Freud's possible motivation for constructing such a scenario, let me quote the following, infamous passage from "On Narcissism," which illustrates the insidious way in which women appear as both inferior and superior on account of their narcissism:

> Women, especially if they grow up with good looks, develop a certain self-contentment. . . . Strictly speaking, it is only themselves that such women love. . . . Nor does their need lie in the direction of loving, but of being loved. . . . The importance of this type of woman for the erotic life of man-

> kind is to be rated very high. Such women have the greatest fascination for men [because] another person's narcissism has a great attraction for those who have renounced part of their own narcissism and are in search of object-love. [Similarly] the charm of a child lies to a great extent in his narcissism, his self-contentment and inaccessibility, just as does the charm of certain animals which seem not to concern themselves about us, such as cats and the large beasts of prey. (1914/1986, 31–32)

The passage is riddled with contradictions: women are too self-absorbed to nurture men, yet their very inaccessibility makes men slavishly attracted to them; women's "charm" is due to a lack of concern for others, yet they contribute to "the erotic life of mankind" by becoming the target for procreation; whereas men are doomed to exist without a narcissism of their own, which is, however, why they are forced to pursue women in the first place. Moreover, women are like "beasts of prey," as if waiting in ambush to attack men, yet they are simultaneously "self-content," causing men to suffer from envy; as Freud explains: "It is as if we envied them for maintaining a blissful state of mind—an unassailable libidinal position which we ourselves have since abandoned." However, he goes on, "the great charm of narcissistic women has . . . its reverse side, . . . the lover's dissatisfaction, . . . his doubts of the woman's love, [and] his complaints of her enigmatic nature" (32).

According to Sarah Kofman, there is the illusion of women's plentitude in "On Narcissism" which differs from Freud's usual depiction of women as "lacking" something (a phallus). What Kofman calls women's "veiling" is usually based on "hiding the fact that she has nothing to hide, for concealing that 'pus-filled cavity' which threatens to contaminate and infect man" (1980/1987, 210), yet here it appears as if woman has something *more* than man. Woman's narcissism, in Freud's essay, is about male loss and, subsequently, envy. Like "His Majesty the Baby," whose parents are said by Freud to dote upon him because he reminds them of what they themselves have lost, the women remind men of their own loss of primary narcissism. Men "have renounced part of their own narcissism" (1914/1987, 32) and women provide the illusion that it could be restored. This emphasis on loss resembles the theory of Ferenczi, where the subject's profound sadness is connected to a loss of primal connection to the mother's womb, as outlined in chapter 1. If one thinks of this female connection in terms of identification, one might go so far as to say that Freud's envy reveals a desire to *be* the "woman" he describes, for it is she who is permitted to indulge in the selfish pleasures of narcissism that are denied to men.

And yet, although it may seem as if women have the better deal, they remain excluded from the ego ideal, which provides access to "the common idea of a family, a class or a nation" (Freud 1914/1987, 43). They seem to roam freely and in opposition to civilization, in which they cannot actively participate. More than likely, it is this very "otherness" that so fascinates Freud.

On a more biographical note, both Kofman and Gast note that there is, in fact, a connection between Freud's frequent allusions to cats and his attraction to his female student, Lou Andreas-Salomé. Freud (like Nietzsche, Salomé's other close friend) had a tendency to compare women with cats, especially during the period he was close to Salomé (how close we do not know). She herself takes up this image in her "charming account of the 'narcissistic cat,'" which I described in chapter 1. Salomé, while arguing along the same biologically determinist lines as her mentor Freud, claimed that women's narcissism was not a shortcoming but an asset, on account of which women were superior to men. Regardless of whether the anecdote of the cat who strays into Freud's office and then dies on him is fact or fiction, it certainly illustrates the frustration Freud must have experienced in the process of becoming attached to both the cat and Salomé—they appear to be more or less synonymous. One might even go so far as to argue that the narcissistic woman appears to be so "dangerous" because she reminds her observer of both his loss and, consequently, his own impotence as a doctor. Freud hastens to state that his "description of the feminine form of erotic life is not due to any tendentious desire on my part to depreciate women" (1914/1986, 32), but the reader cannot help but feel that the author has been let down by both the cat and the woman. According to Salomé's journal, the cat, like a patient in analysis, had "claimed its rights daily to take a place on the sofa" (89), but Freud, the doctor, lost his patient: "One day he found the cat feverish and gasping on the sofa. And although it was most painstakingly treated with hot fomentations and other remedies, it succumbed to pneumonia." Perhaps this is why "primary narcissism," the concept associated with both women and cats, also "died upon" Freud, for in his essay, he could only sustain it as the negative side of the ego ideal and eventually had to abandon it completely.

Ideal versus "Actual" Self

Let me now turn to the other side of the equation: the men who seem forever deprived of narcissistic gratification. According to Freud, "object-love of the attachment type is, properly speaking, characteristic of the male" (1914/1986, 31) so that its predecessor, primary narcissism, is secondary to the ego ideal. However, the ego ideal is defined as a form of "secondary narcissism" which emerges as a result of the repression of primary narcissism. Its position in Freud's oeuvre, as a precursor to the superego, is more prominent than primary narcissism, a concept that did not survive the initial essay—not unlike the cat who succumbed to pneumonia.

Nevertheless, in spite of its being a largely imaginary concept, primary narcissism is essential to the ego ideal: the relationship between those two concepts, like two sides of the same coin, is tautological; the ego ideal exists only as a consequence of (repressed) primary narcissism; and primary narcissism can be deduced only retroactively, by hypothesizing its existence on the basis of having observed its supposed effect, the ego ideal. The problem is that it is unclear how exactly the two concepts are linked or, as Laplanche and Pontalis have asked, "Just how are we supposed to picture the transition from a monad shut in upon itself to a progressive discovery of the object?" (1973, 256–57). According to them, primary narcissism is "characterized by the total absence of any relationship to the outside world," whereas the ego ideal is precisely based on social relations. In fact, Freud himself was concerned with the question "What makes it necessary at all for our mental life to pass beyond the limits of narcissism and to attach the libido to objects?" (1914/1986, 28). He provides an answer in terms of the libido theory: "when the cathexis of the ego with libido exceeds a certain amount [it is] being dammed up" (1914/1986, 28); as a result, libido is released and able to attach itself to others (objects). However, as Laplanche has also observed, the nature of the ego remains unclear: it acts "like an external object, the ego is a love object, charged with libido, 'cathected'" (1990, 73), yet it also pretends to be the subject:

> The ego, even though it is a reservoir of the libido cathecting it, can appear to be a *source;* it is not the subject of desire or wishes, nor even the site in which the drive originates (a site represented by the id), but it *can pass itself off as such.* A love object, the ego "puts out" libido; it supplements and replaces love by positing itself as a loving subject. (74)

Evidently, the nature of the ego was ambiguous enough, within the context of the libido theory, to merit the introduction of a new element, the ego ideal. As a mental image, it need not rely on the old hydraulic metaphor: unlike the metaphor of water, whose fluidity always threatens to transgress boundaries, images lend themselves to greater stability and hence a greater possibility of subject-object differentiation. To explain object relations seems to have been, after all, the direction in which Freud was headed: only three years after the publication of "On Narcissism," in "Mourning and Melancholia" ["Trauer und Melancholie"] (1917), he no longer wrote about primary narcissism as an objectless state but rather about "narcissistic identification" with a lost object, real or imaginary. Unlike "cathexis," the term used within the context of the libido theory, "identification" (as well as its related concepts "projection" and "introjection") entails a process of visualization—the "object" is now imaginary, so the subject can no longer be objectless.

As commentators have suggested, the emergence of the ego ideal is concurrent with Freud's gradual abandonment of the libido theory. Perhaps this abandonment may have been one way not to confront the issue of objectlessness associated with "primary narcissism." Subsequently object relations theorists would become able to argue that "from the subjective point of view . . . the objects that are identified with the self are not part of the self" (Segal and Bell 1991, 162), claiming that the "self" (or "subject") would consist of nothing *but* (imaginary) objects. According to Fairbairn (1986), as noted in the previous chapter, narcissism always involves an object, because in the discourse of object relations, objects may exist in either reality or fantasy—see, for example, D. W. Winnicott's (1986) concept of "transitional objects," such as a teddy bear, taking on the symbolic function as a substitute for the original (Kleinian) object, the mother's breast. From this point of view, objects never do not exist.

However, Freud's original version of narcissism casts a wider net; although he introduces the ego ideal, he never actually defines the "actual" ego, as he calls it:

> We can say that [man] has set up an ideal in himself by which he measures his actual ego. . . . This ideal ego is now the target of the self-love which was enjoyed in childhood by the actual ego. . . . He is not willing to forgo the narcissistic perfection of his childhood; and when, as he grows up, he is disturbed by the admonitions of others and by the awakening of his own critical judgment, so that he can no longer retain that perfection, he seeks to recover it in the new form *of an ego ideal.* What he projects before him as his ideal is the substitute for the lost narcissism of his childhood in which he was his own ideal. (1914/1986, 36)

If anything, it is the *loss* of primary narcissism that defines everything that is *not* the "actual" ego. Presumably the ego ideal is the only thing of substance, for it is only the "ideal ego" that can become the "target of self-love," whereas the "actual ego" remains mysterious: what it consists of remains unsaid, except for the puzzling notion that in childhood, "he was his own ideal." The question arises: How can one be "one's own ideal" if there is no real surface for projection, but only a negative space, defined by the absence and loss of primary narcissism? Primary narcissism, after all, denotes a state in which it is not yet necessary to idealize, a state of nature, in which one is still at unity with oneself. Or is the ego ideal, by any chance, twice removed from the original subject, who sees himself (or herself) in terms of two different images, one authentic, the other superimposed by culture? Most strikingly, there is this discrepancy between the ego ideal as a condition emerging from *within,* via repression, and a dictate from *without,* the "critical judgment" that comes from the "admonitions of others." These others, as the passage says, "disturb" the peace of the hitherto autonomous subject, who must now subject himself to the authority of others, the "parents . . . those who trained and taught him . . . his fellow-men—and public opinion" (1914/1986, 38), as Freud later elaborates, so that really, it is they who shape the subject. Hence it is not surprising that he (or she?) wishes to "recover" from this disturbance by retaining the illusion of primary narcissism—and yet, as Freud makes clear, the ego ideal is a poor substitute, a fake, so to speak, which can never make up for the real thing, the "actual" state of the ego. In what, then, does this "actuality" consist?

In response to this question, it might be helpful to note that Strachey translates as "actual" two different versions of the ego Freud mentions in his original German text: *das aktuelle Ich,* which implies a temporal dimension (the present ego, as opposed to the one of the past or future); and *das wirkliche Ich,* which is, literally, "the real ego." Only the latter seems to have found its way into the translation, yet it is the former, encompassing the notion of temporality, that seems most at stake. *Das aktuelle Ich* is subject to the passing of time, it is never the same from one moment to the next, therefore it cannot be pictured—whereas *das wirkliche Ich* already includes a moment of idealization, of fixity, whereby it anticipates the "ideal ego" (*Idealich*) and, consequently, the ego ideal (*Ichideal*).[1] Judging from Freud's remark that "the most touchy point in the narcissistic system [is] the immortality of the ego, which is so hard pressed by reality" (1914/1986, 34), the function of the ego ideal is to provide an imaginary refuge from mortality, an ego that cannot die because time does not pass. And here is where the two egos truly differ. One represents an eternally fixed image, the other that which is subject to mortality: the body. This difference is consistent with Lacan's assertion that there are "two narcissisms":

> First of all there is, in fact, a narcissism connected with the corporeal image . . . in as much as he is man and not horse. It makes up the unity of the subject. [Then there is] a second narcissism. Its fundamental pattern is immediately the relation to the other . . . the other, the alter ego, is more or less confused, according to the stage in life, with the *Ichideal.* . . . The subject sees his being in a reflection in relation to the other, that is to say in relation to the *Ichideal.* (1975, 125–26)

Based on this assertion, Lacan believes that "the human ego is founded on the basis of the imaginary relation" (1977, 115). According to his views, the "real" is never directly accessible, for it is always already structured by the imaginary and the symbolic. In contrast, object relations theorists have insisted on the priority of biological, physical reality, that is, the reality of the corporeal body. The nature and substance of this "body," it seems to me, are related to the question of its ability to be represented. For example, Charles Sheperdson describes the subject as being essentially ahistorical, therefore "nothing," that is, not representable *as such*:

> The origin itself, the very moment of the emergence of narcissism (the "satisfaction he had once enjoyed") does not appear to lie at the beginning but would seem to emerge for the first time *only through this "later" form.* . . . What Freud is saying here is that it is only on the basis of this ideal ego that the psychic economy is able, nostalgically, to produce for itself a backward glance. . . . The *moment of representation* is the moment of a subject who is not a subject before he sees himself, and who is already lost the moment reflection begins—a subject who is nothing before the image gives him to himself, and who is already something else as soon as the image arrives. (2000, 101–2)

In other words, the subject is "nothing" without the image, an understanding which confirms Lacan's view, yet contrasts with that of object relations theorists who insist on the body as a biological reality. Ferenczi, as I have mentioned, took issue with the notion that one can "neglect the reality of the outer world, to be a fiction" (1913). Instead, he argued, feelings of omnipotence were real, not imaginary, because the fetus in the womb truly does experience omnipotence: after being "cruelly turned out into the world [he is] far from pleased at the rude disturbance of the wish-less tranquility he had enjoyed in the womb [and] *he longs to regain this situation*" (187). Whereas Freud, Ferenczi's mentor, suggested compensation for this loss by way of the ego ideal, Ferenczi did not believe in such a solution, for he felt that such a loss was simply irreparable. Thus, whereas Freud believed in successful repression and future development, Ferenczi envisioned a subject shaped by a fundamental condition of longing for the past (a return to the womb).

Ferenczi insisted that the feelings we experience are based on biological reality, *not* our imagination, and there is a similar tendency in Freud's "On Narcissism" to insist on the "reality" of primary narcissism as the underlying condition which determines everything. However, in Freud, the desire for a fusion with nature, the boundlessness associated with the womb, is thwarted by repression, that is, the male subject's erecting (Freud uses the German *aufrichten*) of the ego ideal. According to Jeanine Chasseguet-Smirgel, Freud's writings exhibit a struggle between the desire to merge with the mother and the necessity to adhere to the law of the father (which must be abolished in order to bring about the fusion with the maternal), a struggle she formulates in terms of Freud's national and religious identity: "The paradox of the Freudian psychoanalytic method resides, I feel, in this conjunction of Romantic German culture and the Law of Moses, in the maternal cosmic dimension and the paternal universe of separation" (1989, 144). Consequently, one might argue that Freud's student, Ferenczi, may have pursued what Freud needed to repress; this assumption is supported by the fact that, according to Gast (1992), the two of them had initially worked together on the project that eventually became Ferenczi's *Thalassa*. As mentioned before, Ferenczi's aim was to draw an analogy between psychic life and biological nature so that all claims to fictitiousness would be replaced by a form of "reality"—which would make Ferenczi the first object relations theorist.[2] Freud's unwillingness to yield to the rather fantastic implications of this claim is evident from the fact that he distanced himself from this project by, apparently, attempting to destroy his writings related to it. However, these writings, according to Gast (1992, 124), have recently resurfaced among the documents of Ferenczi's estate, so that it is possible to assume that Freud's "On Narcissism" is not too far away from the work of Ferenczi, his disciple.

The claim to a boundlessly inflated ego is at the heart of Ferenczi's theory, where the infant's feelings of omnipotence are not imaginary but real. It is also apparent in Freud's "On Narcissism": apart from schizophrenics, women, children, and animals, the subjects of primary narcissism include "great criminals . . . who compel our interest by the narcissistic consistency with which they manage to keep away from their ego anything that would diminish it" (1914/1986, 32). These criminals are larger than life because they manage to transgress all boundaries, that is, rules imposed by the laws of society. When in the beginning of his essay Freud attributes primary narcissism to "primitive peoples," he does so by comparing their mental life to that of children, characterized by "an over-estimation of the power of their wishes and mental acts, the 'omnipotence of thoughts,' belief in the thaumaturgic force of words, and a technique for dealing with the external world—'magic'" (19). Thus, although primary narcissism is complete "otherness," it also denotes a condition where the ego can infinitely inflate itself, to fill up all existing space, so that all differences, all "others," will disappear.

In both Ferenczi and Freud, the subject would like to feel boundless, at the center of the universe, which in turn raises the question of what the universe would look like without any shape or form imposed by boundaries. Presumably, one would feel lost rather than at the center, which is where Lacan's concept of a "mirror stage" is helpful, as it explains how the subject is capable of locating himself (or herself) in space. Lacan's "orthopaedic" image supports the otherwise fragmented body (*corps morcelée*), a theory which derives directly from that of Freud's ego ideal. As far as Lacan's reading of Freud is concerned, everything depends on the construction of this image. This interpretation is consistent with the myth of Narcissus, where the desire to merge with the image must be kept at bay so as to support the life of the subject—any attempt to embrace the "other" by reaching into the water not only destroys the image but may also result in drowning, as some versions of the myth would have it. However, Narcissus's true drama, as Ferenczi also seems to indicate, is precisely his desire to *merge* with his reflection, even at the expense of his own life ("Oh that I might be parted from my own body!"; Ovid 1967, 10). The question thus becomes where to locate the subject's reality: beneath the surface of the water or in the reflection that emanates from it? Freud's primary narcissism, with his positing of an "actual ego" beyond representation, seems to be an attempt to ground Narcissus in some kind of "reality," and yet paradoxically, doing so really depends on fantasy.

Digression: Freud's "Method"

Before I continue my discussion of Freud's line of argument, let me explore the rhetorical nature of his text. Representation, after all, is not just an issue in Freud's thinking "on" narcissism; it also is an issue "of" narcissism if one grants that representation, that is, language, by and large shapes the "content" of any given utterance. For example, positing two egos and two narcissisms, Freud tautologically performs narcissism at the same time that he refers to it. "On Narcissism" not only contains a large number of self-reflective comments but also refers to rhetoric as a method of inquiry, as in this statement: "a science erected on empirical interpretation [will] gladly content itself with nebulous, scarcely imaginable basic concepts, which it hopes to apprehend more clearly in the course of its development" (1914/1986, 21). One such concept, as I have tried to show, is primary narcissism: lacking empirical evidence, it is like a phantom concept, a hypothesis in need of proof, yet essential to all further development. In fact, Freud rarely makes any claims toward scientific method in this metapsychological essay, which he himself admits to be based on the following premise: "in the total absence of any theory of the instincts which would help us to find our bearings, we may be permitted, or rather, it is incumbent upon us to start off by working out some hypothesis to its logical conclusion, until it either breaks down or is confirmed" (21). The "working through" implied by this passage is a rhetorical process, in which language (representation) becomes the essential tool, as opposed to the practice of observing phenomena in the field. Consequently, Freud's rhetoric performs what one could call a "metaphorization" of the biological body, which thereby becomes connected to the realm of fantasy.

To illustrate this point, let me draw attention to Freud's representation of himself as author. Prompted to respond to attacks on his libido theory by Jung, he explains from the very onset why this essay had to be written: he reminds us that, had it not been for Jung's charges, he would have spared himself the trouble of writing what we are about to read: "I have been obliged [by Jung] to enter upon this last discussion, which I would gladly have been spared" (1914/1986, 23). With this initial disclaimer, Freud asserts his authority as a thinker, whose theories are sound enough not to be in need of further explanation; simultaneously, he dramatizes the situation by casting himself in the role of the victim, who is being forced to defend himself. This strategy occurs throughout the essay as Freud leads his reader through a series of largely rhetorical questions whose purpose, presumably, is to convey the impression that he, Freud, already knows the answer, that is, that he has thought "further" than Jung, so that he merely leads the reader through the argument as a courtesy. Still, if one reads the essay carefully, some of the questions precipitated by Jung's attack are legitimate, especially when it comes to differentiating instinct from libido and ego libido from object libido. For instance, Freud asks:

> Why is there any necessity for . . . distinguishing a sexual libido from a non-sexual energy of the ego-instincts? Would not the postulation of a single kind of psychical energy save us all the difficulties of differentiating an energy of the ego-instincts from the ego-libido, and ego-libido from object-libido? (1914/1986, 20)

Instead of an answer, he deflects from the question by referring to a "perceptible uneasiness" (1914/1986, 21) at having to answer such questions in the first place. Revealing the limitations of his theory in the attempt to conceal them, he plays with the reader's expectations of being presented with, ultimately, an authoritative affirmation of his initial stance: "One dislikes the thought of abandoning observation for barren theoretical controversy, but nevertheless one must not shirk an attempt at clarification" (21). This statement makes it seem as if speculation on the part of Freud is not so much a result of his inability to provide proof but rather a result of his having to defend himself against Jung. The rhetorical emphasis of the argument is shifted away from the actual need to provide answers to the assumption that the matter is just "barren theoretical controversy." Such comments reveal to what extent Freud is prepared to "abandon observation," even though he himself claims to dislike this situation. It almost seems as if Freud's rhetorical strategy is to give himself license for rendering hypothetical claims as the "truth"—distracting us from the possibility that Jung's critique may be relevant and that Freud's theory is not as sound as it may appear.

Of course, when it comes to narcissism, appearance is everything. I take this assertion to include the way language can be used to smooth over contradictions, such as the following: Freud expresses the hope that "all our provisional ideas in psychology will presumably some day be based on an organic substructure," yet, at the same time, he wishes "to keep psychology clear from . . . biological lines of thought" (1914/1986, 22). Similarly, he claims that "it is not within the scope of a purely psychological inquiry to penetrate so far behind the borders of physiological research" (27), yet he continues to refer to biology throughout his essay. For example, in the passage on female narcissism, the reader is unsure what to make of his assertion that it must be based on women's "sexual organs," because Freud follows it up with a sentence in which he admits that women's narcissism may also be the result of "social restrictions" (31). Thus, in spite of his apparent self-assuredness, Freud seems confused over issues such as the role of biology in his thinking.

Overall, Freud seems to make an effort to channel biological ways of thinking into "culture," for example, in his similes comparing procreation with man-made laws. The following passage consists of a juxtaposition of scientific and legal terminology:

> The individual himself regards sexuality as one of his own ends; whereas from another point of view he is an appendage to his germ-plasm, at whose disposal he puts his energies in return for a bonus of pleasure. He is the mortal vehicle of a (possibly) immortal substance—like the inheritor of an entailed property, who is only the temporary holder of an estate which survives him. (1914/1986, 22)

The analogy is absurd: nothing could be further from "germ-plasm," which refers to organic growth, than "entailed property," which belongs to culturally determined laws of exchange. And yet, within the context of Freud's explanation of his "method," this passage illustrates the way in which his colorful metaphors deflect from the fact that many of his ideas are not theoretically sound but rather a kind of chain of associations. How else to explain the fact that an almost identical simile in the following paragraph presents the reader with the almost diametrically opposed point of view:

> It may turn out that, most basically and on the longest view, sexual energy—libido—is only the product of a differentiation in the energy at work generally in the mind. But such an assertion has no relevance. . . . This primal identity may well have as little to do with our analytic interests as the primal kinship of all the races of mankind has to do with the proof of kinship required in order to establish a legal right of inheritance. (1914/1986, 23)

Here Freud reverses the previously established analogy and dismisses any further discussion of the previous subject (differentiation of psychic energy) by ridiculing the relevance of his own question, which then appears to be merely rhetorical. One could interpret this tactic as an attempt to deflect the reader's attention from the big picture of biology, which the previous passage about "germ-plasm" so earnestly sets up, but the fact that the passages are related (they both refer to legal rights of inheritance) also makes it seem as if Freud's perspective was consistent. This repetition, in fact, provides a feeling of consistency to an argument which remains, in essence, unclear. Evidently Freud does not have a real answer and therefore directs the reader away from the question. As he himself admits, his "analytic interest" does not consist of a search for "truth" but rather of establishing "proof" in the form of documentation in a system subject to arbitration (law), a system based on language. Language, as I have tried to illustrate, *is* Freud's method, and it is this truth we should keep in mind when looking at object relations, the subject of the next section.

Object Relations

Now that I have drawn attention to the rhetorical nature of Freud's reasoning, let me discuss the central part of his essay: on object relations. This section serves as a bridge (or turning point) between primary narcissism and the ego ideal. Freud begins this middle part of his essay with the admission that narcissism is difficult to study but could be understood indirectly, through "the study of organic disease, of hypochondria and of the erotic life of the sexes" (1914/1986, 25). Compared to schizophrenia, which had been the point of reference for primary narcissism, these three fields of study have in common that they deal with the physical body and the relationships between one's own and other people's bodies. It is through them that Freud addresses the issue of object relations, and it is here that the question of representation arises most forcefully within the overall context of narcissism.

First of all, in the case of "organic disease," libido is said to be withdrawn from others onto oneself, so that an overall "redistribution" of libido occurs within the subject:

> A person who is tormented by organic pain and discomfort gives up his interest in the things of the external world, in so far as they do not concern his suffering. . . . The sick man withdraws his libidinal cathexes back upon his own ego, and sends them out again when he recovers. (1914/1986, 25)

The same principle (i.e., Karl Abraham's *reflexive Rückwendung*) is at work in the second area of study, "hypochondria," which is said to resemble organic disease in everything but the fact that its origin is not organic but imaginary. Here Freud compares hypochondria to neurosis, for example, the highly physicalized symptoms of hysteria, so as to connect the "diseased" to the sexual body: "The familiar prototype of an organ that is painfully tender, that is in some way changed and that is yet not diseased in the ordinary sense, is the genital organ in its states of excitation" (1914/1986, 26). He thus lays the groundwork for his notion of "erotogenicity as a general characteristic of all organs" in support of his thesis that both hypochondria and schizophrenia[3] are characterized by a "damming-up of libido in the ego" (27).

According to Freud, an excess and subsequent "overflow" of ego libido will lead, eventually, to object cathexis (attachment to another person), which in turn provides the rationale for the inexplicable (because hidden) transformation of ego libido into object libido, that is, the shift from primary narcissism to object relations. As Freud suggests, loving oneself may be essential to survival, yet it is bound to lead to illness if libido is not cathected onto objects: "A strong egoism is a protection against falling ill, but in the last resort we must begin to love in order not to fall ill" (1914/1986, 28). With this flip from narcissism to object love, Freud is able to lead into his concept of the ego ideal, which is based on love relationships. As he explains in his discussion of the third area of study of narcissism, "the erotic life of human beings," there are two types of people, the "anaclitic" and the "narcissistic" type, as in the following passage, which is reminiscent of his earlier writings in *Leonardo* and *Three Essays*:

> Psycho-analytic research has revealed a second type, which we were not prepared for finding. We have discovered, especially clearly in people whose libidinal development has suffered some disturbance, such as perverts and homosexuals, that in their later choice of love-objects, they have taken as a model not their mother but their own selves. They are plainly seeking *themselves* as a love-object, and are exhibiting a type of object choice which must be termed "narcissistic." In this observation we have the strongest of the reasons which have led us to adopt the hypothesis of narcissism. (1914/1986, 30)

As I have mentioned earlier, this discovery by Freud is not as "new" as it appears to be—the assumption that homosexual men love "themselves" in the other had been well established (this is one of the very few references to homosexuality in "On Narcissism"); what was new was the finding that now there could be *two* "objects," one's mother *and* oneself.[4] The problem, in other words, was that now one did not only have to think of weaning oneself off one's mother, but also off one's self.

In Freud's "anaclitic" type, a distinction between "sexual instincts" and "ego-instincts" does not yet exist: objects, such as the mother's breast, are identical with the experience of satisfaction they provide, and this satisfaction is, in turn, identical with self-preservation. To argue that the infant's sexual objects are connected to immediate physical satisfaction, Freud refers back to autoeroticism, which he also called "polymorphously perverse" (see Freud 1905/1962, 57). The infant's initial relationship to the world results in a type of object choice based on the model of the nurturing mother, as in the "anaclitic" type (*Anlehnungstypus*[5]): here, the subject falls in love with someone who reminds him of his mother, because he associates this "object" with the satisfaction of his instinctual needs, that is, nurturing. This is the type leading to Klein's version of object relations, where "the development of the infant is governed by mechanisms of introjection and projection. From the beginning the ego introjects objects 'good' and 'bad,' for both of which its mother's breast is the prototype—for good objects when the child obtains it and for bad when it fails him" (Buckley 1986, 40).

However, the second type of "object choice," which Freud introduces as the "narcissistic type," is surprisingly more versatile, as it introduces both the possibility of choice and the strategies of imaginary projection that are so central to Lacan's thinking. Drawn after the old stereotype of the homosexual man who loves his own image, Freud's "narcissistic type" differs from his assumption of primary narcissism in women, as it opens up the possibility of a departure from biological determinism. Now, the issue is not the self but object choice, which is described as indeterminate:

> We have, however, not concluded that human beings are divided into two sharply differentiated groups, according as their object choice conforms to the anaclitic or to the narcissistic type; we assume rather that both kinds of object-choice are open to each individual, though he may show a preference for one or the other. (1914/1986, 31)

Freud's assertion of an essential bisexuality or range of possibilities in regard to object choice broadens the definition of sexuality, so that the "narcissistic type" could be understood as a challenge to the assumption that all sexual relations must be, by definition, heterosexual (i.e., limited to the idea of procreation and therefore exclusive relations with the other sex). Moreover, while helping patients establish successful object relations may be the goal of practitioners of psychoanalysis, "narcissism" undermines the notion that self-love is by definition negative, as it introduces some new possibilities: whereas the anaclitic type loves only "the woman who feeds" or "the man who protects," the narcissistic type has twice as many choices, loving: "a.) what he himself is, i.e., himself; b.) what he himself was; c.) what he himself would like to be; and d.) someone who was once part of himself [mother/child C. R.]" (1914/1986, 33). As Laplanche and Pontalis have pointed out, "these positions are by no means stable but, on the contrary, are caught up in a seesawlike movement which, at the slightest shift of the mirror, can cause an exchange of positions" (1973, 75). Thus narcissistic object choice entails some kind of imaginary projection, including the various possibilities of changes in perspective, whereas anaclitic object choice is reduced to the immediate physical body.

Based on these presuppositions, Freud proceeds with a bold move: he applies his concept of the ego ideal not only to narcissistic object choice but rather to "love" in general. As Lacan has pointed out: "The exact equivalence of the object and the ego-ideal in the love relation is one of the most fundamental notions in Freud's work" (1975, 126). Lacan's observation has been criticized, in particular by Warner (1990), because now narcissism is just as much a function of heterosexual love (the particularity of same-sex desire has been elided). Freud's essay concludes with the statement that "the return of the object-libido to the ego and its transformation into narcissism represents, as it were, a happy love once more; and, on the other hand, it is also true that a real happy love corresponds to the primal condition in which object-libido and ego-libido cannot be distinguished" (1914/1986, 41). In other words, "love" is either a complete fiction or a return to primary narcissism, the state which precedes object relations.

Freud may promote object relations over self-love, yet at the same time, he advocates the ego ideal as the basis of the love relationship, suggesting that object love is successful only when providing us with the illusion that our primary narcissism is restored: "A person who loves has, so to speak, forfeited a part of his narcissism, and it can only be replaced by his being loved" (1914/1986, 30). Based on an economy of exchange, the ego ideal, like currency, works in either direction, a substitute in lieu of the real thing or a way of acquiring it—we either idealize the object that satisfies our needs (as in the anaclitic type) or search for an object that will correspond with our own ideals (as in the narcissistic type). In each instance, our attachment is based on some kind of idealization, where the ego ideal has to match with the love object in order to ensure narcissistic gratification. In this way, a reading of Freud bears out Lacan's view that object relations are not determined by biology but rather by the ego ideal, which is connected to the imaginary and symbolic representations of culture.

Self-Knowledge and Paranoia

On the other hand, the binary opposition of primary narcissism and ego ideal, which I have mapped along the lines of a nature/culture opposition, collapses when it comes to *Selbstbeobachtung,* that is, "self-observation," a phenomenon connected to our critical faculties and related to *Selbstgefühl,* a concept translated by Strachey as "self-regard" (Freud 1914/1986) and, according to Sidney Pulver (1986), often used synonymously with "self-esteem." Self-regard has "a specially intimate dependence on narcissistic libido [as it] appears to us to be an expression of the size of the ego" (Freud 1914/1986, 40); and, as I will show, it is also linked to the physical body, whose role seems more complex than that attributed to it by Lacanian theory (the inaccessible "real"). In accordance with the libido theory, self-regard is presented as measurable in quantitative terms, with an increase in self-love appearing in direct proportion to a decrease of interest in others. Still, as Pulver states in his critique of the use of the term "narcissism" as "a more technical term for self-esteem" in psychoanalytical discourse, this presentation "does not fit the clinical facts. Individuals with high self-esteem are precisely those most able to be more interested in others, while those with low self-esteem are most likely to concentrate upon themselves" (1986, 105). Looking at the way in which Freud's essay arrives at "self-regard," it is less related to the construction of a positive self-image than to the pathological condition called "paranoia" (whose German equivalent, *Beobachtungswahn,* retains the notion of "observation"); which, in turn, is connected to the body itself.

First of all, paranoia is said to arise when it becomes impossible for the individual to ensure narcissistic satisfaction by meeting the requirements of the ego ideal; Freud argues that what we commonly call "conscience" measures the "actual" against the ideal ego and is projected outward, onto others, as a self-critical gaze (he describes this pathology as a form of "rebellion" against the pressure exerted by the ego ideal, i.e., the opinion of parents, teachers, public opinion, etc.). Based on this argument, he identifies "a special psychical agency which performs the task of seeing that narcissistic satisfaction from the ego ideal is ensured and which, with this end in view, constantly watches the actual ego and measures it by this ideal" (1914/1986, 37). This agency, which is essentially related to the ego ideal, is the real precursor to the superego. In paranoia, the self-reflective gaze is directed outward (fear of persecution, the belief that one is under surveillance) but Freud also attributes its characteristics to introspection: "the activity of the mind which has taken over the function of conscience has also placed itself at the service of internal research, which furnishes philosophy with the material for its intellectual operations" (38). Like Tiresias's prophecy in the Ovidian frame narrative, Narcissus's delusion is a form of self-knowledge ("When asked whether this child would live to reach well-ripened age, the seer replied: 'If he never *knows* himself'"; Ovid 1967, 8; my emphasis). On the one hand, seeing becomes synonymous with knowing; on the other hand, the superficial reflection of Narcissus's physique comes to represent more than just his external appearance.

This question of reflection is related to the question of whether the self can perceive itself as "object." Object relations theorists Segal and Bell argue that "when Narcissus gazes at his reflection in the water, he does not know that what he sees is himself" (1991, 162), yet his attraction to the image is precisely the condition of *knowing* that the "other" is a reflection of himself (in Ovid, he cries out "Oh, I am he!"). The question becomes: Is the body secondary to the image, or is the image a mere extension of the body? Depending on whether one places the locus of perception inside or outside the subject or externally, from the position of one who sees *both* the subject and the image, one arrives at the position of a "third," the "monitoring agency" (later known as superego). How exactly does it connect to the physical body?

Let me return for a moment to the libido theory, which posits a psychic apparatus governed by the circulation of libido, a hydraulic model which can be seen, however, as equivalent to the organic body as animated by the circulation of blood. Similar to nineteenth-century representations of the body as a kind of automaton, Freud's mental apparatus appears to be mechanistic, "a device designed for mastering excitations" (1914/1986, 28), whose task is to perform an internal "working-over" of object attachments: objects, real or imaginary, have the purpose of facilitating "an internal draining away of excitations which are incapable of direct discharge outwards" (26), as he explains in his section on object relations. Freud does not at first differentiate between "real" and "imaginary" objects, but he goes on to say that the latter have the potential to lead to the damming up of libido because of a kind of slippage, where the libido "does not remain attached to objects in phantasy, but withdraws onto the ego" (29). Here he distinguishes the ego from other objects, yet he also writes that object libido is withdrawn and reattached to the ego, so it must be some kind of "object." Where Jung had used the term "introversion" (where objects do remain in fantasy) to distinguish between external and internal object relations, Freud introduces narcissism as an objectless state (as described earlier). Now paranoia involves a reattachment of libido onto objects (people perceived as observers and persecutors), and it is described as a transformation of ego libido (which is already object libido withdrawn) into object libido, which Freud calls an attempt at "restoration." Unfortunately, he does not explain how one would be able to tell the difference between paranoia and "normal" object attachments. Paranoia is related to both introspection and object relations, so it becomes difficult to distinguish from "normal" behavior.

Whereas in narcissistic object choice the ego ideal is projected onto the object, paranoia discards the notion of a specific image in favor of the differentiating function itself. This special agency, whose function it is to observe and compare the ego with the ego ideal, represents the position from which the ego may function as an object vis-à-vis the self-observing gaze. According to Lacan, Freud has "spelled out in several places . . . that the fundamental psychic agencies should be primarily conceived of as representing what takes place in a camera, namely as images, which are either virtual or real, produced through its functioning. The organic apparatus represents the mechanism of the camera, and what we apprehend are the images" (Lacan 1975, 123). The ontological status of this "object," the ego, may be uncertain, but there is a connection to the "organic apparatus" that is the physical body, since it is where representation seems to be anchored. Unlike mirror images (reflections) that are fleeting, representations are never identical with their referent, as they include the position of the third, the observer. This position, in turn, would be that of the camera, which records and "fixes" the images so they may be perceived. At least to me it seems that, in the last part of his essay, Freud revises the myth of Narcissus insofar as he focuses on this perspective of a third, whereby the subjectively perceived reflection becomes an actual "object" of representation (we see what Narcissus sees). Like the work of art, this object, the verbal or visual text, may not be real in relation to the three-dimensional reality of the space of the observer, yet it has a physical, material dimension—it is perceived by us, the spectators or readers. The fleetingness of the image becomes fixed and apprehensible through the monitoring agency whose location in Freud is, as I will show in the next section, the physical body.

Reflecting Women

The body and its image, as I have tried to show earlier, are connected, by Freud, to women. The paradox of female narcissism, as Freud defines it, is that the woman is beyond language and representation (the ego ideal), in a state of nature that seems self-enclosed; and at the same time, she is subject to mirroring, to treating her own self as an object, which is evident from statements such as: "It is only themselves that such women love with an intensity comparable to that of the man's love for them. Nor does their need lie in the direction of loving, but of being loved; and the man who fulfills this condition is the one who finds favour with them" (1914/1986, 31). This view not only reiterates the old paradigm of masturbation but also turns the woman's body into the object of the male gaze, where she may either see herself in the mirror or imagine herself being seen by another. It differs from narcissistic object choice as had been ascribed to homosexuality, where one's own physical characteristics are seen in another person, and which can thus be seen as a form of object love; and from the kind of self-observation described earlier, in which there is a third, differentiating function involved. Thus, while narcissism always presupposes the presence of a gaze, narcissistic object choice is not the same as being narcissistic: the former relates to an "other," the latter transforms herself into the "object." Woman's narcissism, in Freud, is between the subject and her own body, gazed at either by herself or by another, and it excludes the position of the third, which is connected to the ego ideal (later superego). Hence, she is in no position to determine what she really looks like:

> We may be tempted to believe a neurotic woman patient when she tells us that it was inevitable she should fall ill, since she is ugly, deformed or lacking in charm, so that no one could love her; but the very next neurotic will teach us better—for she persists in her neurosis and in her aversion to sexuality, although she seems more desirable, and is more desired, than the average woman. (1914/1986, 41)

Here women are portrayed in terms of a confusion between their subjective (internal) self-image and their objective (external) appearance. Although they have been said to be more narcissistic by nature, their neuroses consist in an inability to see themselves in objective terms, for they lack the ability to take on the position of the third, which is instead taken on by Freud. Perhaps through countertransference on the part of the (presumably male) analyst, it is as if his own gaze, which should be (according to him) in a position of objectivity, is "fooled" by these women and their appearances: His assessment of what constitutes neurosis is based on his "discovery" of an inconsistency between self-image and appearance—as if, for some reason, there should be a continuity between people's physical appearance and the way they feel. Freud's likely fear of the attraction the object of his desiring gaze exerts upon him seems apparent: he is "tempted to believe" a woman's statement suggesting consistency between unattractiveness and feelings of worthlessness, then the very next woman "teaches" him a lesson. It is as if his gaze had been corrupted in the process of looking at her and is now in need of correction. In both cases, vision (not what the women have to say) is the measure of all things. Seeing is presented as superior to language, and the issue of who controls the gaze becomes an issue of power in the absence of anything but looks. The cure of the neurotic woman consists of making her see herself as she is seen by Freud, that is, physically desirable (as we have learned before, her biological destiny is to attract men). Freud's women are essentially wanting to be seen as objects, in need of another (male) person's gaze.

In spite of their narcissism, Freud's women seem unable to see themselves as what they truly are: bodies. According to the psychoanalyst Annie Reich, part of women's problems derives from the fact that they often do not have a strong superego (internalized self-reflecting gaze), so they are bound to be insecure and perpetually in need of approval from outside sources. Freud's heterosexual male (whose ego ideal is based on repression) is able to rely on his objectifying gaze to size up women and, if so desired, turn them into love objects—whereas women seem tied to their bodies in ways that prevent them from actually seeing themselves. However, I would argue, the relationship between a female subject and her body is far more complex.

What interests me in the following chapter, on the expressionist poetry of Henriette Hardenberg, is the way in which a woman writer represents a female subject's relationship to her own physical body—for in a way, she articulates the kind of "primary narcissism" deemed mute by Freud; she employs language and representation, which are functions of the ego ideal (superego), to express and represent herself.

Significantly, Freud himself, perhaps unintentionally, discusses "the body" from a slightly different angle, apart from sexual difference and not just in terms of external appearance. Near the end of his essay "On Narcissism," there is a surprising development in regard to the physical body, which Freud, in effect, links to representation. Freud's "body" becomes invested with subjectivity when it is turned into the site of the differentiating function that is to become the superego so that the body is no longer an extratextual, biological entity but rather an active participant in processes of signification. The following passage, which concludes Freud's "discussion of the self-regarding attitude in normal people and neurotics" (1914/1986, 40), is no longer about paranoia but rather about the existence of a "censoring agency" (38) whose location is clearly the physical body itself:

> Silberer, as we know, has shown that in states between sleeping and waking we can directly observe the translation of thoughts into visual images, but that in these circumstances we frequently have a representation, not of a thought-content, but of the actual state (willingness, fatigue, etc.) of the person who is struggling against sleep. . . . If we enter further into the structure of the ego, we may recognize in the ego ideal and in the dynamic utterances of conscience the *dream-censor* . . . self-observation and self-criticism—with such thoughts as "now he is too sleepy to think," "now he is waking up"—[making] a contribution to the dream. (1914/1986, 39)

Freud cites Herbert Silberer's research on dreams (which he also added to a new edition of *The Interpretation of Dreams*) to show that the actual physical state of the dreamer contributes to the content of the dream. Referring to a "dream-censor," the passage confirms the existence of the monitoring agency which had been discussed in conjunction with paranoia. Now Freud suggests that a person's "thought-content" is, in fact, framed by the body, which functions as a container from which its meaning is generated—perhaps not unlike the reservoir in the libido theory, yet with the added possibility that it *is* possible to differentiate by means of representation.

With the body acting as a kind of medium, the "censoring agency" does not only observe but also *translates* "thoughts into visual images." While the reader has been led to believe that the ego ideal represents the internalization of culture in opposition to nature, the body itself is now said to participate in the process so that Freud, in effect, anchors representation in the body.

Dreams, according to *The Interpretation of Dreams* (originally published in 1900), are related to the notion of an "actual self" in that they represent unconscious wishes repressed during waking life. By linking the "censoring agency" to the dreaming body, Freud opens up the possibility of undoing the traditional mind/body opposition. The ego ideal, said in "On Narcissism" to emerge from repression, is now reinscribed into the body in a way that links it back to biological nature, namely, in the form of an individual body. Unlike the sexually determined "natural" body, whose representation is determined by an external gaze, this new body sees itself from within, in terms of its function as a container and transmitter of thoughts—a mediating body to whose perspective, presumably, both men and women have access. The body is no longer determined by sexual difference but rather by its ability to "differentiate" from within, apart from gender.

Freud further developed this notion of a signifying body in *The Ego and the Id* in 1923, where he writes of the ego as "a body ego . . . the projection of a surface" (253, my translation). However, it is here, in relation to narcissism, which is about subject-object boundaries and differentiation, that he represents the body as a locus of agency, where the binary oppositions self/other, subject/object, inside/outside, and so forth collapse, and yet at the same time, representation *is* possible. Just as the hypnagogic state of being "between sleeping and waking" suggests that it is possible to be both conscious and unconscious at the same time, the text that represents the subject as connected to her physical body does not have to be stereotypical in terms of gender but rather may show that "the body" itself is a subjective construct (a text). Like Freud's dreamer, who comes to know what his "willingness, fatigue, etc." *look* like and may "translate" them into his text, the writer attempting to represent his or her "subjectivity" would rely on the physical body, for it is here that the images are generated. At the same time, neither the body nor the image (representation) can be prioritized as an "essence," for there is a continuous interchanging of these two moments: Narcissus knowing and not knowing that the other is himself; seeing and not seeing the image as part of himself; and wanting and not wanting to merge with the image. As will be shown in the next chapter, it is possible to represent this intrinsic connection between the body and representation, even if it may involve, paradoxically, a repudiation of the image.

Part Two : **Avant-Garde Women**

3. A "Body" of Writing: The Voice of Henriette Hardenberg

Beginnings

Freud's concept of "primary narcissism," as I explained in chapter 2, is associated with the primitive, an originary state of nature in which the subject is not yet divided between the body and its image. Unlike Freud's second, more important conceptualization of narcissism, which is associated with the "ego ideal" (and constitutes the basis for Lacanian theory), primary narcissism is beyond representation, that is, language.[1] As a concept, it retroactively constructs a supposed primal unity between oneself and one's surroundings, where the "other" has not yet been brought into existence. This state can be associated, in turn, with the consummation of Narcissus's desire, the experience of merging with the "other" in the waters beneath the reflective surface of the pool. Sandor Ferenczi, as I mentioned in chapter 1, describes it in terms of a fundamental desire to return to the body of the ocean, which he sees as synonymous with the maternal womb. Jeanine Chasseguet-Smirgel, on the other hand, distinguishes between the "maternal cosmic dimension" and "the paternal universe of differentiation" to argue that it is "a question of merging with the mother (of casting off one's Ego in a state of giddy exaltation) by destroying all the representatives of the Father (Reason and Law)" (1989, 142). This distinction is useful insofar as it distinguishes between language and its absence, an issue that particularly concerns me in this chapter, which consists of a series of close readings of poetry by the Jewish-German expressionist Henriette

Hardenberg (1894–1993). As I will demonstrate, Hardenberg's writings not only articulate the "primary narcissism" deemed mute by Freud but also challenge the mind/body opposition that is a dominant paradigm of Western philosophy and, therefore, at the heart of Freud's thinking on narcissism.[2] Hardenberg introduces the body as a landscape, inhabited by a voice that attempts to locate itself in space, engaged in an ongoing process of renegotiating the boundaries that would differentiate it from its environment. Her poetry is about both merging and differentiation, as it represents the fluidity of boundaries associated with water as well as the perpetual motion of the living, breathing body.

Hardenberg was a dancer as well as a poet, and she produced most of her writings when she was very young. Born in Berlin in 1894 under the name of Margarete Rosenberg, she took on a pseudonym when she began to publish her poetry in expressionist journals at age eighteen, in order to obscure this fact from her father, a lawyer. She studied expressionist dance and, at a Dalcroze School performance, met the man who was to become her husband, the expressionist Alfred Wolfenstein. The couple moved to Munich and had a son, and Hardenberg worked as an actor and model. She was befriended by Rainer Maria Rilke, who admired her talent; and in 1918, a volume of her poetry, *Neigungen* (*Inclinations*), was published, followed by further journal publications during the 1920s.[3] In 1930, Hardenberg divorced Wolfenstein and, in 1937, she fled Germany for London to escape from the Nazis, because she was Jewish. Wolfenstein also went into exile, to France, where he committed suicide shortly before the end of the war. Hardenberg remarried, to the German architect and poet Kurt Frankenschwerth and, for over thirty years, worked as a translator and private secretary for an American art historian. Her exile, along with her job as a secretary, may account for the modest body of her work, most of which was produced during her years in Germany. Although she lived until she was almost a hundred years old, most of her writing is from the early part of her life, before her displacement into exile. For most of her remaining life, her work disappeared from the literary marketplace, and it was not until shortly before her death that her work was reedited by Hartmut Vollmer (1988), followed by a posthumous edition (1994) which shows that, in private, she never entirely gave up writing. With the need to survive and support herself, her public voice had become mute and, for all intents and purposes, she seems to have been forced into silence.

In what may be, perhaps, an uncanny harbinger of this development, silence announces itself early on in her poetry, as her voice seeks to transcend the limitations of the physical body by way of exploring the limits of language. According to Marina Krug, who interviewed the poet shortly before her death in London, Hardenberg had always wished to "express her desire for immortality, i.e., for transgressing the limits of her body and her identity"(1994, 7).[4] With this intent, it may not be surprising that there is a parallel between the appearance and "disappearance" of Hardenberg's body as a person, onto and away from the presence on the literary scene of her native language, and the appearance and disappearance of her "body" of work which has, fortunately, now reappeared. Much of Hardenberg's poetry focuses on the body, as it seeks to define its contours within a landscape or to disappear therein—at least one often gets the impression of liminal spaces, of exploring the outermost boundaries of a space that may threaten to swallow an "I" that remains, essentially, indeterminate.

Hardenberg uses what Michael Stark describes as the "lyrical 'I'" of expressionism, which encompasses a split between the "empirical author" and an "anonymous and pre-conscious speaker authority" (Anz and Stark 1982, 632), yet by focusing on the speaker's body, she does not seem to locate this authority outside of the subject.[5] Whereas much of German expressionist poetry is allegorical, representing abstract qualities beyond the immediate image, Hardenberg's text literalizes the body by not treating it as a metaphor.[6] And, while much of German expressionist art depicts movement in the form of anonymous human bodies engaged in athletics or dance, Hardenberg's bodies are not designed to represent something beyond themselves—for example, the hectic pace of modernity—but to draw attention to their own physicality, the strange oscillations between inside and out, upside and down, distant and near, which make up the condition of Narcissus vis-à-vis his reflection. Thus her poetry seems to invoke Freud's "primary narcissism," with its loss of boundaries, yet Hardenberg shows how the body is connected to its representation in language and how language generates and shapes "the body" in turn.

Before I turn to Hardenberg's poetry, let me address the issue of gender that is bound to be at stake in any discussion of the body, which is after all the site of sexual difference. If the body is the place that identifies a given subject as "male" or "female" on the basis of his or her biological makeup, then Hardenberg deconstructs this reductive view of the human subject by refusing to present the reader with a body image, according to feminist philosopher Elizabeth Grosz, "an internalized image or map of the meaning that the body has for the subject [and] for others in its social world" (1994, 39). Whereas culture—including Freud—often reduces women to their physical appearance, Hardenberg's textual bodies are beyond gender insofar as they are never allowed to congeal into the fixity of an image. Here it matters less what the subjects look like from the outside than how they feel within their bodies, whose texture, shape, and size are constantly shifting. Consequently, if "a stabilized body image," as Grosz explains, "requires and entails understanding one's position . . . in space, as well as a set of clear-cut distinctions between the inside and the outside of the body, [and] a position as a sexually determinate subject" (48), Hardenberg's text is in defiance of precisely this position.

Whereas much of her male contemporaries' artistic production seems to be based on "typecasting"—frequently, expressionists created socially marginalized figures, such as the madman, with whom they, as artists, identified[7]—Hardenberg more often than not presents the reader with an "I" whose identity remains unclear. Sexual ambiguity is part of this overall destabilizing of "identity," for in her voice she, at times, "cross-dresses" by using the male persona as a kind of mask, just like her well-known contemporary Else Lasker-Schüler. While I do not believe that women's writing is essentially different from that of men, it may well be that Hardenberg's own experience of being "marginalized as a poet, Jew and woman" (Krug 57)[8] has rendered her more susceptible to the constraints imposed by these social "identities." Beth Bjorklund, in her review in *World Literature Today,* writes that Hardenberg's work not only ranks "among the finest of expressionist prose writing" but is also of "historical interest as the work of one of the few women expressionist writers" (1990, 104). Paul Raabe, Hardenberg's publisher, even goes so far as to claim, in his preface, that Hardenberg, as one of the female expressionists, "corrects our image of this literary period" by introducing us to a "different kind of Expressionism" where "the restrained language of the women Expressionists accompanies the powerfully eloquent revolts of the Expressionist authors."[9] Although the notion of women "accompanying" men seems problematic from today's point of view, it is likely that Hardenberg herself would have agreed with this assessment, since she was among those turn-of-the-century bourgeois feminists who, according to Elke Frederiksen, identified themselves in terms of their biological difference from men—as opposed to proletarian and Anglo-American feminists who demanded social equality to men (Frederiksen 1981, 9).[10] Nevertheless, Hardenberg was not entirely oblivious to her social position, as shown in her 1915 essay, "Nachdem ich Blühers Arbeit über den Antifeminismus gelesen habe" ("After I Have Read

Blüher's Work on Antifeminism"), where she identifies as a working woman to argue for professional equality, against raising girls as mere passive appendixes to their future husbands (1994, 142–44).

If much of German expressionism takes on a decidedly masculine stance, depicting the eruption of powerful emotions and primitive destructive forces as they violently disrupt the surface of nineteenth-century conventions, Hardenberg's writing appears to be softer, more "feminine" in its emphasis on fluidity and shifting boundaries.[11] In accepting these paradigms of "nature," she is certainly guilty of the kind of primitivism that is often attributed to German expressionism, and which is also part of Freud's essay, yet her work also deconstructs such paradigms, as my readings will show momentarily.[12] Thus while Krug interprets Hardenberg's masking of gender identity as a "homoerotic gesture," which she sees in terms of an overall "problematizing of gender identity" (1994, 23), my own interest is to take this kind of reading even further, by demonstrating how Hardenberg struggles to escape "identity" altogether. Considering what one might call a "queer" reading of her poetry, I am interested in the figure of narcissism as a way of drawing attention to the constraints imposed by representation (language) itself.

And, whereas in Freud and Ferenczi narcissism appears to be organized primarily in terms of gender—Freud compares women to children and animals; Ferenczi reduces them to the womb—Hardenberg's text makes this kind of simplistic gender stereotyping impossible by not ever allowing the reader to get a clear "picture" of anything. This, rather than the "desire for a universal connection to humankind" attributed to it by Vollmer (1993, 76),[13] is what constitutes the radical transgressivity of her poetry. At least my sense is that Hardenberg's text simply precludes any such notion of a coherent "self" or "universe."

Her first published poem, "Wir werden" ("We Become"), published in the expressionist journal *Die Aktion* in 1913, is endowed with the rhetorical force of a manifesto, as it combines the first-person perspective of an individual body with the plural of an unidentified "we":

Wir werden herrlich aus Wunsch nach Freiheit.
Der Körper dehnt sich,
Dieses Zerrende nach geahnten Formen
Gibt ihm U e b e r spannung.
Schwere Hüften schauern sich zu langem Wuchse;

Im Straffen beben wir vor innerem Gefühl—
Wir sind so schön im Sehnen, daß wir sterben könnten.
(Hardenberg 1988, 40)

We become magnificent in our wish for freedom.
Our body stretches,
contorting itself toward intuited forms
with t o o m u c h strain.
Heavy hips tremble into growing tall;
Tightening, we quiver with inner feeling—
We are so beautiful in our longing that we could die.[14]

Here beauty does not refer to external appearance but to desire ("longing"). The body is engaged in an effort to transcend itself and is represented through movement rather than as a fixed image. The poem stretches the limits of both language and the body by evoking movement as a means to physical and spiritual transformation. Depending on where one chooses to see its climax—in the visually stressed middle or in the end—it may be either a critique or an affirmation of corporeality.

In fact, the significance of this poem is in the tension it produces between two competing possibilities of interpretation. On the one hand, there seems to be a progression toward the last line, where death is invoked as a kind of ultimate transcendence, a departure (release) from the body. "Too much strain" at the center would then suggest that the opposition between body and mind had to be overcome in favor of another, spiritual dimension. On the other hand, the reader's gaze is drawn toward the central line, which is visually strained to expand through the insertion of extra spaces between letters. This typography makes it seem as if the poem itself were a body continuing to expand; the stress on the middle takes emphasis away from the end. If one sees this line as the focus, it appears as if the poem is really about the tension between two halves.

However, in narrative terms, the poem also tells the story of a transformation from abstraction to embodiment. The shift from an idealistic "wish for freedom" to a subjective state of "inner feeling" is underscored by the shift from a generic "body" to "heavy hips" and a reference to organic "growth." If one sees the central line as the climax, there is a reversal in the narrative: the initially upward movement toward "intuited forms" becomes grounded in a body that redistributes its energy by "trembling," "quivering," and "tightening," as if to condense its substance. In the end, the desire whose "form" had been, at first, only "intuited," appears to be visualized into a self-reflective image that is said to be "beautiful."

Still, while this interpretation may appear to reduce the subject to narcissistic self-reflection along the lines of Freud's view of women, Hardenberg's poem does not provide closure: although the grammatical change from the initial "becoming" (*werden*) and the final "being" (*sein*) would suggest the reaching of a permanent, static condition, the poem ends with the grammatical subjunctive ("we *could* die"). Consequently, it is not so much death as it is the possibility of another (imaginary) space opening up, invoking the possibility of further "stretching" along with the suggestion of a return to the beginning. While it may seem as if the motion of the first half is arrested and fixed into an image, the poem really suggests that the body is involved in an infinite process of "becoming." Rather than reifying the subject into an image ("beauty," which can then be objectified as a property of "femininity"), the text allows us to imagine that her subjectivity cannot ever be contained.

Body/Language

Whereas "Wir werden" resists the figurative by refusing to frame the body from an outside perspective, another 1913 poem, "Requiem," presents the dead body as an image, enveloped by a natural environment. From a first-person perspective, a human figure is transformed into part of the earth in a symbolic burial over the course of the poem:

Meine Mutter sitzt im Blütenschnee,
Vögel in ihren roten Haarbächen spielen Frühling.
Sie läßt sich kosen von Flügeln auf ihrem roten Meere.
Es fließt um sie,
Schüttelt ihren winzigen Körper
Und füllt die alten Augen.
Du, mein rotes Blut im Schnee,
Ich kann nicht zu dir,
Dir nicht helfen aus deinen Lasten.
Du lachst so, Farbe—
Meine Mutter ertrank.
Blüten, küßt ihren Taubenleib,

Vögel, legt euch an sie heran,
Trinkt sie aus, deckt sie zu:
Ihr werdet alle rot, schimmrig braun,
Liebeserde.
(Hardenberg 1988, 14)

My mother sits in a snow of blossoms,
Birds play spring in her hair's red brooks.
She lets herself be caressed by wings on her red sea.
It flows around her,
Shakes her tiny body
And fills up her old eyes.
You, my red blood in the snow,
I cannot come to you,
Cannot help in easing your burden.
You laugh like that, color—
My mother drowned.
Blossoms, kiss her dove's body,
Birds, lie next to her,
Empty her, cover her:
You all are turning red, shimmering brown,
Love earth.

Here the emphasis on the color red, the use of conventional symbols (the "burden" of suffering evoking the figure of Christ; the "dove" symbolizing peace), and the presence of animals that respond to human language endow the body with allegorical significance so that it resembles a kind of religious icon. A requiem for a person, the poem also resonates with past texts from German myth and folklore by using the motif of blood in the snow. For example, in Wolfram von Eschenbach's *Parzival*, Parzival is mesmerized by three drops of blood in the snow because they remind him of his wife; and in the fairy tale "Snow White," the red of Snow White's lips is likened to blood, the whiteness of her skin to snow. In the persona of a daughter, the poet stages her mother's burial in her own voice, which comes into being through the "matrix" of these other texts (which can be seen as having a maternal function). Hence the poem is not only about the physical body, the natural cycle of birth and death, but also about the creation of poetry and symbolic meaning, that is, the way language is "generated" into being. This view is quite in contrast to Freud's version of primary narcissism, where the subject also merges with nature but where language is not at all part of the picture.

The theme of "familiarity" is reiterated, for example, by the shift from *Blütenschnee* (blossom snow) to the phonetically similar *Blut im Schnee* (blood in the snow). The blossoms are turned into blood, whereas the snow becomes the background for the mother, synecdochically addressed as the color red, which takes on human form by "laughing" at the poet. The blood not only suggests the connection between mother and daughter (their "bloodline") but also suffuses the space of the poem in a way that makes it seem as if, metaphorically, the mother's body, which appears at the center of the poem, were "drowned" in it.

The poem's second half explains the mother's cause of death as drowning—which would normally be bloodless—and this part is reminiscent of the "red brooks" and "red sea" from the beginning. The image of water (which Hardenberg uses frequently, as I will show) is reminiscent of the womb; however, it is not, as in Ferenczi, a comforting thought. Considering the extensive use of the color red, it seems as if the mother had actually drowned within her own blood—or as if her daughter, as the poet who creates this text, had buried her with words. To me, it seems as if this "blood" may actually signify poetic language, as it emanates from the central image of the mother's body, which is silent. It is as if the poet attempted to stage the birth of her own creative language from the body of her mother, which in turn disappears into the poem—the last line marks the birth of a new compound word, *Liebeserde* (love earth), an invented word referring to both an abstract human concept and the body of the earth itself.

Hardenberg plays with the tension between opposites: on the one hand, the poem is a requiem, that is, about death; on the other hand, it opens with references to spring, the season of new beginnings. And, although the poem refers to the mother's loss and the speaker's separation from her ("I cannot come to you"), it also invokes the pleasure of composition, as if the poet were to animate the poetic space around her mother's body. At least I would venture to say that the poem evokes the mythical connection to Mother Nature as a self-enclosed narcissistic universe primarily in order to perform its celebration of artistic creation—which would be in keeping with Lou Andreas-Salomé's aforementioned belief that women are more creative because of their narcissism. Here the apparent primitivism is only a means to the end of staging of the coming into being of poetic language. As we encounter the daughter's perspective, it is the poet's desire for self-reflection through representation that is being celebrated here; and in this sense, Hardenberg's "narcissism" is an opening toward, rather than a closing off from, the world.

To support this point, let me compare Hardenberg's active burial ceremony to a similar poem by her contemporary Gottfried Benn, "Schöne Jugend" ("Lovely Childhood") which is part of a compilation of five poems, *Morgue* (1912). Benn's bodies, unlike Hardenberg's, are on display for autopsy; their stories are told from the disengaged perspective of an omniscient narrator and in the past tense:

> Der Mund eines Mädchens, das lange im Schilf gelegen hatte,
> sah so angeknabbert aus.
> Als man die Brust aufbrach, war die Speiseröhre so löcherig.
> Schließlich in einer Laube unter dem Zwerchfell
> fand man ein Nest von jungen Ratten.
> Ein kleines Schwesterchen lag tot.
> Die andern lebten von Leber und Niere,
> tranken das kalte Blut und hatten
> hier eine schöne Jugend verlebt.
> Und schön und schnell kam auch ihr Tod:
> Man warf sie allesamt ins Wasser.
> Ach, wie die kleinen Schnauzen quietschten!
> (Benn 1912, 78)

> The mouth of a girl who had long lain among the reeds
> Looked gnawed away.
> As the breast was cut open, the gullet showed full of holes.
> Finally, in a cavity below the diaphragm
> a nest of young rats was discovered.
> One little sister lay dead.
> The others thrived on liver and kidneys,
> Drank the cold blood and
> enjoyed a lovely childhood here.
> And sweet and swift came their death also:
> They were all thrown into the water together,
> Oh, how the little muzzles squeaked![15]

Like Hardenberg in "Requiem," this poem establishes a connection between nature and the body by positioning it in an animated environment. Again, there are animals that drink blood, but here they are not birds but rats. They drown and are pitied by the poet in the last line, so that we recognize that the title actually refers to their "beautiful youth," not that of the girl. Whereas Hardenberg suggests some kind of mourning, Benn takes an ironic distance to his subject, whose death is described as a biological matter of fact rather than an occasion for spiritual growth. In the last line, the poet's exclamation over the rats' squealing extends this irony, for their death seems gratuitous, considering that they were able to live only by desecrating a human corpse. Benn's poem is devoid of the pathos that often appears in Hardenberg, but he takes a decidedly antihumanist stance, not only by reducing a person's death to part of the food chain but also by using language primarily in referential terms. Although the image is powerful, there are no invented words here, no metaphors or symbols, or any other textual strategies that suggest that the poet is struggling with (or taking pleasure in) language. Instead, this poem seems designed to exhibit the poet's complete control over his material, with the ironic exclamation in the end only adding to the impression of complete detachment on the part of the author.

Benn's poem is shocking because it constitutes both an aesthetic and a moral transgression in a culture whose traditions usually connect death with some kind of spiritual transformation. While, in reality, a viewer who stumbled upon such a scene might avert his or her gaze, this poet takes on the disinterested stance of a scientist to indulge in depicting all the details of the biological process of decomposition, so that the corpse on display seems to be desecrated not so much by the natural behavior of the rats but also by the lack of affect on the part of the observer. Compared to Hardenberg, who mythologizes the body into images of organic wholesomeness, Benn seems to want to decompose the body in a language that dissects rather than connects: instead of burying it, he fragments the corpse into stages, so that one could imagine ever smaller animals, like worms, participating in its disintegration.

According to Walter Sokel, in Benn "nature is . . . reconstructed by the will to demonstrate its hidden essence—total indifference to human values" (1959, 114). Here language becomes a way of stimulating physical excitement, a means to create sensation rather than reflection and thoughtfulness. Benn's horrifying image of a long-dead corpse seems diametrically opposed to Hardenberg's extensive burial ceremony: whereas she plays with and bridges the gap that separates the observer from the observed, Benn widens it by constructing a coldly detached, medical gaze. Language functions as a transport for sensual impressions that appear to be external to it; whereas in Hardenberg, language draws attention to itself.

Hardenberg's body, in other words, expands into language, whereas Benn's reduces itself to shock value.

As I have begun to show in my discussions of "Wir Werden" and "Requiem," Hardenberg's writing represents a desire to transgress the limits of the physiological body (which she has also expressed in her interview with Krug) and, I would argue, the concomitant desire to create an alternative "body" of language. If one considers that women, in this patriarchal culture, are often reduced to their bodies, being thought of as closer to nature and taught to judge themselves in terms of their physical appearance (see my previous discussion of Freud's female patients in "On Narcissism"), Hardenberg's writing shows that the relationship between a subject and her body is complex and shifting. Compared to Benn's text, the body here is not an extratextual, biological referent, but rather a space in and through which the subject struggles to define herself. This struggle, which is ongoing, is represented in the next example, the beginning of the posthumously published 1914 prose text "Eigene Ergänzungen" ("Personal Supplements"), about a dancer named Sran, narrated in the third person:

> Muster drängten nach Erfüllung; sie blieb, ohne sich zu rühren. Sie empfand Druck auf ihrem Körper, jede Lage, Schiene war sie und mußte ihn selbst von sich tragen. Er war ohne Bewegung, mit ihr berührt, und sie wuchs aus sich selbst heraus. Die blauen Farben der Luft schenkten die Angst, und die mächtigen Wiesen drehten sich vorbei; immer war sie deren Mittelpunkt und kannte nicht Entfernung daraus. (Hardenberg 1994, 79)

> Patterns insisted on being carried out; she remained, immobile. She felt pressure on her body, in all positions, a rail she was, on it having to carry away her body, by herself. This body was without movement, in touch with her, and she was growing out of herself. The air's blue colors gave the gift of angst, and powerful meadows passed by in turning; always she was their center and knew no distance from it.

Here Hardenberg describes a process of decentering as the dancer tries to master her body while losing herself in space. Most strikingly, the awkwardness of the language conveys the awkwardness of the dancer's movements, just as if the writer, too, were struggling with the mastery of her medium.

The syntax is unconventional, like German expressionist dance. Compared to ballet, whose orderly structure was designed to give all movements an appearance of ease, expressionist dance is an exploration of movement that may seem erratic and unfamiliar. The kinetic impulse originates from within the body of the dancer, who moves more naturally and in keeping with the way the body is designed. Whereas classical dancers strike poses that seem artificial and outmoded—the vocabulary having remained unchanged since the sixteenth century—modern dancers emphasize organic, less painful patterns of movement. And while classical dancers wear point shoes and jump up high into the air to seem light and ethereal, modern dancers remain barefoot and close to the ground, even when jumping (their focus being on the landing, not on "taking off"). Thus expressionist dance is at once more modern and more primitive than its predecessor, ballet. Hardenberg's poetry, too, is indicative of such an attempt to return to a state of nature. In it "expression" is favored over form, resulting in an archaic grammar. The rhetorical devices used by Hardenberg to achieve this effect are: (1) *parataxis,* that is, the absence of subordinating conjunctions or any conjunctions (so that everything seems to be on the same level), which is mentioned by Bjorklund (1990) as a characteristic feature of expressionist poetry and defined as a property of oral language by Lanham (1991, 108); and (2) *hyperbaton,* a departure from ordinary word order, often in conjunction with the omission of articles, which results in a more dramatic style (e.g., *Schiene war sie* [a rail she was] instead of *Sie war eine Schiene* [she was a rail]). Together they give the impression of a more primitive, immediate language in which the logical relationships implied by grammar are expanded to accommodate the ambiguity of emotional, seemingly irrational ways of thinking. In this sense, the text may be seen as reminiscent of Freud's description of "primary narcissism," which also refers to the primitive; yet here this condition is actually "expressed," that is, performed, not just referred to.

Thus Hardenberg shows her subject to be in search of its own physical boundaries and position in space. The "patterns" that offer themselves are an involuntary body language, making itself felt as "pressure," creating tension from within. At the same time, the dancer seems moved by external forces, as the environment she perceives takes on a life of its own. While the passage locates her at the "center" of the scene, the phrase that she "knows no distance from it" indicates the absence of any periphery that would define the center in the first place. The dancer is decentered, seemingly without physical boundaries (which would differentiate her from her environment)—she seems to permanently negotiate her position in space. However, unlike in Freud and Ferenczi, this is not necessarily a desirable condition.

Clearly, Hardenberg's writing shows the "body" to be at odds with its subject. The dancer is both connected to and alienated from a body that seems rather "unruly," an issue that also extends to her relationship with the surrounding space. If, as Grosz explains, "the body image . . . necessarily involves the relations between the body [and] the surrounding space" (1994, 85), Hardenberg shows these relations to be by no means clear. Instead, she draws attention to the subject's uncertainty—a picture quite different from the supposedly self-satisfied, narcissistic woman Freud had in mind. Hardenberg's dancer is not self-absorbed to the exclusion of her environment—rather, she seeks to establish her connection with the outside world by continually attempting to locate herself in space.

To emphasize the experimental nature of Hardenberg's writing, let me compare it with a 1922 sonnet by Rilke, number 2:28 of "Die Sonette an Orpheus," which is dedicated to the memory of the dancer Wera Ouckama-Knoop, who died young from an illness. There are more similarities between Hardenberg and Rilke than between Hardenberg and Benn, insofar as Rilke seems to have a similar faith in the redemptive power of language. Unlike Benn, who uses language to alienate the reader, focusing on the separation between language and matter, Rilke celebrates the poet with his lyre, whom he portrays as having the power to animate inanimate objects. Like the mythical poet Orpheus, who seeks to bring back his beloved, Eurydice, from the underworld, Rilke does no less than bring back to life the dead Wera through his poetry:

O komm und geh. Du, fast noch Kind, ergänze
für einen Augenblick die Tanzfigur
zum reinen Sternbild einer jener Tänze,
darin wir die dumpf ordnende Natur

vergänglich übertreffen. Denn sie regte
sich völlig hörend nur, da Orpheus sang.
Du warst noch die von damals her Bewegte
und leicht befremdet, wenn ein Baum sich lang

besann, mit dir nach dem Gehör zu gehn.
Du wußtest noch die Stelle, wo die Leier
sich tönend hob—; die unerhörte Mitte.

Für sie versuchtest du die schönen Schritte
und hofftest, einmal zu der heilen Feier
des Freundes Gang und Antlitz hinzudrehen.

Oh, come and go. You, almost a child, complete
for an instant the dance figure, that it be
a pure constellation by which we beat
the order of stupid nature transiently.

Yes, for it was nature that first stirred
fully just to listen to Orpheus' song.
You were excited from the time you heard
and felt it strange when any tree thought long

whether it would go with you by ear.
You still knew where the lyre was raised to call,
Resounding—the unheard-of center. Therefore

you tried the lovely steps and hoped to turn
the eyes and footsteps of your friend to learn
for once the whole and healing festival.[16]

The poem is addressed to Wera, but since she no longer has a physical body, the poet calls her spirit into existence with his use of rhythm and melody. He recalls her from the dead by making her dance to his lyre, so that her body transforms itself into music, as it reappears from beyond the grave. However, unlike Hardenberg's dancers in "Wir werden" and "Eigene Ergänzungen," Wera is not the active subject of her dance but rather an extension of Orpheus, upon whose music her performance depends. Her movements are not spontaneous, motivated from within, but directed by his lyre, so that the poem is not so much a representation of Wera herself as it is a representation of the poet's powers to move and transform. Unlike Hardenberg's self-reflectively "narcissistic" voice, in which we cannot tell the point of view from which the poem is written, Rilke clearly objectifies his dancer (as Freud does his female patients). Wera, unlike Benn's corpse, which is a mere physical shell, is a sign of essence, with her artistry being superior to the *dumpf ordnende Natur* (literally, "dully organizing nature"), yet she is not so much herself creative as she is a performer, a kind of puppet whose dance illustrates the sound of the poet's lyre. Whereas in Hardenberg the dancer's movement seems motivated from within, Rilke's sonnet provides a clear pattern into which she may fit her steps. The rhythm conveys her steps as repeating the back and forth of *O komm und geh'* in the enjambment of the stanzas and the alliterative patterns (e.g., *mit dir/tönend—Mitte/schöne*), and while it may seem as if she were adding her own interpretation to the end rhymes and basic meter, the repeated references to her "listening" (*hören*) clearly denote her as a passive subject.

Like a ballet dancer, who listens and counts her steps, Wera follows the sound of the lyre, which provides her with access to the *unerhörte Mitte*, the center that is "unheard-of." This latter word, in German, has scandalous connotations, so that one gets the impression that something inaccessible ("unheard of") is being accessed and penetrated, primarily through the impact of the poet's lyre. Hardenberg's dancer texts, on the other hand, do not have such phallic connotations, for they do not claim to create a center. Lacking orderly patterns, they are about the subject's decentering and lack of harmony, where there is "too much strain," and seemingly climactic moments lead only to further contortions. Whereas Rilke's musical structure creates a sense of stability and harmony, the bodies in Hardenberg's texts lack the centering effect of an external subject who would control and direct their physical movement. Like Narcissus, and unlike Wera, her subject can never be quite sure where she herself ends and "the other" begins.

In fact, Sran, the dancer from "Eigene Ergänzungen," dances behind closed curtains after the performance is over, and she ends up fighting with her own body to the extent that finally, she erupts into a scream, fearing that her arms might break from the tension of having to carry herself. No such thing could happen to Wera, but then again one cannot be sure that Wera is truly meant to be alive.

At least to me it seems that the issue of what it means to be alive within one's own body is central to Hardenberg's text, which does not shy away from representing the awkwardness of movement, a sense of being dislocated in space, and the feeling that one's body is somehow never quite one's own. Hardenberg shows the impetus of movement to come from within, on impulse, almost involuntarily. Her dancer feels pressure (*Druck*) and "grows out of herself" only as a way to release the tension she has built up inside, not to inhabit some abstract form or image. Again, one might draw a parallel to the comparison between classical ballet, with its predetermined forms (such as arabesque) that have to be compared against the image in the mirror, and expressionist dance, with its emphasis on the internal workings of the body. And again, one might observe the degree to which Hardenberg departs from traditional paradigms of gender. Ultimately it seems that the body as matter is to be transcended in both Rilke and Freud, whereas Hardenberg's work seems really engaged in the effort to verbalize body language, to show that body and mind are connected. It is here that Hardenberg's text seems more sophisticated than Freud's, for his separation between language and "nature" is what renders the body, in effect, inarticulate.

Self–Other

One of my initial claims for this chapter was that Hardenberg's text is in defiance of creating a "body image." Grosz's claim that "the body image is the condition of the subject's access to spatiality" (1994, 85) is compromised by the fact that, in Hardenberg, spaces are largely fantastic. Bodies expand and contract in an unpredictable fashion, and there is the constant reminder that it is language that creates these bodies in the first place. If one thinks of Lacan's assessment, in "The Mirror Stage," that the subject is actually fragmented, having assumed "the armour of an alienating identity" in the form of a body image only because it has been "caught up in the lure of spatial identification" so that the body image is, really, "orthopaedic" (1977, 4), Hardenberg's poetry seems, paradoxically, more true to the subject's physical sense of the subject's body than any image could be. What we are confronted with, in other words, are texts that constitute "bodies" in their own right. This condition is manifested by the fact that Hardenberg's subjects are not self-enclosed, that is, in opposition to their reflection, but rather profoundly engaged with their surroundings.

What interests me in the following section is the relation to the "other," which I have so far not yet addressed in relation to Hardenberg's writings. As long as there is only a single subject present on the scene, matters seem less complicated, but once another is introduced, the question then becomes: How real is it? The question of narcissism continues in regard to what extent the other is merely a reflection of the self and to what extent there is a true "other," which resists assimilation into the self. Let me begin by looking at the following poem, which was published underneath "Wir werden" in 1913 in *Die Aktion* and later came to be titled "Love" ("Liebe"). Written from the perspective of an omniscient narrator, it seems to be about the relationship between two people, a couple walking through a forest and, evidently, tortured by nature and their very bodies:

Zwei gehen nackt durch einen Wald;
Sie schreiten hoch
Und lachen mit den Vogelschreien.
Der wunde rasende Klang würgt ihre Kehlen.
In ihren Häuten brennen sie eisig,
Atemstücke brechen aus verschütteten Massen.
Menschen reißen sich höher:
Ihr Kopf starrt vor;
Augen, die tief bluten,
Stürzen in Schädel zurück.
Arme und Beine sind Stricke;
Sie meistern krachende Leiber.
Zwei fühlen sich breit verschmelzen und berühren sich nicht.
Sie schlingen sich um Bäume
Und brechen entzwei.
(Hardenberg 1988, 31)

Two walk naked in a forest,
strutting highly, laughing with the birds' cries.
The sore, burning sound chokes their throats.
They burn like ice in their skins,
Pieces of breath break away from buried masses.
Humans tear themselves further upward:
Their head staring forward;
Eyes bleeding deeply
Fall backward into skulls.
Arms and legs are ropes;
mastering crashing bodies.
Two feel themselves melting widely into one another but do not touch.
They coil around trees
And break in two.

First of all, it is striking that these "two" appear to be like one, for they are not differentiated except by the grammatical plural—that is, until the last three lines, where the drama of "breaking apart" unfolds through the attempt to "melt into one another" (paradoxically without touching). The poem ends as it began, with *zwei* (which means "two," whereas *entzwei* means "apart"), suggesting both the completion of a circle and an essential division. Obviously, there are biblical connotations of Adam and Eve tasting from the tree of knowledge (around which the lovers "coil" like the snake), to be expulsed from the garden of Eden. However, there is no real before-and-after narrative here; while they seem to be a primal unity as they strut through the forest, their story is anything but romantic: their nakedness makes them vulnerable, and although they act as if they belong to nature by laughing with the birds, their laughter is shrill and painful. In fact, the scene becomes increasingly artificial as it turns out that they are not alone (suddenly, masses of human beings are present) and that their bleeding eyes pop out of their skulls as if they were puppets, alienated from both themselves and one another. The poem's harsh sound pattern also conveys this rather violent atmosphere, with consonant pairs mimicking the sounds of breaking and grinding, such as "-ck," "-rz," "-schr," "-rgt" (that could be attributed to either trees or bones), and vowels that sound shrill and hysterical, such as "-ü" and "-ei," indicating both the cries of the birds and those of the human beings, who seem so tortured that their breaking apart at the end almost comes across as a release. In truth, it seems, primal unity never existed, and the image of the other is merely the self divided.

However, this poem is an exception among the many poems about relationships written by Hardenberg, most of which are decidedly more playful and erotic. Whereas "Liebe" seems to be about self-alienation, the next example, the erotic poem "Gefühl" ("Feeling"), published in *Die Aktion* in 1914, shows how the process of defining a "self" invokes the presence of an "other." The poem uses the image of water, which offers the possibility of merging, yet unlike Freud's narcissistically self-enclosed monad, Hardenberg's "I" is open to the "you," to which it seems profoundly connected without there being the need for symbiotic fusion:

Meine Stirn ist dein großer See.
Du mußt mich lieben.
Meine Linien führe ich an dich heran,
Daß sie dich rühren.
Du bist zu weit zu erreichen an allen Seiten,
Und meine Tiefen dehnen sich langsam;
Ich kann sie nicht bringen,

Wenn ich zart bin.
So schmerzen wir uns immer,
Ich bin dein matter, hängender See,
Dein nasser, glitzernder Abendstern.
(Hardenberg 1988, 41)

My forehead is your large lake.
You must love me.
I am guiding my features toward you,
So they will move you.
You are too wide to be reached on all sides,
And my depths extend gradually;
I cannot bring them,
When I am tender.
This is how we always hurt each other,
I am your weary, hanging lake,
your wet, glistening evening star.

Using the visual metaphor of geometry, the poem suggests the possibility of designing one's own physical shape. The "I" addresses the "you" in terms of lines, sides, and depths. The first line indicates intimate proximity, switching the point of view and expanding the perspective from a part of the speaker's body, the "forehead," to a part of the landscape, a "lake." (Again, the body merges with its environment.) The image of the lake is repeated in the next-to-last line and becomes a metaphor in the last line. The body of the text seems written from the perspective of the lake whose contours suggest the shape of a human body, starting with the "forehead" and extending into "depths." This effect is achieved through the use of verbs from both the register of landscape architecture ("to guide," "to reach," "to bring") and the register of emotions ("to love," "to move," "to hurt"). The relationship between the two spaces, body and lake, is organic. The voice, speaking as the lake, is focused on the other whom it seems to want to envelop.

Again, the relationship between the subject and her body is depicted as complex, a far cry from Freud's patients, who are defined only from an external, objectifying point of view. Beyond the subject's control, on the one hand, the body appears constructed to be rewritten, on the other. Writing is a form of distancing oneself from what one wishes to represent; representations are by definition not identical with their referents. Consequently, after the approach of the other in the first four lines, there is a withdrawal. The "I" and the "you" disconnect and the "I" is transformed into a distant star, a poetic metaphor. The reader is made aware of the discrepancy between an "I" whose existence seems bound up with an other and an "I" that constitutes itself through language, but unlike in Freud, this language emanates from the subject herself. The star is a signifier for distance and differentiation, as well as for the construction of figurative language. Given that the star is catachrestic in relation to the metaphoric "body" represented by the actual poem, it provides the perspective necessary to evoke the illusion of depth, which thus presents the reader with the impression of a three-dimensional body emerging from this process of poetic self-expression. The "other," as I have tried to show, is always already part of this, both in terms of the poem's content, and in terms of the reader who witnesses the subject's workings from within.

As I have mentioned, water figures prominently within the body of Hardenberg's text. The poem I just discussed features a voice speaking in the form of a lake; the next example, also a love story, is the poetic prose text "Tröstung" ("Consolation") also published in *Die Aktion* in 1914. It is worth quoting in full, as it represents the struggle of an "I" to emerge from a preverbal state of nature, thereby dramatizing the shift from a natural to a "written" body; and providing a clear example of an opposition to Freud's "primary narcissism," where the aim is to validate rather than deconstruct "nature":

> Die Kröten schreien im Teich, sie müssen schlafen, es ist Winter. Meine Haut ist starkes Eis, viele Meter um mich herum liegt es einsam, und der Kopf hängt darüber hinaus und schlägt nach allen Seiten auf. Ich denke ganz Bestimmtes, ganz Dasselbe, und der Kopf schlägt langsamer, heftiger. Weit hinten seh ich einen hellen Morgen gehen, der sollte zu mir mit seinem Licht, den Strahlenwald durch meine toten Berge führen, den armen Kopf in seine warmen Täler legen, obgleich es ihnen wehe tut, den abgeschnittenen Stumpf in ihrem frischen Schoß zu halten. Gesund zu wachsen würde er mir helfen, Glieder bewegen, Gedanken rühren in meiner Körperkraft.
>
> Der Sonnenfreund war dicht zu meinem Königshaupt gekommen, und als er das Kranke sah, zog er seine schützenden Tücher auf meinem gefrorenen Körper aus und sagte: ich will auf deinen kalten Flächen gehen, bis du die Arme zu mir legen kannst, bis dein dunkel Seidenauge, in seinen grünen Sümpfen verloren, mir seine Schmerzen zu tragen erlaubt.

Das war meine Liebe, die aus Enge gewachsen war, die herausstieß, die weiter wurde als meine riesenkalten Flächen, die mich einmal besiegte.

Blut fließt, und Menschen, die vorübergehen, schütteln sich. (Hardenberg 1988, 64)

The toads scream in the pond, they must sleep, it is winter. My skin is strong ice, lying lonely for many yards around me, and my head hangs down from above, falling and striking all sides. I think about certain things, the very same things, and my head beats down more slowly, more forcefully. From afar I see a bright morning walking, he should come to me with his light, to lead the forest of beams through my dead mountains, to lay my poor head into his warm valleys, although it hurts them to hold in their renewed lap the stump that was cut off. If it would grow healthily, it would help me to move my limbs, to stir thoughts with the strength of my body.

The sun friend had come close to my royal head, and when he saw where it was ill, he took off his protective cloths, spread them on my frozen body, and said: I want to walk on your cold planes until you can lay your arms toward me, until your dark silk eye, lost in its green swamps, will allow me to carry its pain.

This was my love, which had grown from restrictedness, which thrust out, which became larger than my huge cold planes, which defeated me once.

Blood is being shed and people who pass by are shuddering.

The beginning evokes a primal scene: the world is an organic totality with animals, plants, climate, water, and mountains. It is as if nature itself were speaking, appearing as a creature both human and plantlike, and, somehow, frozen within a pond. It is as if the body *were* the environment, and it remains unclear, grammatically, what "I" and "my body" refer to. Are they identical, or is this the story of an individual "body" trying to break free from the confines of the landscape? Either way, the reader remains confused as to who "I" is. Is "I" part of or different from the landscape it inhabits, and how exactly does "I" inhabit it? Like Freud's autoeroticism, in which the infant cannot yet conceive of itself as separate from its environment, Hardenberg's subject here reenacts a state of nature. However, Hardenberg makes it clear that this state is not at all "natural" in the empirical sense. The reader is quickly reminded that what we are dealing with is a work of art.

Whereas the first sentence is written from an omniscient narrative perspective, the second sentence introduces the narrator ("me"), and it is only in the third sentence that the unmodified, subjective "I" appears. It becomes clear that this is an inner landscape, one that bears no resemblance to external, objective reality.[17] Evidently, the text belongs to the realm of fantasy: the toads can be associated with frogs who appear in fairy tales. The subjective, dreamlike nature of this anthropomorphized landscape is highlighted by the absence of conjunctions, where each phrase introduces a whole new reality (rather than presenting the reader with an ongoing narrative).

However, the text is in generic disguise: like the frog who turns into a prince (or vice versa), it starts out as a prose poem and then gradually turns into an actual tale. Retroactively identified as a love story, it may be read as the story of breaking out of the confines of one's natural body in order to enter the "body" of grammar. In the middle of the text, there is a shift from present to past tense, an intrusion of temporality which marks the point where the voice is liberated by her lover, the morning light. He, too, emerges from the environment to become a separate entity, yet to the "I," who is the landscape, he is an outsider coming in. While the story appears to be romantic, it contains this "rupture" (shift in tenses) in the middle of the text, which forces the reader to recognize the difference between mythical and chronological time (which is preceded by the use of the subjunctive, i.e., *würde* [would] to suggest the difference between fantasy and reality, i.e., the possibility of differentiation).

The next-to-last sentence states that the speaker's love has "defeated" her. The syntax collapses, the "I" disappears, and there is "blood." Suddenly, there are "people" passing by, as if another world (society) had appeared. Hardenberg edited this final sentence from a later publication, perhaps because its effect only increases that of the previous sentence, where the narrator already distances herself from the original scene. Both final sentences create the impression that the story is about the loss of an original state of nature, yet this state is shown not to have existed in the first place, as the reader comes to realize that she or he has been reading a story. As the storyteller reveals her presence, the text retroactively comes to be about "writing." The subject differentiates herself from "nature" by taking the position of an author. The text may be read as a fantasy about the physical origins of one's voice or as an erotic fantasy about writing, considering, for example, that the lover traverses the surface of the subject's skin in a kind of "writing." What it cannot be read as, however, is a straightforward rendering of a subject evolving from a state of nature. Compared to Freud's evolutionary thinking, Hardenberg plays with our sense of reality.

Skin, for example, is a central metaphor in "Tröstung." It demarcates the border between inside and outside, enveloping the body as its outermost layer, a surface suggesting depth, acting as a protective coat, and suggesting, in turn, containment and impenetrability. Spatialized into a site, it eliminates the difference between inside and outside and at the same time, paradoxically, continues to represent the borderline that keeps this difference in place. By representing the body's surface as ice, thin and fragile, Hardenberg suggests that it covers the depth of an invisible life taking place underneath. There is something monstrous about this, suggesting the possibility of an eruption from beneath the surface. The voice, after all, emerges from primal unity and then painfully differentiates herself from the mold into which she has been cast. "Tröstung" can be read as both a liberation from and loss of primal unity with nature. It is about ice that turns into a swamp, a transformation from a form that is too hard into a substance that has no form and thus could threaten to engulf the subject. Perhaps this is why, in the end, the narrator's voice seizes control, making it her story ("das war meine Liebe"), and allowing the reader to realize that what we have been dealing with all along is language. Unlike Freud, who seems similarly conflicted about his relation to biology (yet unwilling to acknowledge it), Hardenberg works through this conflict by showing "nature" to be a function of language. Rather than assuming, as Freud does, that nature is "out there," to be studied and rendered objectively (scientifically), Hardenberg allows us to realize that our image of nature is more often shaped by our own—often culturally determined—fantasies, motivated by desires and anxieties, not empirical reality. In this sense, "Tröstung" is not about "nature" as an extratextual, biological referent, but a tale about storytelling, that is, language. The "skin" resembles the text, a series of signifiers that create a surface (texture); and the "content" of the story (signified) becomes subject to the author's control. Thus Hardenberg shows not only how the body emerges from nature into language but also how language shapes the subject (which, after all, may be the "consolation" the title refers to).

However, contrary to Ferenczi, whose body of water—the great womb of the ocean—is about undifferentiation (and therefore, as Gast [1992] has observed, desexualizes the subject of narcissism), Hardenberg maintains the erotic tension between self and other, the struggle and the pleasure connected to the oscillation between merging and differentiation that constitutes Narcissus's desire. Hardenberg's voice emerges from (rather than merging with) the primordial, mythical realm, namely, by way of encountering an "other" to herself. Compared to Freud's "primary narcissism," which claims that the (female narcissistic) subject is cooped up within herself, unable to develop object relations (relationships to others), Hardenberg shows that there is an essential connection between self and other, and there exists an ongoing erotic tension within narcissism. Narcissism here no longer appears as a distant point in time (to be envied by those who have lost it) but rather as an ongoing characteristic of subjectivity itself. The distinction between primary narcissism and later versions of narcissism (on which I will elaborate in the following chapters) may thus become obsolete.

Expressionist aesthetics, particularly Hardenberg's, allow apparent contradictions to exist side by side, as the logic of spatiotemporal relations is suspended in favor of a more fantastic, artistically created universe. Unlike practitioners of its later incarnation, "abstract expressionism," early German expressionists depicted scenes and figures that resembled reality yet were, in effect, nonrepresentational. While this departure from realism may seem similar to the unconscious language of dreams identified by Freud, expressionists did not consider their work as a result of repressed material coming to the fore (such as the surrealists, whom I will discuss in chapter 5); rather, they were interested in showing that "reality" is what we perceive and that this perception is always also subjective. They thus represent a departure from the objective, scientific paradigm to which Freud continued to adhere in spite of his acknowledgment of the irrational (which he sought to understand and master rather than celebrate).

Let me illustrate this idea with the help of a German expressionist painting, the 1913 work *Glassy Day* by Erich Heckel of *Die Brücke* (see next page), which illustrates this tension between merging and differentiation that characterizes both narcissism and Hardenberg's writing. Here the two halves of the lake and the sky seem to be reflective of one another, yet there is only a thin, seemingly fragile line that separates them from being a single, undifferentiated space. If it were not for this line (which seems reminiscent of the skin in "Tröstung"), it would be difficult to tell where the lake ends and the sky begins. Through the line, however, it becomes possible to differentiate between the two spaces, to see them as reflective of one another. As for the female figure in the lower left-hand corner, she seems to be part

Erich Heckel, *Glassy Day*

of her environment, so it is difficult to tell whether she is to be considered the perceiving subject or one among the objects of the landscape. If one follows Lou Andreas-Salomé's description of Narcissus as someone who "does not see only himself in the water but himself as part of everything around him" (1921, 366), one could call this figure a female Narcissus, yet she does not have eyes to see either herself or her surroundings. Correspondingly, she is the only element in the painting that does not have a reflection (the two extensions below her knees are her calves, as her legs continue into the water). Although human, she seems connected to the surrounding landscape, for example, through her posture, which mimics the angular, geometric shapes around her. Similarly, nature seems to reflect her shape, mainly in the form of the rocks, which look like breasts. Interestingly, it is the female figure's round shape that bears the closest resemblance to actual nature, whose forms in reality tend to be round, not angular. Considering the shapes and colors of the supposedly "natural" elements in the painting, they seem rather artificial, so that, similar to the condition of Narcissus, it becomes difficult for the viewer to distinguish between what is nature and what is art. As I would argue, this play between shifting perspectives and boundaries is the play between fusion and differentiation that also takes place in Hardenberg's writing.

The last example, "Tröstung," in particular, could be read not only in contrast to Ferenczi's model of the subject's desire for fusion (in *Thalassa,* the subject wishes to merge; in "Tröstung," a voice emerges) but, once again, in contrast to Benn. According to Sokel, Benn was a "self-hating" intellectual who considered retrogression into a primordial swamp a viable solution to the problem of intellectual activity:

> By universalizing his personal plight into the plight of mankind and postulating retrogression as an absolute ideal, the poet is not merely enabled to act in revolt, but to establish contact with a deeper layer of life, which corresponds closely to Bergson's vitalist Reality and to Jung's concept of the "collective unconscious." A spontaneous feeling wells up, breaking the crust of a cerebralized self, and beckons like the mirage of the blue ocean in desert wastes. *Südlichkeit* (Southernness) is the leitmotiv of these visions. It is associated with a tropical bliss of inactivity and sensual release. (Sokel 1959, 92)

It seems to be this anti-intellectual concept of "Southernness" (*Südlichkeit*) by Benn that Hardenberg evokes in her 1918 poem "Südliches Herz" ("Southern Heart") which was published in 1920 in *Die Erhebung* and subsequently selected by Benn for his 1955 anthology *Lyrik des expressionistischen Jahrzehnts* (where Hardenberg is the only female author apart from Lasker-Schüler). Vollmer has connected this poem to Hardenberg's feelings for Rilke, which he describes based on her diary entries as "between devoted fascination and revering distance" ("zwischen hingebungsvoller Fascination und ehrfürchtiger Distanz"; Vollmer 1993, 76). While there does not seem to have been a physical relationship between the two of them, the poem appears to be quite erotic, essentially a description of sexual intercourse. What is unusual, however, is that the speaking voice takes on both male and female characteristics so that the poem, in effect, undoes any preconceived notions of sexual difference:

Blüte sitzt tief,
Bergspitzen biegen sich hin,
Wind ausgeruht liegt,
Der Baum steht starr.

Da plötzlich erblüht
Mitten ins Herz hinein
Brennend sitzt du mir im Baum.

Nirgend ist Ruhe in mir,
In Flammen schreie ich auf,
Ein Meer ist in allem bewegt.

Da zucken auch sie,
Blüte und Baum,
Schon rot von ihrer Süße.
(Hardenberg 1988, 53)

Blossom sits deeply,
Mountaintips bend themselves into shape,
Wind lies calmly,
The tree stands rigidly.

Then suddenly, comes into bloom
Right into the middle of the heart
Burning, you are sitting in my tree.

Nowhere inside me is calm,
I cry out from within the flames,
an ocean is moving all over.

Then they, too, are twitching,
Blossom and tree,
Already red from being so sweet.

"Südliches Herz" seems to be about the penetration of an "I" by a "you" in the guise of a tree trunk entering an ocean. The blossom and mountaintops can be read as vagina and breasts, the rigid-standing tree as an erect penis, and the ocean in flames as a female orgasm. However, "you are sitting in my tree" also suggests that the supposedly female speaker *is* the phallus, as she becomes the tree which is, in turn, penetrated.

Once again, the poem decenters the subject. It positions the "I" in a fixed place, at the heart of the tree. The heart being a human reference, it is positioned geographically in the title as well ("Southern"), to appear as part of a landscape. If one reads this landscape as a metaphor of the human body consisting of male and female sexual organs, the title suggests a displacement of the heart southward, to the genitals. Considering the uncertainty over whether they are both in the tree or whether they *are* the tree, one could interpret the encounter between the "I" and the "you" as intercourse within a single body dividing itself, a statement on the ambiguity of gender. Two selves may exist, inhabiting the tree like a body that makes them appear as one, yet it remains possible to interpret the poem literally, so that the objects in the environment remain separate from the speaking "I." In such a reading, the poem would simply describe not a sexual encounter between two entities but a single cataclysmic event in nature that submerges the "I" within a flood of images. There would be a shift in perspective, from a panoramic view to a focus on the heart of the tree; the poem would begin and end with an impersonal, omniscient narrative perspective; and the "I" that appears and disappears in the second and third stanza would be swept away by the greater force of nature. In this second reading, "nature" appears more powerful than the individual, whose subjectivity (and gender) are to remain in the dark—an interpretation which revises Freud's view of nature as associated specifically with the female.

Hardenberg, by creating competing possibilities of interpretation (as in her first poem, "Wir werden"), enables us to see that any interpretation, including Freud's, can be only one version of the "truth." Truth, in Hardenberg, is poetic, subject to shifting interpretations that depend on the reader's expectations and desires. She works with this tension also in "Gefühl," where she draws attention to the issue of language (highlighted by the question of what "I" is speaking); and in "Eigene Ergänzungen" and "Tröstung," where she causes doubt over the body's shape and location in relation to its environment. Clearly Hardenberg's texts upset the spatial boundaries between inside and outside, surface and depth, self and other, with metaphors of movement. Eruption and withdrawal delineate the body in a state of suspense, often in relation to an "other" who enters the internal landscape. Most important with respect to narcissism, her "I" refuses to take on a definitive physical shape that could be visualized by the reader as a "body image."

Depersonalization

One way in which the absence of visualization can be made apparent is, literally, through the depiction of blindness. The following poem, "Blinder Mann" ("Blind Man"), from 1918, is grouped among Hardenberg's antiwar poems and is among those in which the poet uses a masculine persona. Her friend Richard Oehring actually complained about it in a letter: "I do find it rather strange that you write so many poems from the male point of view, considering that, to me, your girlishness, in particular, seemed to be the essence of you" ("Etwas wunderlich finde ich es, daß Sie soviel Gedichte vom Standpunkt des Mannes aus schreiben, obwohl ja gerade erst Ihre Mädchenhaftigkeit so wesentlich mir an Ihnen erschien"; Hardenberg 1988, 147). Oehring seems to have missed the point insofar as Hardenberg precisely did *not* wish to represent an "essence" of gender. Similarly, Bjorklund, who attributes the use of the masculine persona to a supposed "difficulty of saying 'I' for women" (1990, 104), does not seem to have taken into account that the number of texts in which Hardenberg uses a genderless or feminine "I" is disproportionately higher and that most of the poems written in the masculine persona depict the male as injured or disabled, thereby undermining traditional conceptions of masculinity. It seems to me that the act of taking on a cross-gendered persona merely confirms the point made in the other poems as well, namely, that a persona is a kind of mask, behind which dwells a much more complex, often elusive subject, which ultimately refuses to be categorized in terms of any preexisting roles of gender. If anything, this mask provides some kind of stability in what is, essentially, a completely destabilized universe, where blindness becomes synonymous with the absence of stability (i.e., a fixed body image):

Ich ging nur tastend,
Blutige Finger über Leben legend,
Schleichende Füße öffneten keinen Weg.

Auf mir Hügel gebaut,
Durch mich Täler,
Wandern die Hände über gepreßtes Land.

Keine Blicke stürzten in andere hin,
Aus mir standen nicht Morgen auf
Und nicht sanfte Laternen zur Nacht.

Lächeln nicht zum Horizont,
Aus der Welt,
Hinein drang ich auf umringende Wand.

Winterfenster, glitzernd gespannt,
Erwarte ich das Zerrissensein—
Zum Frühling zu gehen,

Bloß wie ein Kind aus dem Mutterleib
Aus mir selbst zu erstehen,
Zu Leben und Tod.
(Hardenberg 1988, 28)

I walked only gropingly,
Laying bloody fingers across life,
Hovering feet did not open a path.

Upon me, hills were built,
Through me, valleys,
Hands wandering across compressed grounds.

Glances did not hurl themselves into others,
Mornings did not rise from me
Nor soft lanterns for the night.

Smiling not toward the horizon,
Out of this world,
Inside I pressed, onto a surrounding wall.

Winter windows, tensely glistening,
I am waiting to be torn apart—
To walk toward spring,

Naked, like a child from the womb
To bring myself into existence,
Into life and death.

Here the figure (who can be identified as male only in the title) experiences a state of bodilessness, due to a lack of visual perception. "Blinder Mann" suggests injury rather than innate blindness: the poem's opening lines present someone with bloody fingers, who has difficulties in finding his way. This lack of external orientation, in turn, seems to lead to the construction of an interior space, yet it remains unclear whether this space provides shelter or confinement. While the poem ends with a reference to birth that could be construed as hopeful ("to bring myself into existence"), it contains a total of five negations (*keinen, keine, nicht, nicht, nicht*), so that the overall impression is hopelessness. This emphasis on the negative would be consistent with the impression that the poem represents an injured soldier, a narcissistic wound if ever there was one (Freud's "The Uncanny," which I will mention in more detail in chapter 5, specifically connects narcissism to the loss of one's eyesight).

Again Hardenberg plays with competing interpretations: for instance, while the division into stanzas of three lines gives the poem an orderly appearance, the blind man's disorientation is reflected in the irregularity of the rhyme scheme as well as the frequent shifts between past and present tense (like the dancer Sran, the blind man seems to be uncertain of his own location in space); and, while the rhythm appears somewhat monotonous, suggesting a kind of linear progression, it remains uneven, as if imitating the blind man's groping movements.

The narrative suggests a move away from the (negative) external space and toward the blind man's subjective inner space, but this escape seems claustrophobic, limited by the surrounding wall against which the blind man must press himself. The image of a simultaneous escape and confinement into interiority relates to discussions of art and utopia among German expressionists, such as Kasimir Edschmid, who stated in his famous 1917 speech "Expressionismus in der Dichtung" ("Expressionism in Poetry") that "that which seems to be external reality cannot be that which is true. True meaning lies deeper . . . it is an image of the world which must be mirrored but: this image exists only *within* ourselves" (Anz and Stark 1982, 48; my translation). This theme of a mirror whose reflection exists, paradoxically, only inside ourselves is also described by the philosopher Ernst Bloch, in his description of an internal mirror, into which we enter and disappear to experience the "gothic chamber of self-awareness," where time stands still and the "whole wide, seemingly real, world" is nothing but a "picture of a harmless memory hanging on the wall."[18] Hardenberg's blind man, on the other hand, finds a window through which, it appears, he will be able to "walk toward spring," so that there is actually an opening between these two spaces (inside and outside). Still, the poem ends abruptly, with a line that seems too short in relation to the previous lines, a reference to life and death without anything else in between. As in Bloch's "gothic chamber," time seems compressed into a single, pregnant moment, yet here there is no picture—the poem simply ends and leaves us bewildered, as in a state of blindness. In this sense, it is reminiscent of the state of Narcissus, who does not "see" that he is deluded.

Once again it seems as if the subject had become alienated from its own body. The final example I will discuss, Hardenberg's short prose poem "Bewegter Mensch" ("Moved Human Being"), written at the end of World War I and published in the *Prager Presse* in 1922, suggests a dissolution of physical boundaries that truly threaten the subject with extinction. Here the self-alienation that is part and parcel of narcissism (and not yet part of Freud's version of "primary narcissism") becomes evident. Nightmarish, the subject ("I") is unhinged from its body, no longer encountering any physical resistance:

> Ich bin ein Fluß, über keine Landstraße gehe ich mehr, die Steine sind versunken. Ich bin ein voller Fluß. Vom Winde werde ich getrieben, ich reibe mich an mir, ich bin so viel ich. In mir die Glätte und der Schein, meine bunte Haut oben ausgerollt. Die Flügel von Vögeln durch mich. Geisterhände an mein Herz. Die Sonne kommt herunter. Ich schreie. Weiß stehe ich auf und bekenne. (Hardenberg 1994, 72)
>
> I am a river, I no longer walk across any country road, all stones are submerged. I am a full river. I am drifting with the wind, brushing myself against myself, I am so much I. Smoothness and brightness inside of me, my colorful skin rolled out above. Wings of birds through me. Ghostly hands at my heart. The sun comes down. I scream. I get up, white, and confess.

Here the "I" is a floating signifier threatened with extinction by the natural world, into which it gradually disappears. Lacking a solid shape, it seems no longer in need of a center or position in space, at least until the subject erupts into a scream, which suggests something terrible has happened. As if the "I" had been at play and now suddenly recognizes the horror of its own bodilessness, the scream marks the reversal from spectral to real voice.

The initial ephemeralness of the "I" designates an unreal subject, whose playful movement among the natural elements (wind, water) is created through linguistic repetition: the recurring linguistic designation "I" provides the illusion of constancy, yet the speaker is in actuality disembodied so that "nature" is anything but a positive force. There is an "inside," yet the "skin" is detached, located "above," marking the speaker's position as elsewhere (below). It seems as if the voice were without skin: "wings of birds" are passing through to indicate that there is no material substance (body) in which it could be anchored.

The appearance of movement through repetition is also undermined by the fact that the text consists mostly of prepositions instead of verbs, creating the impression of a static world.[19] The subject inhabits an uncanny, dreamlike world until "the sun comes down" to mark the passing of time. After this intrusion of temporality, the "I" finds its body, whose physicality expresses itself through the utterance of sound. While the text seems to perform an expansion of the subject ("I am so much I"), it also depicts the subject's struggle with the loss of physical boundaries, that is, a complete lack of position. Hardenberg juxtaposes the supernatural ("ghostly hands at my heart") to the natural (the "heart," which represents both the human body and human emotions) and creates the possibility of a new beginning, a resurrection (*aufstehen,* getting up, is related to *auferstehen,* to be resurrected). The subject becomes corporeal and can be visually identified as "white," yet seems to be in a state of shock over what happened. What the voice chooses to "confess" we never learn.

The scream is a frequently used expressionist device that is connected to a vision of the end of the world (apocalypse). The world of Hardenberg's subject "ends" with the recognition of temporality that includes the body's mortality. Her prose poem describes the horror of being unable to exist without a body but also the inability to fully express oneself *with* a body. If the body is the site of sexual difference, it is the place where the (female) subject struggles to identify herself, so that the body cannot be simply discarded. In regard to the mind/body opposition, this means that neither can be favored over the other, at least not if the subject is to establish a more positive sense of self. What Hardenberg describes is not a spiritual transformation but rather a need to articulate (express) oneself in opposition to the threat of losing one's identity ("I")—a gesture which would certainly be consistent with the subject's fear of being silenced (as mentioned at the onset of this chapter). Compared to Freud's, Hardenberg's is a more subtle representation of the relationship between the female subject and her body (image). Hardenberg's text draws attention to the opposition between language and silence, with which the subject must struggle in order to define herself. Ostensibly, this project fails: the scream is expressive but does not mean anything beyond its articulation; and the text ends before we learn what the voice communicates. And yet, paradoxically, it is language that creates the impression that language cannot articulate the truth of the subject, whose real body seems to be always elsewhere ("beyond" articulation). Thus whereas Freud locates the female subject beyond language, in a primitive realm beyond comprehension (screaming may be all there is), he fails to engage the possibilities of negotiating silence through language. His theory rests on the assumption that narcissistic women are inarticulate, whereas Hardenberg's poetry depicts subjectivity as precisely the attempt to come to terms with one's body through language. And, unlike Freud's "talking cure," which necessitates the presence of the analyst as the ultimate authority, Hardenberg's subject becomes her own "author-ity."

What she tells us may not be as easy to accept as Freud's version of the narcissistic woman. The experience of disembodiment suggested by "Bewegter Mensch" seems disturbing, especially if one considers that the body image is "a ghostlike icon of the subject" (Grosz 1994, 63). Here the subject itself appears to be "ghostlike," perhaps because it fails to produce this "icon," which might, somehow, anchor it in space. "Bewegter Mensch" might represent a form of "depersonalization" that is connected to mental illness, where there exists according to Grosz a

> severe psychical transformation of the body image. [Subjects] may feel a dramatic change in self-conception and in relations to the external world. . . . Not only is the subject's own body treated with disinterest, but the outside world is also flat and disinvested. Depersonalization may in fact account for the phenomenon of out-of-body experiences. (76–77)

Given this darker side, which I will further explore in the following chapters, Hardenberg's writing renders the absence of a fixed body image problematic as much as it celebrates the utopian potential of transgressing all physical boundaries. This situation may be due to the fact that the refusal to define oneself in terms of a fixed body image seems inevitably connected to a refusal to define oneself socially, in terms of sexual identity (difference). While Hardenberg's poetic subject may wish to transcend its body as a way of escaping the social confines of gender, it also runs the risk of entering the space of unreality, or madness. And yet, as Grosz makes clear, "the stability of the unified body image, even in the so-called normal subject, is always precarious" (1994, 43). At the very least, I believe, it is this "precariousness" that is at stake when reading Hardenberg's texts.

To conclude, what makes Henriette Hardenberg's writing unique is her concern with the "I" and the "body" *as* language. She presents us with a textual subject, engaged in an ongoing process of writing and rewriting her corporeal "self," thus drawing the reader into a subjective space that has no particular shape or boundaries, so that her language holds both the promise of escaping the confines of gender and the fear of losing one's "identity" as a result of this transgression. What the "I" that rises from the dead at the end of "Bewegter Mensch" may "confess" is that it speaks from a nonexistent place, a place that could be the threshold of death (silence), as well as a new space, perhaps a language yet to be articulated. In short, Hardenberg's linguistic bodies are fluid and lack a definitive shape because they depict a (female) subject whose identity is uncertain, as it wishes to escape the confines of sexual difference.

In contrast to Freud, Hardenberg suggests that woman's "self-contentment" depends on her ability to express herself rather than on her "good looks" (determined by the male gaze); that she is "inaccessible" only to those who are unwilling to communicate with her; and that she is neither "child" nor "animal." Rather, she creates a voice that survives the vicissitudes of time, as it continues to generate the dialectical tension between different possibilities of interpretation, different "bodies" in motion, and different "selves," all of which refuse to be arrested into the confines of positionality. Related to the motion of writing, which suggests an ongoing displacement of meaning, Hardenberg's desire for transcendence may manifest itself in representations of disembodiment, depersonalization, and death, yet it enables her to represent herself as a subject of language, in her very own voice. As she explores the possibilities of this voice, she shows her subject forever engaged in (re)defining its "body" and "self" through writing—representing, so to speak, an identity always "under construction," never quite yet come into being.

4. Between Birth and Death: The Image of the Other in Djuna Barnes's *Nightwood*

Critical Considerations

The subject of this chapter, Djuna Barnes's experimental novel *Nightwood,* published in 1936, relates to my topic, narcissism, because as I will demonstrate, reflection itself is its governing structural principle. The question of the epistemological status of the object, which I have posed at the onset of this book, is most relevant to this text. Within the context of Anglo-American modernism, Barnes (1892–1982), a journalist and playwright from New York who lived in Paris between the two world wars, belongs to a generation of writers, such as James Joyce, Gertrude Stein, and Virginia Woolf, who experimented with narrative and linguistic technique to draw attention to language and the work of art *as* art (not a "representation" of something else). This performative aspect of Barnes's idiosyncratic, baroque language, with which she creates a dreamlike universe bearing little resemblance to the real world, makes it difficult to read her in referential terms. And yet, *Nightwood* contains numerous references to "race," "blood," "heredity," and "degeneracy" that evoke nineteenth-century biological discourses about race and sexuality—such as that of the "third sex"—which make it equally problematic to approach the novel on purely formal grounds. As my analysis will show, this discrepancy between different modes of representation (performative, referential) is due to the narcissistic structure of the novel itself, whose plot can be divided in two halves, with the second being largely reflective of the action that took place in the first (like a metatext). As if to embody Narcissus's condition of being paralyzed by his own reflection, *Nightwood* turns out to be less about the telling of the actual story itself than about the reflection it generates—a structure which is, as critics have observed, consistent with the figure of "inversion" used to describe homosexuality in the nineteenth century and which I will connect to Freud's concept of "narcissistic object choice" (discussed in chapter 2). As I argue, *Nightwood* invokes two paradigms of homosexuality: the genetically based concept of the "third sex" and images of narcissism. As I will demonstrate, they are juxtaposed against one another in favor of narcissism, which is based on the imagination rather than biology.

As I have shown in the previous chapter on Henriette Hardenberg, the concept of narcissism can function to challenge traditional notions of gender and subject-object relations. My reading of Hardenberg was based on the first part of Freud's essay "On Narcissism" (1914/1986), in which he wrote about "primary narcissism" in relation to "femininity." The present chapter relates to the second part of Freud's essay, where he discusses "object relations." In classical psychoanalytic theory (starting with Freud's *Three Essays,* 1905/1962) "objects" are "the persons or things onto which the biological drives are concentrated," and their role is limited to enabling "the discharge of the drive" (Buckley 1986, xii). With Melanie Klein, "the experience of the object in reality becomes of crucial importance . . . and the internal objects are viewed as reflections of experiences with real persons." Consequently, the debate within object relations theory revolves around nature-versus-nurture questions: "What is biologically innate in the psychology of the individual and what is modulated by direct environmental experience?" (Buckley 1986, xi). Lacan, on the other hand, has revised Freud's theory of the drives into a structure of imaginary/symbolic/real, which no longer relies on biological "instincts" or the hierarchically based model of the "unconscious." This structure makes it possible to think of the psyche as a text, where the "real" exists but can be perceived only in the form of gaps within the subject's symbolic and imaginary structure. *Nightwood,* as my analysis will show, lends itself to both approaches, since its "narcissistic" structure revolves precisely around the ambiguous nature of the "object."

As my discussion of Freud's essay should have made clear, the concept of "object relations" is necessary insofar as it constitutes the bridge between "primary narcissism" and the kind of narcissism determined by the "ego ideal" (which Lacan takes as his point of departure). The reader may recall that Freud initially saw primary narcissism as a state preceding object relations, yet he had to introduce object relations—which he attributed to, in part, "narcissistic object choice"—to account for the emergence of the ego ideal. He then connected the ego ideal to the more prevalent form of adult narcissism which, paradoxically, ended up contradicting the assumption that the "object" could be in any way "real." The purpose of this chapter is to show how everything hinges on this question of the nature of the "object," which Barnes, as I argue, shows to be connected to narcissism in a way that evokes the figure of Narcissus as one who does and does not see the reality of the "other." Rather than attempting to resolve the contradiction, I would maintain, Barnes (like Hardenberg) placed her faith in art and the imagination, in opposition to Freud's biological determinism. At the same time, she reminds us that even imaginary objects possess real physical power—so that even if the beloved does not seem "real" from the point of view of an outside observer, his or her presence will feel quite real to the one who loves.

Before I turn to my analysis of Barnes's novel, let me outline the critical debates that have surrounded it since its inception. First of all, there is the issue of the text itself: T. S. Eliot and Emily Coleman, Barnes's official and unofficial editors, exerted varying influences over Barnes's decision as to where each chapter ought to be. Joseph Frank has shown that—as in cubism, where the object is fragmented and can be seen simultaneously from various angles—the novel's apparent lack of sequential organization can be attributed to its "spatial form," where there is a "continual reference and cross-reference of images and symbols" (1963, 32). However, research into Barnes's earlier drafts (Fuchs 1993; Hollis 2000) proves that the novel's narrative structure was significantly altered. Most critics have based their interpretations on the published version of *Nightwood,* but some have now proceeded to interpret the text based on these earlier drafts. Still, since Barnes herself is known to have been pleased with Frank's reading, which is based on the final, published 1936 version, I am using the 1995 edition by Cheryl Plumb, which retains the 1936 chapter organization but contains minor changes due to Eliot's censorship of sexually explicit content.

In fact, sexuality is what makes *Nightwood* such a radical book, as it seems based, primarily, on the transgression of social and aesthetic norms.[1] Most readers have strong reactions to it, starting with Eliot, who, on the one hand, admits that "when I first read the book I found the opening movement rather slow and dragging" (Eliot 1936/1961, xii) and, on the other hand, ends up attributing to it no less than a "quality of horror and doom very nearly related to that of Elizabethan tragedy" (xvi). Indeed, the cast of characters that inhabits the decadent atmosphere of the "night" in European capitals (Paris, Berlin, Vienna) during the 1920s is anything but "normal": there is the "wandering Jew" (Barnes 1995, 8) with a bought aristocratic title, Baron Felix Volkbein, and his retarded, feebleminded son, Guido; Nikka the Nigger, who exhibits his tattoo-covered body in the circus; the "unsexed" trapeze artist Frau Mann; the puritan American with "some derangement in her equilibrium," Nora Flood; her faithless lover, an androgynous lesbian from the Midwest, Robin Vote; her lover, Jenny Petherbridge, who is "unable to wear anything becoming" because her head and body do "not go together" (58); and, above all, the "god of darkness," "fairy," "queen," and "faggot" (64), Doctor Matthew O'Connor, who secretly dresses as a woman, "haunts the pissoirs" (77), and performs abortions on prostitutes.

Not surprisingly, *Nightwood* has caused a good deal of debate over the issues of racism and anti-Semitism. Barnes refers to dangerous and disturbing stereotypes, yet she does so in the form of parody, with profound sympathy for the suffering of her socially marginalized characters. At least this is what Jane Marcus (1991) and Kenneth Burke (1968) have argued (and I agree with them), yet recent critics have begun to interpret *Nightwood* as racist, anti-Semitic, and even fascist: Karen Kaivola makes an earnest attempt to rescue the novel's "Jews, Africans, and lesbians" from "anti-Semitic, racist, and homophobic ideologies" (as if they were, somehow, not fictional characters but real people to be rescued from the text) to arrive at the unfortunate conclusion that "blacks and Jews are situated as the white lesbian's Others" (1993, 182); Meryl Altman deliberately eschews the question "how all this may relate to . . . an avant-garde conception of subjectivity as disunified or problematic" (1993, 168) in order to claim that authors like Barnes, Joyce, and Proust "inescapably participated in an ongoing European discourse . . . whose most famous grandson is Hitler" (164); and Erin Carlston proceeds to directly align *Nightwood* with "Italian, French, and German fascist thought" to argue that it "cannot be said to have a purely oppositional relation to fascism" (1998, 43). My own sense is that the text's experimental, avant-garde form does matter, since it is too anarchic to allow for the kind of totalitarian vision one would associate with a fascist aesthetics—which I see as centered exclusively around the celebration of power for its own sake (rather than: art for art's sake). *Nightwood's* structure of reflexivity, which is related to the figure of irony, does not allow for any kind of totalizing vision, since it by definition creates a split within the subject.[2]

The third critical issue, which is most relevant to this project from a historical point of view, is homosexuality. As the reader will recall from chapter 1, the history of narcissism is tied up with the history of the "third sex," a term mentioned throughout Barnes's novel. Part of my reading is to show how it is criticized in favor of narcissism as a less biologically determined concept. Homosexuality is connected, as Julie Abraham has noted, to the issue of race: "*Nightwood* indicates that Barnes was aware of the parallel between anti-Semitism and hostility toward gays in the European social context in which she was living" (1991, 256). Some critics (Eliot 1936/1961; Burke 1968) have focused primarily on the figure of the gay transvestite Doctor Matthew O'Connor, with his endless speeches, yet the story really revolves around the same-sex relationship between Nora and Robin which is, as we know, based on the real-life nine-year relationship between Barnes and her lover, Thelma Wood (1901–70). Wood was, according to Barnes's biographer Philip Herring, "the great love of her life" (1995, 156), and many details in *Nightwood,* such as the description of their apartment in Paris, correspond to this relationship; Thelma's last name is part of the book's title, and "Robin" alludes to her pet name, "Bird."[3] And yet Barnes "insisted that she was never a lesbian—she had only loved Thelma Wood" (Herring 1995, 255). Or, as Monique Wittig observed, "Barnes dreaded that the lesbians should make her *their* writer" since "one should not reduce and limit her to the lesbian minority" (1983, 64). However, as she acknowledges, "Barnes is read first and widely by lesbians" precisely because "Barnes cancels out the genders by making them obsolete," and that, Wittig concludes, "is the point of view of a lesbian" (1983, 64).

In regard to my project, the issue of what might be a specifically "lesbian" point of view in *Nightwood* is interesting mostly insofar as it relates to the discourse of narcissism and object relations. According to Teresa de Lauretis, "lesbian desire . . . is constituted against a fantasy of castration, a narcissistic wound to the subject's body image that redoubles the loss of the mother's body by the threatened loss of the female body itself" (1994, 261). This definition, which also relates to my discussion of the precarious nature of the body image in Hardenberg, would account for the rather disembodied nature of Robin and Nora's relationship in *Nightwood.* As Carolyn Allen has argued, "Nora's story [is] a narrative of lesbian erotics" (1993, 177) which is based on a form of "objectless desire," a concept that is directly related to narcissism.[4] Similarly, Victoria Smith (1999) has argued that *Nightwood* is based on a "language of loss," albeit with reference to Freud's later essay "Mourning and Melancholy" ("Trauer und Melancholie"; Freud 1917), which reformulates narcissism away from objectlessness.

Whether or not *Nightwood* is a "lesbian" text, its "narcissistic" structure, as I will show, ultimately undermines all notions of racial, ethnic, religious, and sexual "identities" on which the aforementioned discussions are based. I found that the most useful approach to *Nightwood* comes from queer theorist Frann Michel, whose assessment is that Barnes's work "warns us away from dichotomizing its form and content in service of arguments that it is 'really' lesbian or homophobic" (1993, 54)—and I would add, this warning applies equally to the issues of race and anti-Semitism. Michel's argument is based on the fact that Barnes has had relationships with both women and men, hence needs to be categorized as "bisexual," a position which "is understood as one way of acknowledging the complexity of sexuality [and] serves as a challenge to essentializing dichotomies" (55).

Looking at *Nightwood* from a discourse-analytical point of view, I argue that there are two competing versions of "homosexuality" juxtaposed against one another. The first is centered on the seemingly endless monologues of the doctor, who brands himself as "nature's mistake" and whose rhetoric about the "third sex" evokes the nineteenth-century sexologists with their characterization of the homosexual as a "stepchild of nature," comparable to "someone born with a physical defect" (Krafft-Ebing 1899, 5).[5] The second version is based on the "narcissistic" images of Nora and Robin, which depict same-sex desire in unapologetic terms, based on a romantic ideal of "true love," where gender is not the issue. Considering that Barnes wrote during a period when the Nazis had appropriated nineteenth-century biological paradigms, it may not be surprising that she chose to represent her lovers in terms of narcissism, much as it may be connected to other stereotypes about homosexuality (see chapter 1).[6] Narcissism functions to undermine any kind of biologically based conception of the human subject by insisting on, above all, the imagination and, therefore, art over "nature."[7] And, while Barnes may not have been directly familiar with the writings of Freud or Klein, she lived in Europe during the time when debates over narcissism, homosexuality, and "femininity" took place within the psychoanalytic community as well as in public.[8] She was part of a lesbian subculture, the salon of Natalie Barney, the "Amazone of letters" (who did become a fascist when she went to Italy to join Mussolini), which made her experience firsthand the way in which homosexuality would have been "performed" at that time.[9]

The notion of "performativity" is evident from the fact that *Nightwood* is extremely theatrical: everyone suffers, yet everyone seems concerned primarily with appearances, including costumes, designs, and decor. The novel effectively undermines any conception of what would be "natural" in favor of promoting the reality of art *as* performance.[10] As in Narcissus, it is the surface that creates the illusion of a depth that remains inaccessible.

In fact, an apparent conflict between "nature" and "art" is part of Barnes's biography: she was born "in a log cabin on a mountain overlooking the Hudson River" (Herring 1995, xvi) and grew up in a rustic setting in a relatively poor family. Influenced by transcendentalism, her family educated their children at home, in an environment promoting, supposedly, artistic and sexual freedom. Barnes's father, Walt, openly practiced polygamy, so Djuna grew up in a set of two families, headed by her paternal grandmother, Zadel, to whom she was very close. Zadel once ran a literary salon in London (where she was friends with, among others, Oscar Wilde's mother) and evidently helped Djuna become a writer. In 1915, Barnes was able to move to Greenwich Village and to support herself, along with part of her family, by working as a journalist and playwright. She became associated with Eugene O'Neill's Provincetown Players, for which she wrote a number of plays, and in 1920 was sent to Paris by *McCall's* magazine.

In Paris, in 1921, she met Thelma Wood, who was then the lover of the photographer Berenice Abbott. Like Robin, most of *Nightwood*'s other characters can be traced to real-life people Barnes met in Paris. Matthew, "the Tiresias of *Nightwood* was in reality Daniel A. Mahoney, Barnes' close friend for many years and one of the most sadly entertaining 'characters' in modern Left Bank history. Barnes would sit for hours listening to him, often taking copious notes, which became the basis for O'Connor's monologues in her novel" (Herring 1995, 210). Similarly, the Baron Felix Volkbein is based on a lover of Barnes's friend, the infamous Baroness Elsa von Freytag Loringhoven, whose name was Felix Paul Greve and who "occasionally signed hotel registers 'Baron Volkbein'" (113).

However, while it may be tempting to interpret the novel in relation to the author's life, this autobiographical approach seems counterproductive because it would only reduce Barnes's formal accomplishments to another narrative.[11] Due to its opacity, one might feel the need to supplement Barnes's text with information about the author's life because it seems inexplicable otherwise, yet doing so would only compromise the fragility of its dreamlike structure (for instance, the cryptic final scene, where Robin plays with Nora's dog, is hardly illuminated by the fact that, as Herring writes, the scene was suggested by Barnes's friend Fitzi, who "once, when drunk, playfully pretended that her dog, Buffy, was her sweetheart"; 1995, 168). Barnes's life was interesting enough to have become the subject of several biographies,[12] yet she herself wished to be known on account of her artistic merit, causing her to react with hostility even toward critics who wanted to write about *Nightwood* not primarily in terms of its aesthetics but in terms of its sexual or political content.[13] As might be the case with many women writers who are known more because of their lives than because of their work, Barnes was sensitive to the issue of being misunderstood: she called herself "the century's most famous unknown" (Herring 348) in allusion to the fact that everyone seems to be interested in her person, yet no one seems to really read her work.

In this sense, Shari Benstock may be right that *Nightwood* represents "the tragic effect of woman's estrangement from her own self" (1986, 263). One may only speculate to what extent this description applies to Barnes. Within the milieu of the Paris expatriate scene, photographs from the time depict an elegantly dressed, beautiful woman, whose apparent self-confidence commands attention. In later pictures, however, after her return from Europe, in the early years of World War II, Barnes seems to have aged prematurely, probably due to her severe addiction to alcohol. Less fortunate than some of her contemporaries, such as Gertrude Stein or Peggy Guggenheim, who were independently wealthy (in fact, Guggenheim occasionally helped support Barnes), she eventually had to refrain from the kind of socializing she had become used to in Europe. Back in New York, she rarely left her tiny apartment at 5 Patchin Place (maybe because she had so little money) and became known as a "recluse."[14] During the more than forty years of her life after the publication of *Nightwood,* she never stopped writing, yet she published only a rarely produced play, *The Antiphon* (1958), which deals with her family background in terms of violence and abuse. In 1928, she had published, among other things, a self-illustrated best seller, *Ryder,* in which she parodied her family.[15] Some critics (DeSalvo 1991; Dalton 1993) have interpreted these works in regard to the alleged incest that took place during Barnes's childhood; however, I am not sure such an approach truly helps us understand Barnes's art. Since one of the aims of this book is to examine the role of fantasy in modern art, the close reading of *Nightwood* I will conduct in the following sections is primarily concerned with highlighting the self-reflexive nature of Barnes's narrative technique.

The Birth of the "Great Past"

Nightwood takes place in a Europe of overwrought interiors, statues, castles, works of art, and aristocratic families. In the opening passage, the narrator conveys the impression of a decadent atmosphere in which birth and death coincide:

> Early in 1880, in spite of a well-founded suspicion as to the advisability of perpetuating that race which has the sanction of the Lord and the disapproval of the people, Hedvig Volkbein, a Viennese woman of great strength and military beauty, lying upon a canopied bed, of a rich spectacular crimson, the valance stamped with the bifurcated wings of the House of Hapsburg, the feather coverlet an envelope of satin on which, in massive and tarnished gold threads, stood the Volkbein arms,—gave birth, at the age of forty-five, to an only child, a son, seven days after her physician predicted that she would be taken. . . . She named him Felix, thrust him from her, and died. (Barnes 1995, 3)

Starting with the figure of a year, the narrator endows the birth with the significance of an actual historical event, magnified by a succession of large-scale concepts ("race," "Lord," "people"). The gaudy decor gains weight through its design, and the entire passage seems overwrought. Loaded with references and details, it has a listlike quality and a monotonous rhythm which distracts the reader away from its semantic content, the birth. Retrospectively, it appears as if the birth is the result of a pressure exerted from the accumulation of clauses, from beneath which Hedvig, the grammatical subject, emerges only to find her own end. Unlike Freud, who writes that having a child may open up the possibility of "curing" women from their narcissism, Barnes represents childbirth as purely negative.

Considering that birth and death occur almost simultaneously, this initial scene is emblematic for the novel as a whole: in addition to numerous references to death and disintegration, all narrative movement is followed by stagnation through the insertion of descriptions and reflective commentary. In keeping with this pattern, the passage builds some kind of momentum and then dies down at the very moment of birth. As if the narrator were to remove herself from the grandiose setting she just established, the background no longer works as an introduction to what now appears to be an almost anticlimactic event, related in a matter-of-fact tone. Whichever action *Nightwood*'s plot advances, it is bound to be reflected by such distancing moves. Descriptions become self-fulfilling prophecies, and a seemingly downward-spiraling syntactic structure is connected with the novel's overall theme of "descent." Matthew's wish, "How more tidy would it have been to have born old and have aged into a child, brought finally to the brink, not of the grave, but of the womb" (1995, 83), can be read as a paradigm for the way in which the novel revolves around the notion of retroactive growth. Throughout, time itself is described in terms of death.

Compared to Freud's scientific notion of positive development, Barnes's novel is organized around the idea of physical decay, the cultural references here are characterized by "descent." A discourse of culture (history) is connected to a discourse of nature (biology) in the way in which Hedvig "thrusts" her newborn from her as if she were an animal, quite in contrast to the artificiality of her environment. What marks Hedvig herself as human is her name and the fact that she names her son before she dies. The name, Volkbein, appears in conjunction with the House of Hapsburg as yet another sign of the pretense to historical truth into which Felix is born. Unlike the House of Hapsburg, the Volkbein coat of arms is fictitious, but the reader, ironically, does not learn what it looks like. Translating *Volkbein* into the image of a "leg of (the) people," the compound word appears to be related to the German word *Fußvolk* (footmen/infantry). Appropriately situated between the words "stood" and "arms" (the latter connoting weapons and human limbs), the name suggests a pompous militarism which dominates the design of the entire bed, including its content, Hedvig.

Compared to Freud, who romanticizes nature as an inaccessible point of origin, Barnes insists on the importance of art and culture by depicting things in terms of their surfaces (rather than their "essence"). The narrator frequently describes people submerged by the texture of their environment, as in the case of the trapeze artist Frau Mann, in whose "face was the tense expression of an organism surviving in an alien element" and whose body "seemed to have a skin that was the pattern of her costume" (1995, 12). Just as she is described in terms of her profession, Hedvig is described in terms of her reproductive capacity, a capacity which seems, however, vital to the environment in which she appears.

Hedvig's death is accompanied by a reference to time in terms of accurate predictability by a physician, performed according to the requirements of historical continuation in that she continues the family line. As if to mock the emphasis on descent, however, Felix carries on the family name and title as an orphan who drifts about aimlessly and desperately wishes for an heir without being himself in any historical "place" by virtue of his "blood." Having briefly recounted the family's history, the narrator skips ahead thirty years: "what had formed Felix from the date of his birth to his coming to thirty was unknown to the world, for the step of the wandering Jew is in every son" (1995, 8). Felix continues to pursue the illusion of aristocracy, like his Jewish father who, as we learn, married Hedvig on account of her Aryan heritage and obliterated his Jewish background with a "pretense to a Barony . . . a coat of arms that he had no right to and a list of progenitors (including their Christian names) who had never existed" (5). In contrast to his father, Felix feels most comfortable in the company of circus people, being so fascinated by glamour that he does not care whether what it represents is real or not. However, he ingratiates himself by bowing to anyone in sight who seems superior (which is, to his mind, almost everyone), and "his embarrassment took the form of an obsession for what he called 'Old Europe': aristocracy, nobility, royalty" (9). Left with two life-size portraits of his grandparents that turn out to be reproductions of "two intrepid and ancient actors" (7), Felix is attracted to the masquerade of the circus people because they adorn themselves with false aristocratic titles. His need for pretense is reminiscent of the description of the bed in which he was born, in which items like the "feather coverlet" of satin with the "massive and tarnished gold threads" are on the same level as "history." A stereotypical product of his environment, Felix only confirms the narrator's initial "suspicion as to the advisability of perpetuating that race which has the sanction of the Lord and the disapproval of the people" as having been, unfortunately, "well-founded."

Subjected to this vicious circle, Felix does not have a place in the novel, either. Except for another brief appearance in chapter 6, his character is limited to being a husband and father to Robin before she meets Nora. When Barnes's editor, Coleman, wondered why Felix was not edited out of the novel, Barnes replied, in a letter of November 8, 1935, that his function was to counter the belief "that women would not fall in love with one another if a man had slept with them, if they had been well f—— and had borne a child" (Barnes 1995, xviii). A leftover from an earlier project by Barnes, "a book in progress whose chief figure is an Austrian Jew" which she decided to abandon when starting to work on *Nightwood* (ix), Felix is an orphan on a metatextual level as well. Not "related" to the rest of the novel, he may also be seen as providing a point of departure to question the concept of personal and cultural "history": his story sets up an opposition between history as narrative movement and stagnation (i.e., "death"), which the rest of *Nightwood* sets out to undo. The whole first chapter (appropriately titled "Bow Down") sets up an atmosphere cluttered with objects and mistaken identities, showing Felix to be confused between his racial background and a proliferation of signifiers denoting "culture." Partially because of Felix, who may or may not "fit in," the novel raises the question what exactly constitutes a "story."[16]

From the beginning, the concept of "generation," including the generation of meaning through signs, becomes a questionable enterprise when it is carried out upon the sacrifice of Hedvig's body. Felix wishes to have "a son who would feel as he felt about the 'great past'" (1995, 37). Like his father, he looks at his future wife only in terms of "the destiny for which he had chosen her: that she might bear sons who would recognize and honour the past" (42). However, his obsession with descent takes its toll: his son, Guido, turns out to be retarded.

After dropping Felix from the story, the narrator parts with the concept of narrative as history: the "plot" is reduced to the story of Robin and Nora finding each other, separating, and finding each other again. Here narcissism becomes a most prominent trope for the way in which Nora imagines Robin; and the book itself is organized to thwart any notion of narrative progression. Most of the story is over by the middle of the book, and the book's second half consists mostly of repetition and recollection. In fact, the narrative flow is interrupted for more pages than those in which the narrative itself takes place: for example, the relationship between Nora and Robin, which is said to last ten years, is narrated in as few as ten pages, but Nora's coming to terms with it in her two lengthy meetings with Matthew takes up more than fifty pages. The narrator skips ahead with large "cuts" in which time is condensed (for instance, between Felix's birth and his "coming to thirty") and then uses her characters to reflect upon the time in between in flashbacks. Dialogues take place in so-called real time without any action so that the plot becomes an endless process of reflection.

As the death in childbirth suggests from the beginning on, the novel, which concludes with an image of madness, is a departure from the idea of creation and growth, both of which are shown to take place only to a limited extent. Birth is the point at which death begins by way of deterioration, and the next child in the novel is already dead, a doll given to Nora by Robin as their "child." Most of the action takes place in dark interiors: Hedvig's overly decorated chamber, Robin's seedy hotel room, the bars she frequents at night, the doctor's tomblike apartment, Nora's house and decayed chapel, and so on. The only time the characters move through open space is when they are desperately trying to find something or to escape from something: Robin escaping from her child or Nora's jealousy; the doctor looking for male prostitutes; and Nora traveling frantically to find Robin. All are motivated by some kind of desire for self-destruction, and the initial scene of death in childbirth, like a kind of omen, foreshadows a conclusion of tragic proportions. As the doctor quotes, supposedly, the metaphysical poet John Donne: "We are all conceived in close prison, in our mother's wombs we are close prisoners all. When we are born we are but born to the liberty of the house—all our life is but a going out to the place of execution and death" (Barnes 1995, 82). Clearly, this philosophy differs from Freud's, where the ego ideal functions as an imaginary refuge from mortality, helping the subject repress the knowledge of death on which Barnes's doctor loves to dwell.

The God of Darkness

Doctor O'Connor's first name is Matthew, the name of the author of the first Gospel in the New Testament, the "Gospel to the Jew" which emphasizes the fulfillment of the prophecy that the Messiah has come. It is designed to prove that Jesus is the Messiah and contains parables about his life, including his teachings. The Matthew of *Nightwood,* in contrast to his historical predecessor, tells parables about figures like the mad, homosexual, Bavarian king Ludwig of Wittelsbach, and his philosophy comes from the "underworld" (Barnes 1995, 31). Preaching a gospel of death instead of birth, his rhetoric plays upon the discourse of religion but will always return to himself: "Jehovah, Saboeth, Elohim, Eloi, Helion, Jodhevah, Shadday! May God give us to die in our own way! I haunt the *pissoirs* as naturally, in search of my man" (77). Describing himself as having "a face like a squirrel's" (27) and "a face on me like an old child's bottom" (77), Matthew is self-deprecating: "by his own peculiar perversity God has made me a liar . . . one who, in common parlance is called a 'faggot'" (64). Calling himself "the Old Woman who lives in the closet" (115), he knows the night, which is why people should listen to him: "No man knows it as I know it, I who am the god of darkness" (106).

When Felix meets Matthew at a party in Berlin, he quickly feels "that the evening is already lost . . . and that the whole affair was to be given over to this volatile person who called himself a doctor" (1995, 16). This assessment turns out to be true: Felix recedes into the background as soon as the doctor appears on the scene, and the novel continues to be dominated by the doctor's presence. The following passage introduces Matthew:

> Standing about a table at the end of the immense room, looking as if they were deciding the fate of a nation, were grouped ten men, all in parliamentary attitudes, and one young woman. They were listening, at the moment of the entrance of Felix and the Duchess of Broadback, to a middle-aged "medical student" with shaggy eyebrows, a terrific widow's peak, over-large dark eyes, and a heavy way of standing that was also apologetic. The man was Dr. Matthew O'Connor, an Irishman from the Barbary Coast (Pacific Street, San Francisco) whose interest in gynecology had driven him half around the world. He was taking the part of host, the Count not yet having made his appearance, and was telling of himself, for he considered himself the most amusing predicament. (Barnes 1995, 13)

Like Felix, Matthew is portrayed in broad strokes, as a caricature, with his physical appearance reduced to the main features of his face and his posture. He, too, carries a false title: calling himself a doctor, when he is, actually, a "middle-aged 'medical student.'" Later, the narrator confirms that he "was not a licensed practitioner" (1995, 34) and we learn that his "interest in gynecology"[17] is also of a personal nature:

> Am I to blame if I've turned up this time as I shouldn't have been, when it was a high soprano I wanted, and deep corn curls to my bum, with a womb as big as the king's kettle, and a bosom as high as the bowsprit of a fishing schooner? . . . For, no matter what I may be doing, in my heart is the wish for children and knitting. God, I never asked better than to boil some good man's potatoes and toss up a child for him every nine months by the calendar. Is it my fault that my only fireside is the outhouse? (Barnes 1995, 78)

As this passage shows, Matthew is a member of the "third sex," with the soul of a woman in the body of a man (Ulrichs 1994), with which he explicitly identifies later on in the novel. As if to emphasize this Matthew's feeling of being physically trapped within the wrong body, the narrator also tells us that he lives in a "relatively small square, through which tram lines ran in several directions, bounded on the one side by the church and on the other by the court" (Barnes 1995, 30), and in a room "so small that it was just possible to walk sideways up to the bed, it was as if being condemned to the grave" (68). Due to these limitations, it is not so much Matthew's body as it his mind that "is always wandering" (88). However, his philosophy reduces everything to the physical body: "I, as a medical man, know in what pocket a man keeps his heart and soul, and in what jostle of the liver, kidneys and genitalia these pockets are pilfered. There is no pure sorrow. Why? It is bedfellow to lungs, lights, bones, guts and gall!" (17); and "No man can find a greater truth than his kidney will allow" (72). According to Matthew, life consists only of the biological cycle of birth and death, with everything else in between being only a source of misery. He is so negative and ashamed of himself that Nora accuses him of being "already dead," which is consistent with his view of the "third sex" as "lifeless," since he focuses only on the possibility of reproduction. Later on, when he learns that Nora and Robin have given each other a doll as a symbol for their union and "the life they cannot have," he says that "the third sex . . . contains life but resembles the doll" (123) and calls himself "The uninhabited angel!"[18] In fact, after trying to discourage Nora from loving Robin, he drowns his sorrow in drink to become full of self-pity: "I've done and been everything that I didn't want to be or do . . . I stand here, beaten up and mauled and weeping, knowing I am not what I thought I was. I'm . . . a coward. . . . I've never been one thing that I am. . . . And what am I? I'm damned" (132). Clearly, this self-alienation attests to Matthew's having to live in the closet and suffering from it. Thus, unfortunately, Matthew is victim to his belief that everything can be reduced to sexuality and procreation: "Man learns only by what he has between the one leg and the other! Oh that short dangle! We corrupt mortality by its industry" (116). Since for him, there is no other way of looking at the world (because this is what he has been reduced to by the world), love is out of the question: "I know no one loves, I least of all, and that no one loves me" (122).

A parody of a prophet who suffers from knowing too much, Matthew is lonely, and "telling of himself" is the only way he can relate to people. In the passage that introduces him, the narrator illustrates the power of his speech by the way she presents his listeners, "in parliamentary attitudes." In fact, as it turns out, Matthew's speeches are crucial to the development of the novel, and yet except for the fact that he speaks from a grammatical first-person point of view (and that there are quotation marks around his monologues that often last several pages), his style seems identical with that of the narrator.[19] As Donna Gerstenberger observes: "The reader of

Nightwood experiences O'Connor largely *as narrative*. The novel inscribes him by story and narrative act (i.e., not to be confused with Barnes or the implied narrator of the novel but as a creator within the larger narrative), whose stories often seem to exist for their own telling" (1989, 136). Usurping the position of the narrator, Matthew's presence draws attention to the narrator's absence, which is exactly how he is introduced: keeping the "guests" (i.e., readers) entertained in lieu of the "host." Turning the novel into a gathering of speakers and listeners, Matthew is in a position to subvert the concept of narrative as a succession of actions governed by cause and effect. His soliloquies are performances of a language consisting of epigrams and obscure allegories. They relate to the events of the story mostly in the abstract.

Not surprisingly, it turns out to be his relationship to Nora, the subject of the novel and his main listener later on, which "troubles" (1995, 130) Matthew. Nora becomes one of "the people in my life who have made my life miserable, coming to me to learn of degradation and the night" (133). She is first introduced by the narrator before him, as the anonymous "one young woman" in the group. A couple of pages later, she introduces herself by approaching him with a question about language to which he responds, literally, by paternalizing her:

> The young woman, who was in her late twenties, turned from the group, coming closer to Felix and the doctor. She rested her hands behind her against the table. She seemed embarrassed. "Are you both really saying what you mean, or are you just talking?" Having spoken, her face flushed, she added hurriedly, "I am doing advance publicity for the circus, I'm Nora Flood." The doctor swung around, looking pleased. "Ah!" he said, "Nora suspects the cold incautious melody of time crawling, but," he added, "I've only just started." Suddenly he struck his thigh with his open hand. "Flood, Nora, why sweet God, my girl, I helped to bring you into the world!" (Barnes 1995, 16)

Presenting himself as a midwife to Nora, the doctor positions himself prior to her, even though the narrator mentions her before mentioning him. Instead of answering her question, he asserts his position as a storyteller, regardless of whether his audience is interested or not. His attitude is that of a preacher, and he later explains that "I talk too much because I have been made so miserable by what you are keeping hushed" (135). Nora, as her question indicates, does not seem to be impressed. As we learn later, she "was an early Christian; she believed in the word" (47). For her, the issue is to find a language that can bridge what she perceives as a discrepancy between internal "truth" and social "appearance." In her capacity of "doing advance publicity for the circus," she represents rather than performs. To her, rhetoric must also represent, namely, a greater power whose essence is, however, nonverbal; talking cannot be the frivolous occupation that it seems to be for the doctor. What her question fails to address is that "just talking" is vital to Matthew. Since he is so lonely, his main objective is to manipulate others into listening to him. Nora's question seems irrelevant to him, and the two linguistic categories she establishes are meaningless because "meaning," to him, is speaking. At the end of the party, she admonishes him: "You argue about sorrow and confusion too easily" (19), but she is again mistaken: his language turns out to consist of self-fulfilling prophecies and determines even Nora's reality within the universe of the novel.

Addressing Nora as a "girl," he situates himself at the origin of the narrative, a strategy he repeats when called upon to "find" Robin, who has passed out in a hotel room. The story of Nora and Robin seems to become Matthew's "story," even though he is not directly involved. He is the matchmaker for the brief and unhappy marriage between Robin and Felix in the second chapter, and his prediction that "Nora will leave [Robin] some day; but . . . one dog will find them both" (1995, 89) comes true. Each of these instances constructs Matthew's presence as integral to the novel so that he seems to "create" the book from inside its covers. As a representative of the "third sex," he holds on to the biological paradigm that precedes narcissism so that he can be understood as a counterpart to Nora and Robin's narcissistic relationship (which I will discuss shortly).

Matthew's prophecies can be read in reaction to other characters. For instance, when Nora forces him to listen, he walks out, unable to deal with her lament. He predicts "the end—mark my words—now *nothing but wrath and weeping*!" (1995, 136; Barnes's emphasis), as if to punish her for transgressing his domain (language). When Felix, at the party, laughs at Matthew's phrase "time crawling," Matthew puts him in his place in regard to history: "'The last muscle of aristocracy is madness—remember that—' the doctor leaned forward 'the last child born to aristocracy is sometimes an idiot, out of respect—we go up—but we come down'" (38). The narrator only has to follow along: "as time passed it became increasingly evident that his child, if born to anything, had been born to holy decay. Mentally deficient, and emotionally excessive, an addict to death" (90). The figure of time is central to the way in which Matthew operates: arguing that "we all carry about with us the house of death. . . . Time is a great conference planning our end" (109), he places himself in a position prior to time, making it possible for himself to speak endlessly and thereby perpetuate the novel. Nora's resistance to Matthew, in this sense, could be read as an opposition to narrative itself, which is confirmed by the fact that she becomes primarily invested in images of Robin that are poetic, that is, do not have a narrative.

Time, in Matthew's philosophy, contains its own undoing: "In the acceptance of depravity the sense of the past is most fully captured. What is a ruin but Time easing itself of endurance?" (1995, 101). He perceives Nora's desire for Robin as ruinous early on: "The doctor, seeing Nora, out walking alone, said to himself . . . 'There goes the dismantled. . . . Out looking for what she's afraid to find—Robin" (54). He then expands the metaphor of Nora's dismantlement:

> You went about the house like someone sunken under lightness. You were ruined and you kept striking your hands together, laughing crazily and singing a little and putting your hands over your face. Stage tricks have been taken from life, so finding yourself employing them you were confused with a sense of shame. When you went out looking for someone to go mad with, they said, "For God's sake, look at Nora!" For the demolishing of a ruin is always a fine and terrifying spectacle. (Barnes 1995, 119)

As his "reading" of Nora shows, the doctor positions himself to judge the other characters according to his own philosophy of decay and "degeneration" (deterioration). Like Freud, the analyst, he occupies the position of the third, the observer. Acting as an audience to their emotional dramas or "spectacles," he takes on a position of detached superiority within the economy of the novel that seems to be narrated, at times, entirely through him. Hence he describes himself in grandiose terms, as a "god" and a "liar" (implying that he is able to get away with this self-aggrandizement—like Freud's narcissistic criminal) as well as a madman: "I was in on what was wrong with the world . . . and I went mad, I'm like that." Madness, to him, is performance, for example, when he talks about the Bavarian king Ludwig: "if wanting a theater all to yourself is madness, I'm madder than most" (1995, 23). He perceives the other characters as if on a stage, and when Nora's own "madness" over losing Robin causes her to have tears and nightmares, the doctor maintains his distance. His verbose reflections allow both to connect him to and separate him from others, as this is his way of making time: so long as he continues to speak, the action cannot continue—Nora sits listening to him, instead of going out to search for her beloved (which she eventually does, near the end of the book). Hence through speaking, the doctor expands the moment yet leaps into the future and the past as if he were not locked into any present situation. This atemporality, if anything, is related to the static quality of the "ego ideal," which is fixed in time to provide the illusion of immortality to the subject who suffers from knowing that, eventually, his life will come to an end.

However, in spite of his self-aggrandizement, the god of darkness is human, not always in control: when Felix spots him in the streets, he "instantly . . . threw off his unobserved self, as one hides, hastily, a secret life" (1995, 92); and when they talk in a café, he at some point "had 'deteriorated' into that condition in which [Felix] had seen him in the street, when he thought himself unobserved" (97). The sad truth of Matthew's life is that he must live in the closet, which is why his divine place in *Nightwood* must be shared with the other member of the "third sex," Robin Vote. As the object of desire, she is caught up in Nora's narcissism (Nora makes what Freud would call a "narcissistic object choice" by falling in love with a woman) and thus becomes part of the novel's paradigm shift from "third sex" to narcissism.

A Wild Thing Caught in a Woman's Skin

Compared to Matthew, Robin's powers are of a different kind, which seems to make language itself obsolete. In the second chapter, "La Somnambule," the reader is introduced to her and she becomes the actual center of the novel, around which everything else revolves. Robin is found by hotel personnel as an anonymous "lady in twenty-nine who had fainted and could not be brought out of it" (Barnes 1995, 33) and thus first presented to us via the gazes of the doctor and Felix:

> On a bed, surrounded by a confusion of potted plants, exotic palms and cut flowers, faintly oversung by the notes of unseen birds, which seemed to have been forgotten, left without the usual silencing cover (which, like cloaks on funeral urns, are cast over their cages at night by good housewives), half flung off the support of the cushions from which, in a moment of threatened consciousness she had turned her head, lay the

young woman, heavy and dishevelled. Her legs, in white flannel trousers, were spread as in a dance, the thick lacquered pumps looking too lively for the arrested step. Her hands, long and beautiful, lay on either side of her face. (Barnes 1995, 34)

This scene reiterates the novel's opening: the subject of the sentence is introduced only after a series of descriptive clauses and both scenes feature a woman on a bed (as if to parody this repetition of women in beds, the doctor, at a later point, also appears in a "narrow iron bed . . . in a woman's flannel night gown" (69). However, the atmospheres differ: whereas the Hedvig scene posited a certain point in time and introduced cultural references to identify her, the Robin passage starts with the location of a body. The opposition between nature and culture, to which Hedvig is subjected, is mellowed, as "potted plants, exotic palms and cut flowers" suggest a domesticated nature, enveloping its inhabitant like organic furniture. The narrator compares this image to a painting by Le Douanier Rousseau to explain that Robin "seemed to lie in a jungle trapped in a drawing room" (34) so that nature and art, around Robin, are intertwined. In fact, art now replaces "history" if one compares Hedvig's with Robin's setting: whereas Hedvig gives birth, Robin is asleep, thus representing the timelessness of death, as she will continue to do throughout *Nightwood*. And, while "nature" determines Hedvig only in part (her environment locks her into culture), Robin seems to be in complete harmony with it: like the birds who are forgotten, "left without the usual silencing cover," she is lying "flung off the support of the cushions," physically present but unconscious; and her posture evokes dance along with their song. The scene is devoid of action, and the "arrested step" only highlights the absence of any dramatic impulse at the present time. As the title of the chapter tells, Robin is "La Somnambule" ("The Sleepwalker") and this imagery continues even after the doctor has awakened her with a splash of cold water. In this amazing passage, Robin's primitive nature is connected to mythical time, which progresses cyclically, by way of return:

> The girl was sitting up. She recognized the doctor. She had seen him somewhere. . . . She closed her eyes, and Felix . . . found himself seeing them still faintly clear and timeless behind the lids—the long unqualified range in the iris of wild beasts who have not tamed the focus down to meet the human eye. The woman who presents herself to the spectator as a "picture" forever arranged, is for the contemplative mind

> the chiefest danger. Sometimes one meets a woman who is beast turning human. Such a person's every movement will reduce to an image of a forgotten experience; a mirage of an eternal wedding cast on the racial memory . . . as the unicorn is neither man nor beast deprived, but human hunger pressing its breast to its prey. Such a woman is the infected, carrier of the past—before her the structure of our head and jaws ache—we feel that we could eat her, she who is eaten death returning, for only then do we put our face close to the blood on the lips of our forefathers. (Barnes 1995, 36)

Robin resembles a mythological figure, but she does not actually represent or embody anything. Conceived of in terms of reflection, whoever looks at her will see himself, in this case Felix, who falls in love with her on account of her ability to be a "carrier of the past." As the narrator explains, "his love for Robin was not in truth a selection; it was as if the weight of his life had amassed one precipitation. He had thought of making a destiny for himself. . . . Then with Robin it seemed to stand before him. . . . He was taken aback to find himself accepted, as if Robin's life held no volition for refusal" (1995, 40). Passively, Robin destroys Felix's life by doing exactly what he wants her to do: she gives birth to his son and then leaves him and the child. When Felix asks the doctor, "Why did she marry me? It has placed me in the dark for the rest of my life" (95), he fails to recognize that Robin's "chiefest danger" is precisely that of being a "picture": she offers herself to the gaze, but she reflects back only the desires of those who look at her. This quality is reminiscent of Sheperdson's "moment of the emergence of narcissism" which I quoted in chapter 1: "the moment of a subject who is not a subject before he sees himself, and who is already lost the moment reflection begins—a subject who is nothing before the image gives him to himself, and who is already something else as soon as the image arrives" (2000, 102).

Paradoxically, Robin "represents" reflection. She is a projective surface, a reflective image which only seems to have depth on account of its ability to absorb the viewer into his or her own fantasies. Truly oblivious to others, Robin lives in her own world and eludes even the reader's grasp. Rather than being a character, she is a figure, an object on whose "possession" the novel may focus but who forces those who look at her (the "contemplative mind") to look, really, at themselves. Only Matthew is immune to her, because he himself lives in the "night world" in which Robin exists. Naturally, they recognize each other from the cafés they frequent.

However, although Robin represents nothing, the main metaphor used to describe her is that of a "beast turning human." Even during the daytime, she appears in connection with a primitive animality:

> Removed from her setting,—the plants that had surrounded her, the melancholy red velvet of the chairs and the curtains, the sound, weak and nocturnal, of the birds,—she yet carried the quality of the "way back," as animals do. . . . She was gracious and yet fading, like an old statue in a garden, that symbolizes the weather through which it has endured, and is not so much the work of man as the work of wind and rain and the herd of the seasons, and though formed in man's image, is a figure of doom. (Barnes 1995, 39)

In keeping with the previous description as part of a painting, Robin is compared to "a statue in a garden" (an image that is later reiterated), and her nature combines nature and art, whereby she comes across as both unself-conscious and overly refined. Acting as an "essence," Robin does not depend on her environment, since she does not orient herself in space through visual perception; Felix is frightened by "the sensuality in her hands" because "when she touched a thing, her hands seem to take the place of the eye" (1995, 40). While magnetically attracting the gaze of others, Robin herself is blind, with her gaze described as having "the long unqualified range in the iris of wild beasts that have not tamed the focus down to meet the human eye." Wild and with "no volition for refusal," she does not appear to be the agent of her own destiny, yet her weapon is the way she yields to the gaze, to fatally draw the viewer into her world.[20]

On the one hand, Robin dominates the novel, and on the other hand, she escapes definition. In fact, on the part of the author herself, there seems to be a struggle over how to articulate her, for she appears to differ with each new description (she appears to be an "essence" in some scenes and a "surface" in others)—Robin is nothing "but human hunger pressing its breast to its prey" (1995, 36). However, it is the texture of her clothes that seems to determine her identity:

> Her clothes were of a period that [Felix] could not quite place . . . heavy silks that made her seem newly ancient. One day he learned the secret. Pricing a small tapestry in an antique shop facing the Seine, he saw Robin reflected in a door mirror of a back room, dressed in a heavy brocaded gown which time had stained in places, in others split, yet which

was so voluminous that there were yards enough to refashion. (Barnes 1995, 40)

Robin's clothes come to represent the "newly ancient" way in which she embodies the past, yet this is not due to the fact that the gown is from a different period but rather that "time" itself has "stained" its fabric. Like a magic gown, it has the capacity to renew itself, just like Robin, who seems forever engaged in wandering through the novel, with "yards enough to refashion." It is as if, literally, the gown "covers" her up instead of revealing what may be underneath. However, Robin does not seem to have any substance, so her very nature seems to consist of what she wears. Felix, who believes to discover her "secret," learns nothing about her, except that she is contained by her own texture. What he sees is the reflection of the surface, because Robin's "secret" *is* her appearance. Just like the gown, her presence in *Nightwood* yields enough fabric, that is, language, to be refashioned so that she not only represents the reflective surface onto which the other characters' desires can be projected but also the texture (fabric) of the novel itself.[21]

If the gown is indeed a signifier for the text that represents Robin, it is not surprising that her language also differs from that of the narrator and the other characters. Robin rarely speaks, and when she does it is in a primitive language of prayers, curses, and songs. Much less eloquent than the others, she expresses herself only in situations of physical intensity, for example, when giving birth to Guido: "Amid loud and frantic cries of affirmation and despair, Robin was delivered . . . looking about her in the bed as if she had lost something . . . she kept crying like a child who has walked into the commencement of a horror" (1995, 44). Compared to Hedvig's giving birth, Robin's gestures and nonverbal utterances are powerful, and in spite of her apparent passiveness, she is capable of expressing great rage: "One night [Felix] found her in the darkness . . . her chin thrust forward that the muscles in her neck stood out. As he came toward her, she said in a fury, 'I didn't want [the child]!' Raising her hand she struck him across the face" (45).

In spite of her assertiveness when cornered, Robin is "unable or unwilling" to represent her whereabouts to the other characters (and the reader). This task is left to the doctor, whose function in the novel, as I have explained, is to appear as if he were at the origin of the narrative. Not only because they are both members of the "third sex" but also because he competes with Robin for the reader's attention, he becomes the only one who is not subject to her destructive powers. After Robin has left her family to suddenly reappear without an explanation, the reader learns where she was through Matthew:

> For three or four months the people of the quarter asked for [Robin] in vain. Where she had gone no one knew. When she was seen again in the quarter, it was with Nora Flood. She did not explain where she had been, she was unable or unwilling to give an account of herself. The doctor said: "In America, that's where Nora lives, I brought her into the world and I should know." (Barnes 1995, 45)

Thus it is he who circumscribes and tells their story, as the next chapter takes place "in America" in a flashback (and through it, the connection between the three main characters—Matthew, Nora, Robin—is established, although they are never together at the same time). Matthew, in his function as a "narrator" who "gives birth" to characters and their stories, tries to control Robin, yet she eludes his as well as the reader's grasp. While he tries to act as a representative for her, by giving words to her silence, her nonverbal presence makes his rhetoric seem false, as if language were simply not able to capture her. Ultimately Robin's visual presence seems to exert more power than all the verbiage spilled by the "god of darkness." In fact, Burke calls her "an 'unmoved mover' . . . the *eromenon,* the *loved,* a God that moves us not by paternal or paternalistic participation in our affairs, but purely as an impassive destination for us to aim at, like a target or a beacon" (1968, 243).

What makes Robin so elusive is that she embodies a combination of opposites: although she is a "vamp," she is also a creature of "primitive innocence" (Barnes 1995, 100) who lives in "perpetual childhood" (113). She has "the troubling structure of the born somnambule, who lives in two worlds—meet of child and desperado," and this structure is complemented by her having the physical characteristics of both genders: she is "a tall girl with the body of a boy" (43). Her androgynous physical appearance (which corresponds to that of Thelma Wood; see photograph no. 13 in Herring 1995) combines both sexes, yet ultimately remains beyond gender, as it is really adolescent.[22]

Robin's sexually ambiguous image is also that of a madwoman: representing a form of self-enclosed "primary narcissism," she seems to suffer from hallucinations and a split personality. The narrator describes her as "a figure of doom [with] the face of an incurable, yet to be stricken with its malady" (Barnes 1995, 39); "she was really like those people who, coming unexpectedly into a room, silence the company because they are looking for someone who is not there" (94). It is as if Robin were "in her own nightmare" (121): her "engagements were with something unseen" (138). This madness is transferred onto Nora, who loves Robin in a way Freud would term "narcissistic object choice": "She is myself. What am I to do?" (108). In her capacity to destroy those who love her, Robin is like "a practised whore who turns away from no one but the one who loves her" (51). Oblivious to Nora's feelings, Robin drives her insane, although Nora realizes that they are dependent on one another: "If I asked her, crying, not to go out, she would go just the same, richer in her heart because I had touched it, as she was going down the stairs" (125). Subject to Robin's cruelty, Nora fails to see the narcissistic nature of her own involvement, since Robin seems to reflect primarily Nora's need to suffer and feel sorry for herself. Providing the illusion of being a real "other," Robin *is* Narcissus's reflection, so Nora's drama consists of her longing and wanting to merge. Robin's narcissism seems to have been transferred onto Nora, who has now become Robin's prey. Or, as Matthew puts it, Robin is like a cat "smiling sideways . . . with canary feathers to account for" (86).

An Image Is a Stop the Mind Makes between Uncertainties

Robin is like Narcissus: when Felix first sets eyes upon her, it is "as if this girl were the converging halves of a broken fate, setting face, in sleep, toward itself in time, as an image and its reflection in a lake seem parted only by the hesitation in the hour" (Barnes 1995, 37). Later he confesses to Matthew: "I find that I never did have a really clear idea of her at any time. I had an image of her but that is not the same thing. An image is a stop the mind makes between uncertainties" (93). Making images of Robin without having a "clear idea of her" is what everyone in *Nightwood* seems to do. Unlike Felix's, Nora's visions of Robin are not limited to her clothes or a potential place in the family tree but rather intimately connected with her own physical and emotional self. Nora, in her longing and suffering for Robin, becomes the emotional center of the novel, with which the reader is likely to identify (more than with the ironically detached attitude of the doctor).[23]

Like Felix, Nora has a background before she meets Robin (whose background we do not learn; she is like a "found object"): she has introduced herself as a publicity agent for the circus early on, but it is in chapter 3, "Night Watch," which is ostensibly about her relationship with Robin, that she is fully introduced by the narrator. More than Robin and the doctor, Nora seems typically American (the only European among the main characters is Felix), and she is presented among a group of misfits in a gothic wilderness:

> The strangest "salon" in America was Nora's. Her house was couched in the center of a mass of tangled grass and weeds. Before it fell into Nora's hands the property had been in the same family two hundred years. It had its own burial ground, and a decaying chapel in which stood in tens and tens of mouldering psalm books, laid down some fifty years ago in a flurry of forgiveness and absolution. It was the "paupers" salon, for poets, radicals, beggars, artists, and people in love; for Catholics, Protestants, Brahmins, dabblers in black magic and medicine; all these could be seen sitting about her oak table before the huge fire, Nora listening, her hand on her hound, the firelight throwing her shadow and his high against the wall. Of all that ranting roaring crew, she alone stood out. The equilibrium of her nature, savage and refined, gave her bridled skull a look of compassion. (Barnes 1995, 46)

Compared to the European gatherings in the previous chapters, the purpose of Nora's salon is to provide sanctuary, not entertainment. Nora projects an image of strength, consistent with her later relationship to Robin, for whom she provides a home. But she is also a source of darkness and silence, magnified by a "shadow" that includes her hound. The whole setting, as underscored by the hound, makes Nora come across as a kind of witch. Considering that the dog is the same one that finds Robin in the "decayed chapel" on Nora's property at the end of *Nightwood,* this image foreshadows the lovers' reunion. In fact, from a psychoanalytic point of view, one might call the dog an externalized "partial object" of Nora's self, which she needs to recover through Robin. Nora's shadow seems inextricably linked with that of her dog, which is consistent with the description of her personality as mastering the "savage" to achieve "the equilibrium of her nature." However, the narrator goes on, "there was some derangement in her equilibrium that kept her immune to her own descent" (1995, 47).

Puritanical and selfless, Nora "rob[s] herself for everyone" (47) only to realize, through her involvement with Robin, that "there's something evil in me, that loves evil and degradation—purity's black backside" (113). In this sense, the "shadow" with which she is here depicted may symbolize the "shadow" she carries within herself.

And, while Nora appears to be Robin's victim (their relationship ends over Robin's unfaithfulness), it is her own double standard that forces Robin into the role of the villain. As Matthew puts it: "You were a 'good woman,' and so a bitch on a high plane" (1995, 121). This statement refers to Nora's puritanical attitude in regard to sexuality, yet Matthew fails to see that something else is at stake for Nora. Attracted to Robin's "otherness," she loves her as a way of compensating for her own lack of self-love: "I thought I loved her for her sake, and I found it was for my own" (125). If Robin had been a way of dealing with the weight of history for Felix, she now functions as a way for Nora to uncover her own hidden fears and desires. In fact, before she met Robin, Nora was emotionally numb: "The world and its history were to Nora like a ship in a bottle; she herself was outside and unidentified. . . . Then she met Robin" (48). Robin releases her from this condition by bringing her to life with emotions.

In fact, while Robin is the one said to be in the habit of "wandering," it is Nora who manages to draw her into her orbit to "possess" her: when they first meet, it is at a performance of the circus in New York; and when they meet again in the end, it is on Nora's property, in her chapel. Nora seems powerful, but she is neither privileged nor likable: "She was by fate one of those people who are born unprovided for except in the provision of herself" (1995, 48). She seems blind in a way that fits perfectly with Robin's wandering, for her eyes have "that mirrorless look of polished metals which report not so much the object as the movement of the object" (48). Rather than actually seeing Robin, Nora imagines her in a series of images that may be seen as representing her own unconscious so that Robin functions like a medium for her. At least this is how I would interpret the following passage, where Nora is waiting for Robin to come home at night:

> Love becomes the deposit of the heart, analogous in all degrees to the "findings" in a tomb. As in one will be charted the taken place of the body, the raiment, the utensils necessary to its other life, so in the heart of the lover will be traced, as an indelible shadow, that which he loves. In Nora's heart lay the fossil of Robin, intaglio of her identity, and about

it for its maintenance ran Nora's blood. . . . Nora's mind . . . became so transfixed that, by the agency of her fear, Robin seemed enormous and polarized; all catastrophes ran toward her, the magnetized predicament; and crying out, Nora would wake from sleep, going back through the tide of dreams into which her anxiety had thrown her, taking the body of Robin down with her into it, as the ground things take the corpse, with minute persistence, down into the earth, leaving a pattern of it on the grass, as if they stitched as they descended. (Barnes 1995, 51)

Imagining the "heart" as a "tomb," Nora buries Robin inside her body in what seems to be a reverse birth, with the heart acting like a womb. When Robin becomes a threat from growing too large in Nora's imagination, Nora takes her "down with her into" her subconscious (the "tide of dreams") and expands the initial metaphor to bury both of them in the larger womb of the "earth." What seems significant about this passage is that it uses Matthew's favorite tropes—"descent," "death," "decay," "blood"—to describe a process connected to art, not nature. Nora's "blood" animates the "fossil" of Robin in her heart not as an actual, biological process but as a metaphoric, subjective rendering of her feelings. The body is evoked figuratively, not literally, which is underscored through the reference to a particular technique of representation: the text refers to an "intaglio," according to *Webster's* "an engraving or incised figure in stone or other hard material depressed below the surface of the material so that an impression from the design yields an image in relief."[24] The lovers' descent takes place as a form of "writing," a process of pressing the image into the surface in a way that could be read as a metaphor for embroidering, that is, "stitching a pattern," which would also be the opposite of engraving. This apparent reversal of modes of representation—which illustrates the principle of reflection at work throughout *Nightwood*—frames Nora's taking action to fend off the threat of Robin's engulfment of her. Introducing the element of vertical movement transforms the "tomb" into an active burial, with Nora recasting herself in a different role. Her physical incorporation of Robin could be called a form of "narcissistic object relations," yet the text draws attention to its own artificiality so that, given the uncertainty of Robin's nature, the "object" seems imaginary to begin with.

After this passage, Nora and Robin are described like Narcissus and his reflection: "sometimes, going about the house, in passing each other, they would fall into an agonized embrace, looking into each other's face, their two heads in their four hands, so strained together that the space that divided them seemed to be thrusting them apart. . . . To keep her . . . Nora knew now that there was no way but death" (1995, 54). It seems that Nora's entire being is sustained by looking at Robin, and through this intimate proximity, she is threatened by the fear of loss. As a way of keeping Robin, vision itself functions as the most tangible reality for Nora, for example, in the following dream, which repeats and expands upon the metaphor of a "strained" gaze:

> Nora dreamed that she was standing at the top of a house. . . . Nora looked down into the body of the house, as if from a scaffold, where now Robin had entered the dream, lying among a company below. . . . A disc of light, that seemed to come from someone or thing standing behind her and which was yet a shadow, shed a faintly luminous glow upon the upturned, still face of Robin who had the smile of an "only survivor," a smile which fear had married to the bone. . . . The louder [Nora] cried out the further away went the floor below, as if Robin and she, in their extremity, were a pair of opera glasses turned to the wrong end, diminishing in their painful love; a speed that ran away with the two ends of the building, stretching her apart. (Barnes 1995, 55)

Again Nora desires to hold Robin and thus imprisons her in her gaze, which here manifests itself in the form of an architectonic construct that, like a substitute body, contains them both. The dream differs from the previous image of their descent into the earth, not only because Nora sees Robin escaping from her gaze but also because her position implies a hierarchy in which they are no longer on the same level. Having placed herself "on top," Nora may have saved herself from the depths but also sees herself in danger of losing Robin. Robin is no longer "inside" Nora and now clearly marked as a vision by the "disc of light," with the gaze itself taking on substance. Suddenly visual perception becomes painful because it is connected with Robin (and vice versa). Or, as the doctor has observed in a previous scene, where he saw Nora searching for Robin in the streets: "She sees her everywhere. . . . Out looking for what she's afraid to find—Robin" (1995, 54). Again this scene is marked as fantasy (a dream), and it seems that the moments Nora is most strongly attached to Robin are when she is, in fact, absent.

The dream ends with Nora's recognition that "something [is] being done to Robin, Robin disfigured and eternalized by the hieroglyphics of sleep and pain" (56). In the following scene, reality sets in as yet another painful vision, this time no longer a dream. When Nora wakes up, she gets up to look out of the window and sees Robin in an embrace with another woman:

> She saw a double shadow falling from the statue, as if it were multiplying; and thinking perhaps this was Robin, she called and was not answered. Standing motionless, straining her eyes, she saw emerge from the darkness the light of Robin's eyes, the fear in them developing their luminosity until, by the intensity of their double regard, Robin's eyes and hers met. So they gazed at each other. . . . Nora saw the body of another woman . . . her arms about Robin's neck, her body pressed to Robin's. . . . Unable to turn her eyes away, incapable of speech, experiencing a sensation of evil, complete and dismembering, Nora fell to her knees, so that her eyes were not withdrawn by her volition, but dropped from their orbit by the falling of her body. (Barnes 1995, 56)

The difference between what takes place in Nora's imagination and what she now really sees is marked by her physical reaction: unlike the darkness of the earth, in which a visual pattern emerges only in retrospect, trailing behind the bodies, or the "disc of light" which illuminates Robin but is separate from Nora herself, the power of vision now really seems to have taken over Nora's body. In order to see more clearly, Nora is "straining her eyes" and, when seen by Robin, is "unable to turn her eyes away," until the involuntary "falling of her body" pulls her away from the vision. And, whereas the earth and the house are spaces which appear to be part of herself and can contain Robin, the scene in the garden expulses Nora from the illusive paradise of her imagination by presenting her with Robin's betrayal, the truth Matthew said she has been "afraid to find." Nora is physically cut off from the gaze that connects her to Robin and sustains her entire being when her body involuntarily "falls" to the ground so that this gaze reveals itself as substantial. What began as a way of trying to "hold" Robin, a way of visually representing her during her absences by carefully "stitching" or gradually "stretching," has now turned into a "dismemberment," a separation from Robin which cuts apart the connection between them: when Nora's eyes "drop from their orbit," she loses control over herself and her body.

Considering "narcissistic object choice," one could say that it is here that the object reveals itself to be real. Looking back at Nora, Robin resists

Nora's incorporation by actively returning the gaze and by distinguishing herself from the static figure, the statue, into whose mold she seems to have been cast. When Nora sees a "double shadow falling from the statue, as if it were multiplying," she is first led to believe that this figure is Robin alone, with the other shadow coming from the statue itself. Only after Robin looks back at her does Nora realize that there is another woman present. Either the embrace between the two women is so tight that they appear as a single shadow or the statue itself does not have a shadow—in both cases Nora's perception would have been momentarily subjected to a trompe l'oeil. Tricked by the very sense through which she constitutes her subjectivity in regard to Robin, it takes Robin's return of the gaze for Nora to fully grasp the situation, that is, perceive the other woman. Their mutual stare, in fact, seems to hold Nora, forcing her to focus and notice the other woman in the periphery. Thus, even within the dismantling of the gaze, Nora is shown to be at the mercy of Robin, whose power now becomes fully apparent.

Seeing what she sees and being held captive by it, Nora can avert her gaze only by going down on her knees (in the end, Robin will be on hers). Humbled and humiliated, her feeling of dismemberment is based on the fact that she has been split apart from what now appears to have been a totalizing gaze. The "intensity of their double regard" sustains the gaze but makes it impossible for Nora to remain in control, so that the "descent" she had previously imagined together with Robin must now take place without her.

Whether or not Robin is "real" does not seem to matter as much as the fact that Nora needs her to hold herself in place. In this sense, Robin might represent not so much the "love object" but the "ego ideal" of which Freud writes (and which is subsequently taken up by Lacan). The main reversal of this scene consists in the fact that Nora is overwhelmed by being looked *at* by Robin, at a moment when she believes herself to be unobserved in looking at her. Lacan, in *The Four Fundamental Concepts,* describes a split between "the eye and the gaze . . . in which the drive is manifested at the level of the scopic field" (1981, 73). This fundamental split is profoundly disturbing to the subject insofar as it involves an apprehension of the "real": in phenomenological terms, Lacan argues, the subject recognizes that the eye "is only the metaphor of . . . something prior. . . . I see only from one point, but in my existence I am looked at from all sides" (72). If the eye is only a metaphor, the gaze, on the other hand, is "the thrust of our experience, namely the lack that constitutes castration anxiety"(73).

Robin's return of the gaze can be read as the intrusion of an "other" into Nora's narcissistic gaze (which then causes her to feel her entire world falling apart). The fact that she is forced to her knees by this experience highlights her dependence on the gaze. It shows that maintaining the visual connection to Robin is more than just an illusion: seeing Robin proves to have been essential to Nora's entire being.

Consequently, the moment that separates Nora from this connection is the moment at which she realizes that, in order to live, the gaze must be restored. Unlike in Matthew's philosophy, where everything is said to live or die with the actual, physical body, Nora tries to restore and preserve the image of Robin in her imagination: she comes to see the doctor to talk about Robin; and she continues to send letters to her long after they have lost touch. Like Narcissus, she is unable to turn away from the image of her beloved, yet having lost the actual, physical connection to this image, she must set out to recover Robin for real. As this emphasis on the physical effects of the imagination and gaze in *Nightwood* shows, vision is more than just a matter of appearances—compared to the doctor's biologically oriented discourse, where body and mind are separate, the image of the beloved can have a very real, physical effect.

Love Is Death

The "other" woman, Robin's lover Jenny Petherbridge, is introduced in *Nightwood*'s fourth chapter, appropriately titled "The Squatter," as "one of the most unimportantly wicked women of her time" (Barnes 1995, 60). Like Felix, she is a minor character, who exists primarily to take Robin away from Nora. The chapter refers back to the initial meeting between Jenny and Robin, which has taken place in the presence of the doctor, and ends with the garden scene, concluding with the abrupt statement that "it was not long after this that Nora and Robin separated; a little later Jenny and Robin sailed for America" (67). As it turns out, the chapter has only restated the events of the previous chapter, albeit in more detail, and from the doctor's perspective. Subsequently, the narrator returns to Nora, who now suffers from the breakup and comes to see the doctor for advice. This longer fifth chapter, called "Watchman, What of the Night?" consists of their conversation about "the night," including "the one particular night" when Robin met Jenny. Following the brief insertion of a sixth chapter (where Felix and Matthew meet to talk about Robin as well), the conversation spills over into the seventh chapter, "Go Down Matthew," where the doctor has visited Nora and they continue to talk. Nothing happens anymore until the very short final chapter, "The Possessed," where Nora recovers Robin, and it seems as if the entire second half of *Nightwood* is dominated by the conversation between Matthew and Nora, which can be traced as follows.

When Nora asks the doctor about "the night," it is clear that she has no idea about the world he and Robin inhabit. Matthew enlightens her: "Well, I, Doctor Matthew-Mighty-grain-of-salt-Dante-O'Connor, will tell you how the day and the night are related by their division. . . . Every day is thought upon and calculated, but the night is not premeditated" (1995, 70). He explains how the "night" is related to a fear of the unknown, to which Nora responds: "I used to think . . . that people just went to sleep . . . but now . . . I see that the night does something to a person's identity, even when asleep" (70). Matthew confirms this: "Let a man lay himself down in the Great Bed and his 'identity' is no longer his own" (70), but he makes distinctions: "The nights of one period are not the nights of another. Neither are the nights of one city the nights of another. Let us take Paris for an instance . . ." (71). Now the night appears to be about more than sleep, and Nora is prompted to ask about Robin: "I never thought of the night as a life at all—I've never lived it—why did she?" (71). Instead of answering Nora's question, Matthew explains that there is a connection between fantasy ("night") and reality ("day"), to argue that history is transformed into imagery: "Take history at night. . . . All through the night Rome went burning. Put that in the noontide and it loses some of its age-old significance, does it not? Why? Because it has existed to the eye of the mind all these years against a black sky. Burn Rome in a dream, and you reach and claw down the true calamity. For dreams have only the pigmentation of fact" (74). Accordingly, he continues, the night is outside real time, yet exists along with it: "The sleeper is the proprietor of an unknown land. He goes about another business in the dark—and we, his partners, who go to the opera, who listen to gossip of café friends, who walk along the boulevards, or sew a quiet seam, cannot afford an inch of it" (74). Having thus defined the night as more powerful than the day, Matthew reverses Freud's paradigm of repression by bringing the world of the unconscious out into the open. He explains the night's significance to "the lover," that is, Nora, as a space of betrayal: "For the lover, it is the night into which his beloved goes. . . . When she sleeps is she not moving her leg aside for an unknown garrison? Or in a moment, that takes but a second, murdering us with an ax?" (75). Those who, like Nora, claim to be innocent of any knowledge of the night, are part of this destruction: "There is not one of us who, given an eternal incognito . . . would not commit rape, murder and all abominations" (75).

Having thus introduced the night to Nora, Matthew differentiates between night people, like himself and Robin, and people like Nora who "would have the night combed with the great blind searchlight of the heart" (79). He accuses Nora of being naively romantic and includes her, "the lover," into the group of night people:

> And though your normal fellow will say all are alike in the dark, negro [*sic*] or white, I say you can tell them, and where they came from, and what quarter they frequent, by the size and excellence—and at the Bastille (and may I be believed) they come as handsome as *mortadellas* slung on a table. . . . And it's the same with girls . . . those who turn the day into night, the young, the drug addict, the profligate, the drunken and that most miserable, the lover who watches all night long in fear and anguish. These can never again live the life of the day. When one meets them at high noon, they give off, as if it were a protective emanation, something dark and muted. The light does not become them any longer. They begin to have an unrecorded look. (Barnes 1995, 80)

The message is that night people do not constitute a homogeneous group and that Nora, although not as much "in the know" as Matthew, can never be in the position of "your normal fellow," since she now knows and loves Robin. She is "that most miserable, the lover who watches all night long in fear and anguish." The night Matthew refers to is primarily one in which sexual fantasies can be acted out (the "handsome" mortadellas, i.e., smoked sausages, seem to be code for male genitals). Unlike Freud, who pathologizes homosexuals, Matthew attributes a certain superiority to the night people, as if he and Robin were privileged to provide Nora with access to a realm of secret knowledge. However, he is right in that Nora must first acknowledge the power of the night. From the beginning, she has been shown to have some darkness inside her (the shadow), and now that she has been with Robin, there is no turning back: Nora must realize that "Love is death" (1995, 115) and that "Robin's love and mine was always impossible, and loving each other, we no longer love. Yet we love each other like death" (116). As Matthew explains, "night people do not bury their dead, but on the neck of you, their beloved and waking, sling the creature, husked of its gestures. And where you go, it goes, the two of you, your living and her dead, that will not die" (76). Once Nora has entered Robin's world, she is forever caught, even after she has told Robin to leave: "Once, when she was sleeping, I wanted her to die. Now, that would stop nothing" (108). The initial wish to kill Robin was motivated by Nora's need to possess her: "Die now, so you will be quiet; so you will not be touched again by dirty hands . . . die now, then you will be mine forever" (120). However, now Robin is constantly on her mind, and this "possession" is described as madness: "I was going mad because I was awake and seeing it, unable to reach it. . . . I had struck her sleep away, and I went mad and I've been mad ever since" (121). As in Hardenberg, we encounter the connection between narcissism and madness, yet here this madness is presented as a function of desire (for the absent object), not as a form of mental illness (as in Zürn, the subject of my next chapter).

Through talking to Matthew, Nora begins to understand her madness in relation to Robin's: "She knew she was driving me insane with misery and fright . . . she falls into everything, like someone in a dream. . . . A shadow was falling on her—mine—and it was driving her out of her wits" (1995, 128). Again she and Robin appear interconnected, as in Felix's statement which could also apply to Nora: "[Robin] wanted darkness in her mind—to throw a shadow over what she was powerless to alter—her dissolute life, her life at night" (129). Nora adopts Matthew's allegory of the "night" as the origin of madness, but Matthew is unable to help her, as she constructs a circular argument and becomes engaged in a vicious circle of self-reflection: every observation serves only to confirm the fact that she and Robin are hopelessly intertwined, as in Matthew's analogy of "the poor beasts that get their antlers mixed and are found dead that way, their heads fattened with a knowledge of each other they never wanted, having had to contemplate each other, head on and eye to eye, until death: well, that will be you and Jenny and Robin" (85).

What hurts Nora most is not that she has seen Robin with Jenny in the garden but that Jenny has a "child" with Robin, in the form of a doll she saw when having visited Jenny in her apartment:

> "I kept thinking, what else is it that is hurting me, then I knew—the doll; the doll in there on the bed. . . . We give death to a child when we give it a doll—it's the effigy and the shroud; when a woman gives it to a woman, it is the life they cannot have, it is their child, sacred and profane; so when I saw that other doll—." Nora could not go on. She began to cry. (Barnes 1994, 118)

Nora interprets giving dolls as "giving death" by explaining that the doll is "the effigy and the shroud": a three-dimensional object, it is more than an image, and it becomes uncanny as one projects life into it. Unlike a picture or a statue, a doll can be held, yet it carries with it the "shroud" of inanimateness. It is up to its owner to breathe life into it so that it, unlike a reflection, becomes a creature in its own right, dependent on the person who animates it. While Narcissus tries to embrace his reflection in vain, the doll is an "object" that *can* be embraced, so one can have the illusion of fully possessing someone like oneself. And, since the doll stands in for "the life they cannot have," it includes the concept of "creation," like the work of art. As in the beginning, when Hedvig gives birth; and in the doctor's ruminations about death, procreation is represented as an absent or destructive force.

To Nora, the sight of this other doll has been so traumatic that retelling it causes her to interrupt her self-analysis by crying. Evidently the vision in the garden was not what caused her to throw Robin out (instead, she must have gone to see Jenny); it is only after the vision of the "double shadow" that the vision of the doll's "double" has triggered their actual breakup. The doll is what seems to have marked their relationship as "real," yet in its capacity as an inanimate object it is also a mere symbol, whose "sacred and profane" character is based only on its proprietor's willingness to suspend her disbelief. Unlike a real child, the doll "dies" when the stage conventions are violated, so the relationship between Robin and Nora seems little more than a "performance." And yet still, as I have tried to show, the continuation of this performance is vital to Nora, so the question arises whether all relationships are, really, dependent more on images and symbols than on "bloodlines." Clearly, Barnes's text can be read as a critique of the kind of biological thinking that reduces love and sexuality to the ability to procreate.

A Couple of Velvet Dogs; or, Dolls That Looked as if They Had Been Up All Night

The economy of reproduction that shapes Felix's and Matthew's respective worldviews is compromised through the existence of the doll. In Nora's conversation with Matthew, we learn that one night, Nora found Robin in a position of "holding the doll she had given us—'our child'—high above her head, as if she would cast it down, a look of fury on her face" (Barnes 1995, 122). This scene mirrors the earlier one, where "one night, Felix, having come in unheard, found [Robin] standing in the center of the floor, holding the child high in her hand as if she were about to dash it down" (44). Although "she brought it down gently," whereas she "picked up the doll and hurled it to the floor and put her foot on it, crushing her heel into it; and then . . . kicked it, its china head all in dust, its skirt shivering and stiff, whirling over and over across the floor" (122), the impulse seems the same. In fact, one could argue that Robin's neglect of Guido, her leaving him with Felix, is analogous to this physical abuse of the doll. Clearly, Robin is not interested in motherhood, a trait that coincides with Matthew's representation of the "third sex" as sterile and connected to "death":

> The doll—yes, target of things past and to come. The last doll, given to age, is the girl who should have been a boy, and the boy who should have been a girl! The love of that last doll was foreshadowed in that love of the first. The doll and the immature have something right about them, the doll because it resembles but does not contain life, and the third sex because it contains life but resembles the doll. (Barnes 1995, 123)

Drawing an analogy between the doll and "the third sex," Matthew shows the interconnectedness between animate and inanimate "nature," which, like night and day, are inseparable. He defends Robin by accusing Nora of being puritanical as well as heterosexually oriented, since she does not seem to understand that Robin, by belonging to the "third sex," is like the doll (hence the abuse she stages may be representative of that which she herself may have experienced). While Robin represents death, Matthew redeems her by saying that there is "something right" about her. He describes the "third sex" as "lifeless" on account of its not procreating, but this is also where his philosophy seems limited, for he cannot conceive of a more positive queer relationship.

When Matthew raises the question "what is this love we have for the invert, boy or girl?" (Barnes 1995, 114), Nora's answer is phrased in terms of narcissism, which now appears to be a more positive way of thinking about homosexuality: "A man is another person—a woman is yourself, caught as you turn in panic; on her mouth you kiss your own. If she is taken you cry that you have been robbed of yourself. God laughs at me; but his laughter is my love" (119). To this, Matthew reacts with hostility: "Love of woman for woman, what insane passion for unmitigated anguish and motherhood brought that into the mind?" (66). If Carolyn Allen is correct in her assessment that "the mother/child trope figures most crucially in *Nightwood*'s palimpsest. Like positions of gender, mother/child stereotypes abound in discussions of lesbian relations" (1993, 186), Matthew only reinforces this stereotype when he addresses Nora as "you, who should have had a thousand children and Robin, who should have been all of them" (Barnes 1995, 85), and Nora herself remembers Robin as "my lover and my child" (1995, 129). However, his view of their relationship revolves around the (im)possibility of motherhood, whereas Nora realizes that the doll is not merely a substitute "child" but also the signifier of a different relationship—it marks the presence of that "other" world, the night, where nature and art are no longer separate and where it is possible to live in accordance with one's nature and desires. If Robin is indeed Nora's "child," as the stereotype suggests, but also the "doll" that represents the "third sex," as Matthew suggests, then she takes on the function of that which is lacking within Nora.

In contrast, biological motherhood, in *Nightwood,* results in either a loss of life (death in childbed) or mental retardation (Guido). The doll, ostensibly connoting the "joy" of motherhood or the "sadness" of sterility, is more than a poor substitute for the real thing, for it cannot be assimilated into either discourse. Matthew himself mixes metaphors when talking about people at a fair who were purchasing "a couple of velvet dogs, or dolls that looked as if they had been up all night" (1995, 87). What comes across most clearly is that nothing is what it seems to be, so that the novel, in effect, represents a kind of "madness." Inanimate objects are endowed with life, and living creatures can be already "dead," like Matthew, who says: "I'm an angel on all fours, going down face foremost, drinking the waters of night at the water hole of the damned, and I go into the waters, up to my heart, the terrible waters!" (81). Breaking through the surface of the water, he enters the space of darkness that is related to madness, where "representation" ceases to exist and the text itself becomes illegible.

At the very end, the reader is confronted with a cryptic image, after Robin has found her way onto Nora's property and Nora appears, once again, in her house, this time next to a lamp instead of a fire. Nora hears her dog—who has now left her shadow—whining and running about and, finally, she walks into "the night," to the chapel where she finds Robin:

> At the moment Nora's body struck the wood, Robin began going down, down, her hair swinging, her arms out. The dog stood rearing back. . . .

> And down she went, until her head swung against his, on all fours now, dragging her knees. The veins stood out in her neck, under her ears, swelled in her arms, and wide and throbbing, rose up on her hands as she moved forward. . . . Then head down, dragging her forelocks in the dust, she struck against his side. He let loose one howl of misery and bit at her, dashing about her, barking. . . . Then she began to bark also, crawling after him—barking in a fit of laughter, obscene and touching. Crouching, the dog began to run with her . . . until she gave up, lying out, her hands beside her, her face turned and weeping; and the dog too gave up then, and lay down, his eyes bloodshot, his head flat along her knees. (Barnes 1995, 139)

In what seems to be an image of Robin's "possession," Nora's gaze is restored to contain the "object" that is her beloved, which she now "repossesses." If one interprets the dog (as well as the doll) as part of Nora's self, this ending is not as unhappy as it may seem, for it suggests that they get back together on the same level, having "given up" their struggle so that they can, finally, rest with one another. Their reunion is mediated through the gaze, in which desire and fantasy are connected, so that it also relates to the "madness" which is part of narcissism. Distinctions between what is "real" and what is imaginary are no longer possible, for what counts is desire itself—Nora's perspective becomes identical with that of the narrator and we, the readers, see what she sees. In this sense, *Nightwood* is Nora's story, not Matthew's—and Robin is an "object" that belongs, in truth, to Nora's own self. Matthew's attempts to provide rational explanations for the relationship between the lovers, to force them into stereotypical discourses about the "third sex," have failed—he has drowned himself in drink at the end of the previous chapter, never to be heard of again. *Nightwood,* like Robin, who performs "animality" in this final scene, has presented itself as a spectacle, a "play" between lovers that is less connected to Eliot's "Elizabethan tragedy" than to Shakespeare's comedy *A Midsummer Night's Dream,* where men are transformed into beasts and being "mad" means being "madly in love."[25] Thus the novel's playful depiction of madness differs from that of Freud, who seeks to understand mental illness by connecting it to primary narcissism (schizophrenia) and the ego ideal (paranoia). Pathology will be the subject of the next chapter, on Unica Zürn, where the confusion between reality and fantasy takes on the form of hallucinations, leading both to the creation of art and real, physical self-destruction.

5. The Violence of Merging: Unica Zürn's Writing (on) the Body

Case/History

In the previous chapter, I discussed the structure of Djuna Barnes's novel *Nightwood* in terms of an opposition between a discursive frame and a series of images in relation to Freud's concept of "narcissistic object choice." In this chapter, I will focus on a text connected to the third and final concept in Freud's essay, the "ego ideal." When *Nightwood* ends, it remains impossible to tell to what extent the "other" is real or imaginary so that the text opens up toward a playful kind of madness. Similarly, madness is at issue in Unica Zürn's *The Man of Jasmine: Impressions from a Mental Illness,*[1] yet here it is no longer playful but rather based on the author's attempt to transform her own, real-life experience with mental illness into a work of art: the images here are no longer fictitious but said to represent actual hallucinations; and the narrative seems to coincide with the life of Zürn, who was confined to a series of mental institutions and committed suicide in 1970, the year *The Man of Jasmine* was first published. Zürn, who was born in Berlin in 1916, was of a later generation than Hardenberg and Barnes, and she was associated, after World War II, with the surrealists. Compared to the expressionists and the Anglo-American modernists, the surrealists saw themselves in opposition to the bourgeois commodification of art, which they countered with artistic practices intended to tear down the barriers between "life" and "art."[2] Zürn's work is indicative of this practice, which is also connected to "performance art," where the body of the artist is part of the work of art, and which takes place in real time. An extreme example of performance art would be the case of a Viennese artist, Rudolf Schwarzkogler, who in 1969, as part of the movement Destruction in Art, killed himself in the name of art, after performing a series of self-mutilations on stage (Volckmann 1982; Ursprung 1999). Zürn, as I have argued in my introduction to my translation of her 1969 novella *Dark Spring,* made it seem as if her suicide was "scripted" and her madness "constructed." As critics have observed, it is difficult to separate her life from her work, for they seem inextricably interwoven.

Marketed as a "case history" by Ullstein Verlag in Germany, where it was published in 1977—seven years after its initial appearance in France—*The Man of Jasmine* is an artist's text which does not actually represent the spontaneous outpourings of a madwoman it appears to be. Rather, it "performs" madness for the reader: it conveys the impression of a split consciousness, yet it exhibits too much control to have been written by someone truly *in* that condition (which is what distinguishes it from *Art Brut*).[3] Through the use of the grammatical third-person perspective, the text represents the protagonist, a nameless "she," as suffering from paranoia and hallucinations while, at the same time, the narrator tells us her story in realistic, logical sequence. However, the intimate proximity between narrator and protagonist is indicated through the use of the present tense, which gives the impression that the events are recorded simultaneously while they are taking place. The reader is drawn into a text which, on the one hand, offers a consistent, omniscient narrative perspective and, on the other hand, allows us to enter the mind of the unreliable and confused protagonist, for example through the use of *erlebte Rede* (*style indirect libre,* or indirect free style). The effect is that we can never be sure whether what happens is real or imagined. Moreover, while the text appears to be autobiographical, as it is based on the author's real-life experiences and contains frequent references to real places and events, it does not correspond to Lejeune's (1982) definition of "autobiography" insofar as author, narrator, and character are not identical. The reader is tempted, as Sigrid Weigel has observed, to read the "she" as an "I" (1987, 211); yet Zürn's subject claims a more objective point of view for herself, in which "she" becomes an artistic creation, that is, a character invented by the author. According to Emile Benveniste (1971), the grammatical third person represents an impersonal perspective (*non-personne*), in contrast to the I / You dichotomy, and Zürn's use of it may be seen as an attempt to "objectify" her own self, to transform it into more than just an individual "case history." Zürn attempted to live her life "in the name of art," and the question then becomes: Which is which?

According to Zürn's friend and translator, Ruth Henry, "Unica herself is a poetic creature, someone really authentic, and this is what gives her book this striking ring of truth" ("Unica est une créature de poésie, quelqu'un de vraiment authentique, ce qui donne à son livre cet accent de vérité qui nous frappe," Zürn 1970, 256). This claim to an authentic, poetic form of madness can be dangerous: like her predecessor, Antonin Artaud, with whom she identified and whose 1942 collection *Lettres de Rodez* (1978) attests to his miserable condition in the asylum, Zürn ended up being subjected to treatments worse than the condition for which she had been hospitalized.[4] In part her project was to draw attention to this problem, as Brinkmann has also noted (Zürn 1988–99, 4.3:104). To understand madness from within, she wrote, "the reader should allow himself to become interested, if he possesses the beautiful gift of becoming mad, so as to experience what happens in such an institution" (Zürn 1988–99, 4.2:420, my translation). This positive validation of madness as a poetic force, which is combined with a critique of the institution of psychiatry (not to be confused with psychoanalysis), can be seen within the context of both surrealism and the antipsychiatry movement during the 1960s, to which Lacan also belonged (his connection with surrealism is documented by David Macey [1988]). André Breton—who had himself been a psychiatrist during World War II—defined surrealism in his first manifesto as "the future resolution of two states which seem to be contradicting one another, namely, dream and reality, into a kind of absolute reality" (1924, 23).[5] *The Man of Jasmine,* which is often compared with Breton's *Nadja* (1928),[6] is consistent with this premise. It can be placed in the literary tradition of German romanticism and nineteenth-century French authors, such as Gérard de Nerval and Lautréamont, and should be seen in conjunction with the many links existing between surrealism and psychoanalysis (Lomas 2001; Swarbrick 2000). In fact, Zürn went to sessions with Artaud's former psychiatrist, Gaston Ferdière; and what gave her the idea for *The Man of Jasmine* was a psychiatrist's suggestion to contribute an article from a patient's perspective to an institution's journal—later, she dedicated this text to "Monsieur le prof LACAN," who, according to Jean-François Rabain, held his 1961 seminar at Saint-Anne close to (i.e., "a few meters from") her room: "Lacan tenait alors son séminaire à quelques mètres de la chambre d'Unica, dans l'amphithéâtre du service" (Rabain 1998a, 233).[7]

It is thus not surprising, perhaps, that *The Man of Jasmine* forces the issue of what constitutes "madness." More important for this project, it raises the question of to what extent madness is connected to representation (art). While it seems to have a cathartic function, it is also connected to self-destruction, making it seem as if "she" were to produce her illness in order to be able to write about it: "She is so closely connected to her work that she gives death to her own soul. . . . Her crises of madness . . . are the reasons why she loves her illness" (Zürn 1988–99, 5:128, my translation). Zürn's text operates along the lines of Foucault's paradox that "*where there is a work of art, there is no madness;* and yet madness is contemporary with the work of art" (Foucault 1965, 288). It highlights the relationship between the self and representation that Freud describes in terms of the "ego ideal." Unlike the image of an "other"—like Robin in *Nightwood*—the "Man of Jasmine" is an image created by the self for the self. Like the ego ideal, he is connected to paranoia and delusions of grandeur; however, unlike the ego ideal, he is a hallucination, that is, he does not remain internal.

What makes the ego ideal so powerful is that it is not limited to the individual but rather connected to society at large. As Freud writes:

> In addition to its individual side, this ideal has a social side; it is also the common ideal of a family, a class, or a nation. . . . The want of satisfaction which arises from the non-fulfillment of this ideal . . . is transformed into a sense of guilt (social anxiety). Originally, this sense of guilt was a fear of punishment by the parents. . . . Later the parents are replaced by an infinite number of fellow-men. (1986, 43)

As I will show, Zürn's text represents an investigation of this image in relation to the physical body. Unlike Hardenberg's "body," where subject-object boundaries are fluid, Zürn's subject remains separate from its body. Like Narcissus, "she" takes the image for reality and thus comes to rely on the materiality of representation (art). Zürn's writing, in effect, deconstructs the boundaries by which we commonly define subjectivity (fact/fiction, truth/fantasy, etc.) and in the end leaves us questioning just what *is* the difference between a body and a text. For example, language is made "real" by being inscribed into the body of the writer when the protagonist "cuts a 6 on the palm of her left hand with the sharp tip of a nail-file" (Zürn 1994, 40). It is said to be a reversal of her "lucky number," the 9, which is the image of "a person standing erect, his gaze turned to the left" (28). Here the signifier for a "person" is inscribed back into the body of the subject (person), who then becomes the subject of "writing." This fusion of body and text seems paradigmatic for Zürn's oeuvre, which is based on the confusion between representation and reality, and the concomitant desire to overcome the discrepancy between words and things by *merging* body and sign. This merging, which I have discussed in relation to "primary narcissism" (Ferenczi 1913; Hardenberg 1988, 1994) is no longer envisioned as an organic process, connected to images of water, but rather related to film and mechanical reproduction. In Zürn, the "body" is mutilated and fragmented in conjunction with images that seem, ultimately, disconnected from it.

Like many of the female surrealists who joined the movement after World War II as companions of older male artists, Zürn was introduced to surrealist techniques by her companion, the artist Hans Bellmer, whom she met and followed to Paris in 1953.[8] Bellmer's sculptural and photographic oeuvre is well known, and has provoked ongoing debates about fascism and the representation of the female body. His "doll" sculptures consist of adolescent female bodies that have been taken apart at the joints and put back together into grotesquely contorted positions; they may consist of only breasts and buttocks or a second pair of legs in place of a head. According to Bellmer, who immigrated to France in 1938 because he disagreed with Nazi politics, they are a critique of fascism because they invite the viewer's own sadistic gaze. This view is shared by art historian Hal Foster (1993) and, more recently, Thérèse Lichtenstein (2001), who has placed Bellmer's dolls in opposition to Nazi images of the "Aryan" body. However, as Susan Suleiman has asked, "How are we to distinguish Bellmer's sadism from Nazi sadism, both of them directed against 'feminine'?" (1998, 135); and as psychoanalytically oriented critics such as Sue Taylor have pointed out, "it is difficult . . . to accept the pitiful dolls . . . as anything *but* embodiments of female passivity and victimization" (2000, 5).

Bellmer's misogyny seems evident in his treatment of Zürn, whose body he tied up with strings in 1958 for a series of photographs entitled *Unica Ligotée* (*Unica Tied Up*), one of which was published on the cover of the surrealist magazine *Minotaure.* Bellmer's intention was to turn the body into a "landscape" and to alter its contours, for example, by creating additional "breasts" of flesh along the stomach. In what must have been a painful procedure, Zürn's body is reduced to a mountain of flesh, with her head remaining invisible. The fetishizing of the female body among surrealists is well documented (Gauthier 1971; Caws 1989), and Bellmer is often quoted for comparing his fragmentation of the body with the fragmentation of a sentence, "which seems to invite us to decompose it, so that an infinite chain of anagrams may re-compose the truth it contains."[9] Zürn, who adopted the technique of composing anagrams from Bellmer (she published two volumes of anagrams), seems to have been complicit with Bellmer's "fragmenting" of her body as well—if only, as Brinkmann suggests, because being thus tied up would allow her to occupy the position of a victim. According to an unpublished 1998 manuscript by Alyce Mahon cited by Brinkmann, " 'Unica Ligotee' . . . may be seen as allegorical of the traumatised victimized feminine body in Nazi Germany. [Zürn's] body acts as a site of ideological resistance" (Zürn 1988–99, 4:47–48). Certainly, Zürn and Bellmer's representations of the body as fragmented (which may be related to Lacan's *corps morcelée*) differ from Hardenberg's early expressionist depiction of a body that lacks boundaries yet retains an overall integrity.

Zürn's life before meeting Bellmer included the experience of living in Nazi Germany. She had been raised in a villa in Berlin-Grunewald as part of a family of writers (a childhood she has documented in *Dark Spring*); but when her parents divorced in 1931, the villa was sold because her father had gambling debts. Zürn, who chose to stay with her father, left high school to become a secretary, and in 1934, she began working as script girl for the Ufa (Universal-Film-AG), where she was eventually promoted to dramaturge. The Ufa produced all of the Nazi propaganda films, but Zürn worked in a department that produced animated commercials for products such as shoes and cigarettes (Zürn 1988–99, 4:397). Although she was not directly connected to the production of propaganda films and did not join the NSDAP, either, she did not openly disagree with Nazi policies. For example, the department she worked for was headed by Wolfgang Kaskeline, a well-known director, who was forced to resign for being "half-Jewish." Fortunately, he received permission to work for another film company (he was able to prove that he was "only quarter-Jewish"), but Zürn, like most Germans, remained silent until after the war, when she briefly mentioned Kaskeline in one of her texts (4:289). In another text, written shortly before her suicide, she compared the inmates of a mental institution with the victims of concentration camps during the Holocaust. Certainly, as Margret Eifler (1991) has observed, such descriptions are not based on any serious reflection about politics, nor on any "collective" feelings of guilt; they simply act as metaphors for Zürn's own personal anxieties. However, ironically, there is a real link: the Karl-Bonhoeffer-Heilstätten in Wittenau, where Zürn had been held for some time, was actually used by the Nazis to conduct euthanasia on mental patients.

By all accounts, Zürn was not interested in politics. Her goal in life was to be a writer, like her father's first wife, Orla Holm, who had supposedly committed suicide by jumping from a window of the Dresden asylum, the method Zürn herself eventually chose to end her life. In 1935, Zürn published her first article about her voluntary labor service (*freiwilliger Arbeitsdienst*) in a youth magazine (Zürn 1988–99, 3:230). Her mother, Helene, was herself a prolific writer, yet their relationship was difficult. In 1931, Helene had married Heinrich Doehle, who in 1942 became undersecretary of state in the National Socialist *Reichspräsidialamt.* When Zürn left her job at the Ufa, also in 1942, to marry the wealthy industrialist Erich Laupenmühlen, she and her husband regularly spent time with her mother and stepfather (4:51). Then, in 1949, Zürn and Laupenmühlen were divorced and Zürn distanced herself from her mother. Helene Doehle's unsympathetic report about her daughter, which she wrote in 1960 for the Karl-Bonhoeffer-Heilstätten (Zürn 1988–99, 4:322–30) confirms the picture of her mother as "selfish" that Zürn painted in *Dark Spring.* Zürn's own experience as a mother was cut short by the fact that Laupenmühlen, who continued to maintain good relations with the Doehles, was able to gain custody of their two children by paying Zürn a lump sum of DM 3,000 (Zürn 1988–99, 4:305), a decision she regretted throughout her life.

Zürn then moved into her own apartment and reconnected with her friends from before her marriage, mostly artists she knew from the film industry. She supported herself by writing short stories for Berlin newspapers and began a new relationship with an artist, Alexander Camaro. The gathering place for artists in Berlin, which was then divided into four occupied zones, was the cabaret and jazz club Die Badewanne, which was modeled after the existentialist bars in Paris. As Zürn wrote shortly before her suicide, the "*Badewanne*-period," when she was able to actually make a modest living as a writer, was the happiest time of her life, "like a window into another world."[10]

In 1953, she met Bellmer at an art opening and followed him to Paris only two months later. There she was able to meet in person the surrealists she had admired in Berlin, such as Breton and Marcel Duchamp; her favorite poet, Hans Arp; Man Ray, who took pictures of her; Meret Oppenheim, who befriended her; Max Ernst; and Leonora Carrington, who in 1946 had written a first-person narrative, *En Bas* (*Down Below*), about her own experiences of having been confined to a mental institution. Although Bellmer and she were living in poverty, Zürn began to draw and, as Renée Riese Hubert points out, "the seventeen years spent as Bellmer's companion coincide almost exactly with the most productive period of her life" (1994, 141). Her drawings were exhibited at the gallery Le Soleil dans la Tête in 1953 and 1957; and she published a volume of anagrams, *Hexentexte* (1954), as well as a 1958 art book, *The House of Illnesses: Stories and Pictures from a Case of Jaundice,* a combination of text and drawings that could be seen as a predecessor of *The Man of Jasmine.*

In 1960, Zürn had her first emotional breakdown. After an argument with Bellmer, she returned to Berlin and was arrested and committed to the Karl-Bonhoeffer-Heilstätten, where the staff diagnosed her as "schizophrenic"—a diagnosis which was eventually retracted (as will be discussed subsequently) but which set up the link between creativity and pathology that was to become the focus of all of Zürn's work. Apparently, she had made a scene in a hair salon, where she refused to pay her bill. Over a mandatory confinement period of three months, she was treated with a battery of psychiatric drugs that left her crippled and suicidal.[11] When her case was reviewed, Bellmer and her friends succeeded in having her released, yet the court considered taking away her rights so she would enter a plea of "not guilty by reason of insanity" in response to the criminal charges (the unpaid hairdresser bill). After this episode, Zürn was afraid to return to Germany; only seven months later, she was again institutionalized, for almost two years, at the Hôpital Saint-Anne in Paris. Subsequently, in 1964, it was Bellmer who had her committed to La Fond; in 1965 and 1966 she was at Saint-Anne again; and in 1966 and 1970 at the Maison Blanche, from where she was moved to her final destination, the Clinique Psychiatrique Le Chateau. The relationship to Bellmer became increasingly difficult, yet she did not have any other place to go, and he himself seems to have been emotionally dependent on her.[12] She did not speak French very well, but when after seventeen years in France Bellmer requested that she be returned to Germany, she did not want to go. Bellmer, who had become paralyzed from a stroke in 1969, felt unable to take care of her. He offered to pay for her keep in Germany, but that would not be necessary: on October, 17, 1970, while visiting on a furlough, Zürn placed a chair against the railing of the balcony of Bellmer's sixth-floor apartment and jumped to her death.

Seeing and Not Seeing

Given this extreme relationship, one might assume that the figure of the Man of Jasmine is modeled after Bellmer. However, Zürn herself attributed the beginning of her mental illness to her 1957 meeting with the Belgian artist and poet Henri Michaux (1899–1984). Michaux did not see himself as a surrealist, but he was fascinated with madness, and he experimented with altered states of mind through hallucinogenic drugs (e.g., his "mescaline drawings" of 1956). His method resembled "automatic writing," and he combined the media of drawing and writing:

> Whether he threw ink onto paper with his fingers or flung it from the pen . . . born on the white page were "letters" without an alphabet, signs without referents, works without titles, and simple movements of the hand rendering calligraphic notations. (Michaux 2000)

Zürn's description of the number 9 as "a person standing erect, his gaze turned to the left" evokes Michaux's 1926 "alphabet" drawings; and her drawings of fantastic, surreal creatures covered with "tattoos" of abstract geometric patterns make it seem as if their "bodies" consisted of writing."[13]

The Man of Jasmine describes the meeting with Michaux as a shock: "she experiences the first miracle in her life: in a room in Paris she finds herself standing before The Man of Jasmine. The shock of this encounter is so great that she is unable to get over it. From this day on she begins, very very slowly, to lose her reason" (Zürn 1994, 27). This loss of reason, in turn, is accompanied by an altered artistic production. While "she" wants to be a writer, she feels "too weak, too small to endure a great emotional shock with pride and manage . . . to erect a work on the basis of this upheaval" (73). However, "she" becomes inspired by the Man of Jasmine, the "encounter" (*Begegnung*) with whom the narrator compares to that of Herman Melville—the protagonist's (and Zürn's) favorite author—with an Irish lady in a post coach. This encounter, as the narrator tells us, was what inspired Melville to write *Moby Dick* (1851) and, perhaps in reference to this text, the Man of Jasmine later comes to be called "the white man" (like Moby Dick, the white whale). As will become clearer over the course of this chapter, it is this figure that precipitates the series of "paranoid-schizophrenic" delusions that we may see as connected to Freud's "ego ideal."

Based on the shock of meeting the Man of Jasmine, "she engrosses herself in a manuscript 'in honour of the number 9' with the aim of . . . forgetting reality" (Zürn 1994, 27). This action leads to the production of "the manuscript *In the House of Illnesses*" (29), which corresponds to Zürn's 1958 book publication. It contains drawings of body parts that represent rooms in a hospital: the "cabinet of the solar plexuses," the "room of eyes," the "hall of bellies," the "bosom room," the "chambers of hands," the "vaults of the head," and the "suite of the hearts."[14] The accompanying text is focused on eyes, a motif used frequently by the surrealists:[15]

> "Look me in the eye," Doctor Mortimer said. But my eyes wandered sideways to the left and farther to the left, until they froze. As if pulled by strings, my sight took off into the distance, into the left distance and above the little tree across the horizon and a little farther and beyond, as far as into the white sky where my sight came to a halt. "You should try to look me in the eye," Doctor Mortimer said. Only with effort was I able to retrieve my distant sight—it moved so slowly—until I arrived again before Doctor Mortimer's eyes. But there, my eyes closed from exhaustion. Doctor Mortimer lifted my eyelids, first one, then the other. "Bull's eye," he said sadly but with admiration, "the two hearts in your eyes have blown right through your chest. Bull's eye" [my translation].

Here the perceiving subject (I /eye) is seduced by the new space of unreality, in defiance of the doctor's authority. Wandering, the eyes come to inhabit the landscape by which they have been attracted, yet the subject is punished by the loss of her physical integrity (she loses her "eye-hearts"). This scenario (which is reminiscent of Hardenberg's loss of boundaries, albeit in visual form) anticipates *The Man of Jasmine,* where the pleasure taken in visions (hallucinations) repeatedly leads to being straightjacketed, incarcerated, and medicated, yet "she" continues to hold on to it because she enjoys her madness: "If she is mad . . . the most beautiful, incredible ideas start to blossom, like jasmine" (Zürn 1994, 48). In other words, madness here is not the frightening, abject condition which has been described by psychoanalysts working in a clinical context (see, e.g., the description of a schizophrenic patient by Abraham in chapter 1). Rather, importance is placed on what the subject sees.

In Freudian terminology, with which Zürn was probably familiar, the fear of losing one's eyes is equivalent to castration anxiety, that is, the loss of one's power.[16] And, according to Samuel Weber, "eyes are the bodily organ to which the expectation of bodily unity is traditionally attached [because] what can be seen with 'one's own two eyes' can be identified" (2000, 14). The destruction of bodily unity, along with attempts to re-create it by means of "visions" (hallucinations) becomes the main theme in *The Man of Jasmine,* where madness is presented as a creative and self-destructive force.

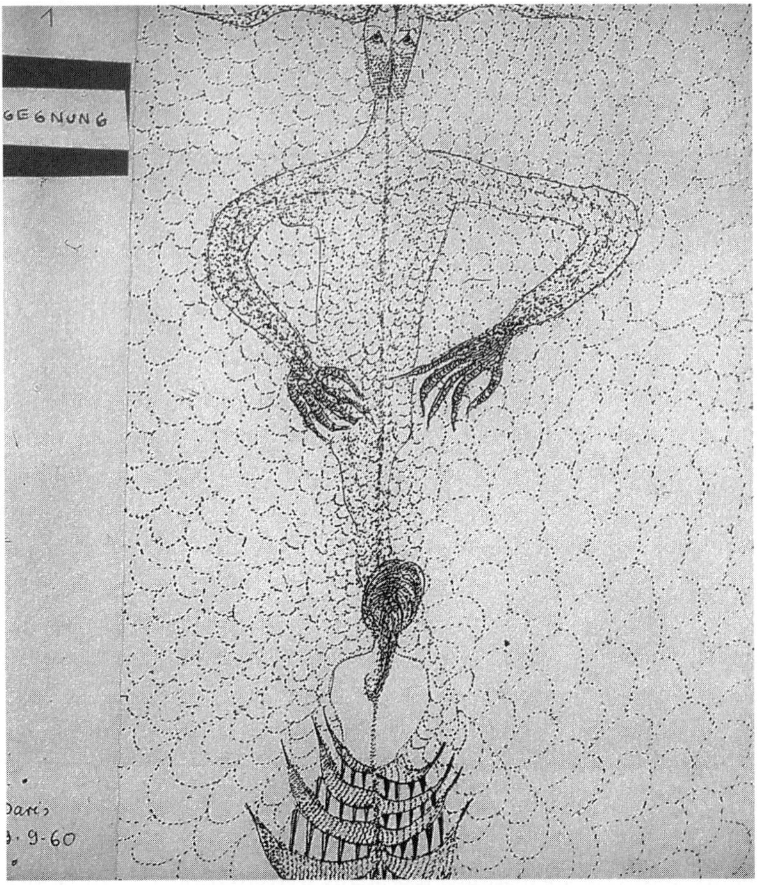

Unica Zürn, *Begegnung* (*Meeting*)

Still, the protagonist's madness includes an obsession with signs and numbers, and there seems to be a competition between them and visual imagery. In a set of drawings dated "19.9.60" (see figures, this page and next), Zürn represented her shocking "encounter" with the Man of Jasmine/ Michaux/madness in conjunction with the number 9. The first drawing is titled *Begegnung* (*Meeting*) and depicts a female figure confronted by a huge creature with claws and bull's horns; it seems to have grown out of her and now threatens to overpower her (like the Man of Jasmine). The second drawing is titled *Berührung* (*Touching*); here, she seems to have been absorbed into the creature; and the light background pattern from the first drawing has mutated into a proliferation of number 9s, which seem to engulf the creature in turn. Numbers are stable signifiers—they mean exactly what they say—but in the paranoid-delusional universe of *The Man of*

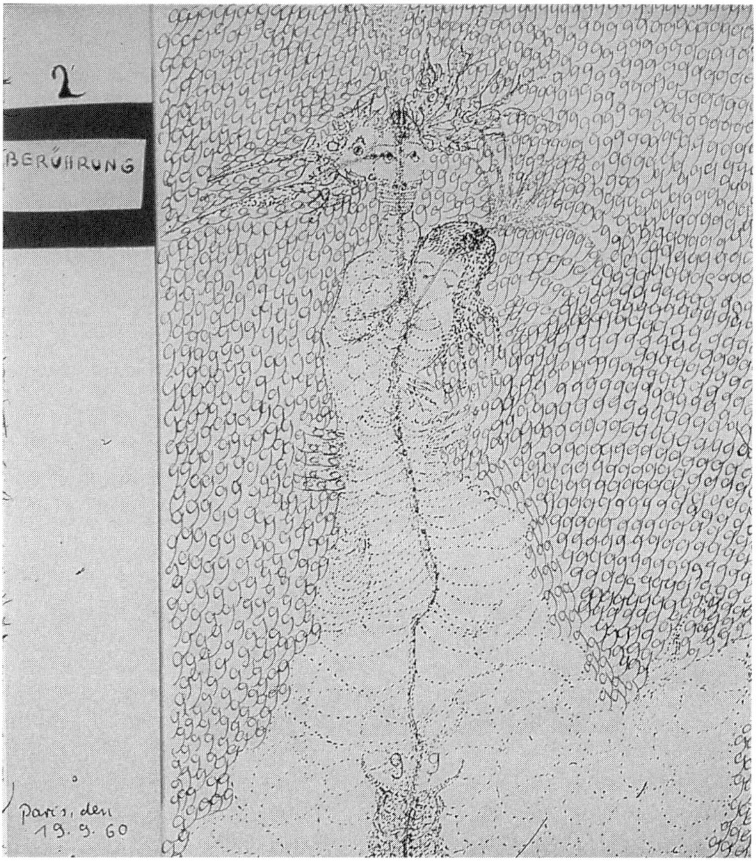

Unica Zürn, *Berührung* (*Touching*)

Jasmine, they turn into signifiers that represent or participate in the construction and destruction of visual images. Perhaps that is why their movement must be "arrested" by gestures as violent as inscribing them into the palm of one's hand.

When the Man of Jasmine "hypnotizes" the protagonist and sends her telepathic messages, "she" loses the ability to interpret signs: "She thinks she can decipher messages to her in almost every advert, in almost every title of the plays and films" (Zürn 1994, 93). Language loses its ability to signify, and everything becomes connected to everything else. Again, this apparent inability to differentiate suggests an experience of a lack of boundaries, which in turn might be connected to schizophrenia; yet Zürn's subject does not completely lose the ability to differentiate. The rearrangement of signifiers is intimately connected to the protagonist's artistic production, which consists of composing anagrams. They are defined by the narrator as "words and sentences which are created by re-arranging the letters in a word or sentence. One may only use the letters which are available, and not draw on any others" (Zürn 1994, 35). A once popular genre adopted by the surrealists, anagrams represent a form of "automatic writing," where the composer acts as a medium for a meaning that reveals itself by chance yet, paradoxically, becomes a "message" tailored to the individual.[17] According to Ferdinand de Saussure, anagrams reveal "a language underneath language" (Starobinski 1980, 49), which may be interpreted as a deeper truth, so that the anagram takes on a mystic, oracular function. For example, when an anagram results in the question: "Is it a madwoman?" the narrator comments: "Obviously she had related it to herself" (Zürn 1994, 36). Language becomes a self-fulfilling prophecy and is perceived by Zürn's protagonist to have a real physical impact, as represented by the drawing dominated by the number 9. Composing anagrams involves making choices on the part of the subject, who is confronted with a seemingly infinite number of possibilities: in a computer calculation, an initial line of only sixteen letters yields 871,781,312,000 possible permutations (Scholl 1990, 261). And yet, while new meaning seems to be created, it is not a creative act but rather consists of recycling what is already there. One may have to feel "inspired" to rearrange the letters in any meaningful way, yet what one comes out with is limited by what has been given so that really, one just reproduces one's own preconceptions.

Perhaps due to this extreme contrast between, on the one hand, infinite possibilities and, on the other hand, severe limitations, the activity of composing anagrams demands a great deal of mental discipline. In *The Man of Jasmine,* it is described as a "dangerous fever" (Zürn 1994, 118) from which the protagonist suffers.[18] The first anagram the protagonist produces is based on a line from the Bible: YE WOULD HAVE PLUCKED OUT YOUR OWN EYES (Gal. 4:15). Out of this line, "she" makes:

The dictum of your day: hard.
Of your eyes: being.
Your skin is song—your advice: understand.
Your house is masked. Your victories close.
Your deed: a resting place united with a coffin.[19]

The anagram begins with a reference to language ("dictum") and daily labor, which may be the production of anagrams itself. Eyes are equated with "being," which then turns into its opposite, death, that is, darkness (absence of vision). The anaphoric repetition of "Your" echoes biblical language; and, most interestingly, the central line equates the body ("skin") and poetic language ("song"), which seems indicative of the close relationship between writing and the body in all of Zürn's work. It is here, I would argue, that Zürn differs most from Hardenberg, for the connection is violent and necessitates, eventually, the author's own self-destruction.

It seems difficult to interpret these anagrams any further, since they mainly repeat, on a very reduced level, what can be found in all of Zürn's text. The significance of the anagrams does not lie in the possibility of interpretation—already, it would be complicated by the problem of their intranslatability (the translation in the foregoing passage obviously is not anagrammatic)—but in their drawing attention to the process of production itself. Their main "content" seems to be the process coming into being, that is, the activity of production connected to them. For example, in what one might call the description of producing an anagrammatic drawing in *The Man of Jasmine,* "she" is asked by a psychiatrist why she was covering "the entire surface of the paper right to the edges? On the others you've left the space around the motif white"; and she responds: "Because I couldn't stop working on this drawing, or didn't want to, for I experienced endless pleasure while working on it. I wanted the drawing to continue beyond the edge of the paper—on to infinity" (Zürn 1994, 103). The drawing is, in fact, designed to exceed its frame. It cannot "contain" anything. The title "she" gives it is "Rencontre avec Monsieur M (Ma Mort)," or, "Encounter with Mister M (My Death)"—naturally, we cannot even begin to guess what it may depict. Compared to the states of narcissism depicted by Freud, Hardenberg, and Barnes, the subject here faces the condition beyond self-reflection which equals death, that is, the absence of all representation.

Points of Origin

What seems most disturbing about Zürn's text is that it points outside itself only to refer back to its own textual origin. On page 92 of *The Man of Jasmine*, the protagonist "gets it into her head to write down the story of her illness," and the reader is suddenly confronted with the fact that he or she is not only reading a book about something or other but a book about the production of that very book itself. The protagonist, who is featured *in* the book, becomes suddenly identifiable as the author *of* the book, as if the book were written from inside its own covers. As we become aware that the book "she" writes in the story is the same book we are currently holding in our hands, we recognize that we no longer read an actual story but rather the evolution of that story itself: not only does the fictitious "story" reveal itself to be "real" but rather there really *is* no story, at least not apart from the one about how the story came into being.

The void created by this kind of conceit seems most disturbing, for it also points to the fact that there is no "subject" apart from the text (which is no longer referential or performative but rather just exhibiting its own "textuality," the mechanism by which it operates). Here the work of art not only displays its fictionality but also restages the conditions of its own making ad infinitum. Zürn used this technique as early as 1953, the year she met Bellmer, in her posthumously published children's book *Katrin: Die Geschichte einer kleinen Schriftstellerin* (*Katrin: The Story of a Little Writer;* see Zürn 1988–99, 3:67–210). Named after Zürn's daughter, it tells "the story of a little girl who wanted to become a writer and really became one." Much of it is a fictionalized autobiography, recounting Zürn's own early experiences in wanting to become a writer. It ends happily, with Katrin sitting down to write her story and thus having become an author. The story she sets out to write *is* "the story of a little girl who wanted to become a writer and really became one" so that not only does the end turn into the beginning but she herself becomes a character in her own book, a book about writing a book in which she becomes a character, and so on. In what seems to be an endless loop, Katrin multiplies as her own fictitious creation in what is, essentially, a mise en abyme: Katrin has no identity apart from her text, a condition which seems to uncannily foreshadow Zürn's own predicament. And although this book, which is not about madness, may be construed as an affirmation of authorship, it also makes it quite clear that Katrin is *nothing* but her text. There is no *hors du texte,* no subject apart from the process of production, and therefore no "person" that could be separated from the text.

It is here that the myth of Narcissus becomes relevant again, for it relates directly not only to the confusion between fiction and reality but also to the danger of absolute inseparability on the part of the subject, who then falls into madness. And, while the fantasy of having total control over one's own self-representation may be exhilarating, it is also airtight because it is self-produced and self-perpetuating: "'I feel as though I am in prison,' she says to a psychiatrist on one occasion. And he answers: 'You are your own prison.' 'I am trapped in a never-ending circle,' she says to another psychiatrist. And he answers: 'I do not believe in this circle.'" (Zürn 1994, 125).

In terms of narcissism, it seems that the oscillation between the self and its image (text) becomes like a funnel that draws the subject deeper and deeper into the void. As in *Nightwood,* there is a vertical movement, but compared to its characters' gradual "descent" into a night indicative of fears and desires, Zürn's textual madness is structured in terms of a sudden "fall" (*Sturz*) into nothingness. Perhaps in anticipation of the *Fenstersturz* (fall from the window) in *Dark Spring,* which retroactively functions as an omen for the author's own suicide through "falling," the structure of the protagonist's illness is described as follows: "she has already disappeared halfway into the abyss of a new, deep depression, as if that were the law of this illness. A few unusual days, a few nights filled with the shattering experiences of hallucinations, a short upward momentum, a feeling of being extraordinary—and afterwards the fall, reality, the realization that it all had been an illusion" (Zürn 1994, 113). As in *Nightwood,* the oscillation between points by which narcissism suspends temporality leads to narrative stasis, yet in *The Man of Jasmine,* there is no longer a dramatic interaction between characters but rather the mere disembodied machinations of a text that gradually erases its own subject.

The Body of Flesh

However, the disappearance of the subject into her text does not take place without extreme physical resistance, for in *The Man of Jasmine*, the reality of the "flesh" seems to return with a vengeance. As I will demonstrate in the following discussion, Zürn's depiction of what would be, ostensibly, a representation of the "ego ideal" is far more nuanced than Freud's; and it includes the physical body. The above-described is evident from the very beginning, which, in a kind of primal scene in the form of a flashback to the protagonist's childhood, sets up the opposition between the inaccessible, material body of the mother and the imaginary, projective-identification body of the Man of Jasmine. The protagonist's own body, on the other hand, remains suspended in what appears to be a kind of limbo between reality and dream:

> One night in the sixth year of her life, a dream takes her behind the tall mirror which hangs in a mahogany frame on the wall of her room. This mirror becomes an open door through which she steps. . . . The

impression of this dream is so strong that she gets up in order to push the mirror to one side. She finds the wall and no door. Filled this morning with an inexplicable loneliness, she enters her mother's room in order to get into her bed and return, if possible, to whence she came so as to see nothing more. The mountain of tepid flesh which encloses this woman's impure spirit rolls over on to the horrified child, and she flees for ever from the mother, the woman, the spider! She is deeply grieved. Then her vision appears to her for the first time: The Man of Jasmine! Boundless consolation! Sighing with relief, she sits down opposite him and studies him. He is paralysed! What good fortune. He will never leave his seat in the garden where the jasmine even blossoms in winter. This man becomes her image of love. . . . And she marries him. The loveliest thing about it is that no one knows. And this is her first, her greatest secret. (Zürn 1994, 25–26)

This passage contains a sequence of three kinds of visions, as in a cinematic montage. First is the dream, in which the protagonist (like Alice in Lewis Carroll's *Through the Looking Glass*) leaves both her body and its image behind by passing through her own reflection. While her material body remains, presumably, asleep in bed, "she" is now completely without form or shape, an experience which also prefigures later hallucinations, where "she" becomes, apparently, bodiless. Unlike the subject of Hardenberg's poetry, however, the physical body in Zürn does not disappear but rather, as we shall see, makes its presence known.

In the aforementioned opening sequence, the protagonist's walking through the mirror frame into another space relates to the German word for being "mad": *ver-rückt,* which means, literally, to be "dis-placed." However, this adjective does not apply to the narrator, who remains in control of telling the story. As the dream is organized into a narrative, the dreamer-protagonist enters a dream that consists of being led along a certain path to arrive at a moment of revelation that is thwarted by her awakening.[20] However, whereas "she" is said to have left the room, the narrator returns to details of the furniture in the second half of the opening sentence. As a result, the text not only leads the reader into the dream but also suggests that "reality" continues to exist within the same textual space, namely, through the ongoing presence of the narrator. This strategy is consistent throughout *The Man of Jasmine* where, apart from isolated moments of slippage between narrator and protagonist, the duality between the narrator, who maintains control over the narrative, and the protagonist, whose state of mind becomes increasingly destabilized, remains. One might even say that the only reason why the protagonist can be recognized as "mad" is because the narrator occupies this omniscient position.

In fact, the protagonist is presented as a passive follower: said to be "led" by the dream ("führt sie ein Traum"), the child is a passive subject. This passivity corresponds with the position of the dreamer as described by Lacan: "Our position in the dream is profoundly that of someone who does not see. The subject does not see where it is leading, he follows" (1981, 75).[21] This description is indicative of the later relationship between the protagonist and the Man of Jasmine, whom she follows blindly and to whom she attributes all responsibility for her actions: "It is not she who is responsible for the actions which finally brought her into prison and the mental hospital, but he" (Zürn 1994, 66). Literally a "dictator," he sends her hallucinations so that she must write about them. Since her identity depends on writing, she must depend on him, and when he withdraws, she becomes depressed and suicidal—they are, literally, "wedded" to one another. In this regard, the Man of Jasmine has a stabilizing function, as he counteracts not only depression from withdrawal but also the subject's "dispersion," which marks the difference between daydream (fantasy) and "night-dream":

> In the daydream the position of the dreamer appears to be unified and set apart from the spectacle. . . . In the night-dream, by contrast, the position of the dreamer can not be assimilated to that of a detached observer. . . . The dream is both distant and all too close. Indeed, distance and proximity are no longer mutually exclusive. . . . The "I" of the dreamer . . . finds itself scattered throughout the dream. (Weber 2000, 7)

Before the Man of Jasmine appears on the scene, however, something else takes place. The second movement of the opening sequence contains a vision more disturbing than any nightmare, for it is real. Searching for comfort in the dark, to get away from dreaming, "she" seeks out her mother's body to "return to whence she came so as to see nothing more." This desire to return to the womb, here defined as a space of darkness (rather than, as in Ferenczi [1913], a liquid space), is thwarted: she is confronted with the real-life vision of a huge, inaccessible, "mountain of tepid flesh." Unlike Bellmer's *Unica Ligotée*, in which the flesh is bound in order to produce what may also be seen as a kind of "writing on the body," this pile of flesh seems boundless and abject—it cannot be read, understood, or assimilated.

Like Felix in *Nightwood*, whose story remains part of the text only by virtue of its conspicuous absence after the first chapter, the mother disappears without a trace from the remainder of *The Man of Jasmine.* She appears but once, in the very beginning, yet she sets in motion all else to come. The shape of her body reappears in the form of the protagonist's fellow inmates at the mental institutions: "lying on the beds are mounds of white, wheezing flesh" (Zürn 1994, 119); and the concurrent realization that "she herself had been just such a mound of dead, ugly, foul-smelling flesh during the worst moments of her mental stupefaction—in her total depression" (119). Here the shock of the "primal scene" is revisited and placed in contrast to the light, flexible body of the hallucinations, which I will discuss in a moment.

To return to the beginning: Clearly, the mother's body is disgusting, and "darkness" is not an option. "She" is driven straight into the arms of the Man of Jasmine, and this action, in effect, constitutes the third image of the sequence. Sculpturelike and immobile, he sits in a beautiful garden, and everything about him suggests that he is a work of art. There seems to be no threat emanating from him, since he is paralyzed (as Bellmer was, eventually, and as Zürn herself would be at times, due to excessive medication). In this way, he offers refuge from the terrifying onslaught of the moving, breathing pile of flesh. A seemingly two-dimensional image, he exists only in the secret "garden" of the protagonist's mind, that is, until she "encounters" him in reality a few paragraphs later, when the narrator jumps ahead to 1957 (when she "experiences the first miracle in her life"). Here is where her madness truly begins: in the shape of a man "she" meets in Paris—identified by Zürn as Michaux—he appears to her "in the flesh," as he enters her own, three-dimensional space. However, both "she" and the reader know that this appearance is not "real" in the same way as the mother's body, to which he continues to function as an alternative throughout the narrative. Having emerged as a synthesis between dream and reality, his presence continues to bridge the gap between the two, as if to mend the rift in perception that has been created by the initial appearance of the pile of flesh. It is as if access to "real" reality, anticipated as the absence of vision (darkness), had been barred by this impenetrable mountain of flesh so that the little girl is doomed to suffer from visions forever after.

Throughout the book, the Man of Jasmine occupies these two spaces: reality and hallucination. Once "he" has stepped out of his frame, neither "she" nor the reader can ever be sure whether he does or does not exist. In fact, this duality is anticipated almost from the beginning when, in the transition bridging the gap between childhood and adult life, the narrator tells us: "Over the coming years she sees The Man of Jasmine behind every male shoulder she leans on. She remains faithful to her childhood marriage" (Zürn 1994, 26). It seemed only a matter of time for him to actually appear, for "she" has remained stuck in childhood. In Zürn's iconography, "childhood" and "art" are often connected (the Man of Jasmine resembles the imaginary playmates invented by the author during her own childhood), and his presence serves as a guarantee that nothing will change. He preserves the mythical garden of childhood, where time does not seem to pass because things do not change (like jasmine, which "blossoms in winter"); and, as "art," he continues to protect the subject from the onslaught of "the flesh" she fears.

In psychoanalytic terms, one might see him as a father figure as well as a mother, since he is presented as nurturing in his function of sending the protagonist hallucinations, thus enabling her to sustain herself. Zürn evokes the cliché of an engulfing, overly physical woman and a distant man who imposes his law (they wed); her text seems to correspond to the Oedipal drama, which is based on "a desire for the death of the rival—the parent of the same sex—and a sexual desire for the parent of the opposite sex" (Laplanche and Pontalis 1973, 282). However, *The Man of Jasmine* reverses these gender roles, as the mother is shown to reject whereas the Man of Jasmine is said to embrace with what appears to be a form of unconditional love. Moreover, it is the mother's body that is represented as phallic (massive, impenetrable) whereas the Man of Jasmine seems dispersed, appearing everywhere and nowhere, and taking on the characteristic of being all-encompassing that is commonly associated with "femininity."

More to the point, "he" does not exist except as a figment of the imagination that emanates from within the protagonist's own mind. Although the mother does appear at the beginning, we learn nothing about the protagonist's childhood, and it is the dream that occupies the prominent position of the text's opening. Unlike *Dark Spring,* which clearly is about family (it begins with a reference to the father), *The Man of Jasmine* is about art. As a figure, I would argue, the Man of Jasmine is not so much a representative of either mother or father (as would be, for example, an internalized "object"), nor of Michaux or Bellmer, but rather of the protagonist's own desire to write—the "author-ity" against which she struggles is her very own. Like Freud's ego ideal, Zürn's Man of Jasmine is a kind of authorial superego, yet his origins are difficult to trace. They can be traced, perhaps, to the absence of vision (the impossibility of returning to the darkness of the womb) or in opposition to the utter illegibility of the mother's body as a mountain of flesh; yet this "negativity" is constructed by the text itself. As I have tried to show, in comparison to Freud, Zürn posits different levels of the imaginary. As I will show in the following section, with respect to a Lacanian view of the subject, her writing, in spite of its references to a seemingly autobiographical subject, resists psychoanalytic interpretation—the only origin it points to is art itself, in the form of "visions."

Motion Pictures

What seems to have taken over everything is the technological "body" of the text itself. Returning to my initial question regarding the epistemological status of the "object," Zürn's text confronts us with a situation in which it becomes impossible to tell how real anything is. In this case, one's perception of one's self becomes utterly unreliable as well and is, if anything, contingent upon one's surroundings: "It is quite clear to her that she is here in a mental hospital . . . and therefore that all the women in the room are mad. If, then, she herself had felt that she had been hypnotized from afar by the famous Man of Jasmine, or his actual living image, didn't that mean she had been crazy now for some time?" (Zürn 1994, 61). The reader shares this confusion, and the question remains unanswered: Is she or isn't she crazy? On the one hand, Zürn deconstructs madness as a matter of institutional discourse, where people are "labeled" by diagnoses; on the other hand, her language illustrates that there may be a real confusion on the part of the subject as to what her condition really is. Is "she" hypnotized or does he really send her messages? What does it mean to say "his actual living image"? Is he the same as or different from his image?

The reader remains in the dark as to the exact nature of the phenomenon said to be "the Man of Jasmine," and this phenomenon continues to shift shape throughout the text. As I mentioned in chapter 1, his existence resonates with the finding of Lacanian analyst Guy Rosolato, who also treated Zürn, that "the rise and fall of *imaginary companions* contradict the loss of the object. They are but projected shadows of the object" (1980, 288), which is the mother. Once the object has disappeared from the scene, only the shadows remain. This unreality is symptomatic of the effects of a technological device with which Zürn was quite familiar, namely, the cinema. As in the movies—or now, the virtual reality of the Internet—we are confronted with what *looks like* reality but isn't; and, unlike in the theater, where space is three-dimensional and things are happening in real time, celluloid images are a recycling of reality, for they are only reproduced.

As I have mentioned, what makes Zürn's text "realistic" is its constant reference to people and places that existed in the author's life. At the same time, *The Man of Jasmine* constructs uncanny resemblances, where what appears to be "real" turns out to be a fiction and vice versa. Through the medium of film, Zürn shows this confusion between reality and fantasy in scenes such as the following, where the narrator backtracks to a time before the "encounter" with the Man of Jasmine:

> Why did she move to France? 1953, in Berlin, she sees the same French film three times in order to get drunk on the sight of a particular face. . . . She identifies so strongly with this masculine face that suddenly she is told "you resemble him." A few days later she meets a man and recognizes his face as the one in the film which she herself has come to resemble. Highly surprised, she hears someone say: "That man resembles X in the film." This confirmation, as well as his request that she should accompany him to Paris, spurs her decision to leave Berlin. (Zürn 1994, 31)

Ostensibly, this scene refers to Zürn's meeting with Bellmer: apparently, she really had gone to see *Les Enfants du Paradis* and become fascinated by the resemblance between Bellmer and the actor Jean-Louis Barrault. The passage makes ironic reference to the confusion between art and life by evoking the cliché of the movie star—the "man of one's dreams"—who literally descends from the screen to join the viewer in real life—as if a dream came true. However, the movie itself is set in Paris, and it also deals with the confusion between life and art: Barrault, himself a mime in real life, plays a mime whose character on stage spills over into his real life so that the confusion goes on on several levels at once. The word "face" is repeated five times as if to emphasize the intoxicating effect repetition has upon the viewer; and it prefigures the hallucinations to come: the word for "face" in German is *Gesicht* and is related to "sight" (*Sicht*), which is etymologically connected to an old German expression for having hallucinations: *Gesichte haben* (literally: "having sights").

Thus Zürn deconstructs our idea of a subject who acts based on a continuous, coherent self—as in Lacan, the subject is always already split, defined from the start by its relation to the mirror image (in this case the man "she" sees on screen). As if to explore the implications of Lacan's example of the "psychic agencies . . . as representing what takes place in a camera" (Zürn 1994, 123) to the subject, whose body in turn *is* the camera, Zürn suggests that our perception of "reality" is shaped by what we see on film.

Through the use of resemblance and repetition, she not only evokes an excessively identificatory relationship between Bellmer and herself but also draws attention to the mechanics of the cinematic medium that appear to determine this relationship in the first place. It is as if the subject were somehow "moved" to Paris involuntarily, through the effect of technology—in fact, as the Wittenau hospital file confirms, Zürn's first crisis of madness, in 1960, was triggered by a British movie (*Holdup in London*) she had gone to see. In this regard, it may be interesting to note that critics often point to Bellmer's photograph of himself and Zürn holding one of his life-size dolls in her arms, whose face resembles her own. Bellmer's doll was inspired by Olympia, the female automaton in Jacques Offenbach's opera *The Tales of Hoffmann*,[22] which was based on E. T. A. Hoffmann's tale "Der Sandmann" (1960). In this story, the protagonist mistakes a doll for a real woman because he wears a pair of special glasses ("eyes") given to him by the antagonist to drive him insane. Bellmer's photograph also evokes an uncanny resemblance between the woman and the doll, but it is Bellmer who appears as the "puppeteer" in back. What interests me in regard to Zürn's text is that here, the role of mechanical reproduction itself seems to replace the puppeteer. Paranoia, as both Freud and Lacan have pointed out, becomes a function of the internal "monitoring agency," that is, the self-observing gaze, rather than a real external agency.

The problem, of course, is that the subject is not aware of the difference between what is "real" and what is "imaginary." Throughout *The Man of Jasmine*, there are hidden links between Bellmer and the Man of Jasmine, even though they are, ostensibly, separate individuals. Bellmer appears as a character named "the friend" (there is, however, one occasion in the original manuscript, where his name appears), and he seems supportive of the protagonist's efforts: he "tells her about anagrams and shows her how to compose such poems. He also discovers her gift for automatic drawing and encourages her," as if through practical support he could counteract the detrimental effects of the "white man's" influence—who sends her the less "productive" hallucinations. However, as we know from Bellmer's definition of anagrams, they are related to physical fragmentation, and the "white man" may be seen, in turn, as counteracting this influence. Although there seems to be competition between them—for example, when the protagonist begins to "write down the story of her illness. Her friend warns her of the possible dangers of dwelling on this subject [and makes] entreaties to desist from writing the manuscript" (Zürn 1994, 92)—they both seem engaged in helping along the protagonist's self-destruction. At the same time, we realize they both delude her into thinking that "she" is well taken care of.

As a matter of fact, it is never quite clear to what extent they are not to be taken as the same person. When "she" interprets the initials on the pillowcase of the Hotel Minerva, H. M., as those of her favorite writer, Herman Melville, and becomes obsessed with them because they are also the initials of the Man of Jasmine (Henri Michaux), there is a slippage that extends to the initials of "the white man," which in French is *homme blanc*, and he shares his initials with Hans Bellmer (Scholl 1990, 89).

This constant slippage of signifiers, based on relationships of resemblance and contiguity, is also represented in relation to cinematic technology, as in the following scene, where the Man of Jasmine suddenly shows up in a movie theater:

> The first crisis starts in a cinema. She sees him enter as the lights dim. He takes a seat several rows away from her at the same time sitting directly behind her. An advertising spot for a certain oil begins. Bottles filled with oil *keep appearing one after another* until their sight becomes unbearable to her. The bottles *turn into the symbol* of the male member—the sight gives her such a feeling of nausea that she fears she must vomit. (Zürn 1994, 30; my emphasis)

Here Zürn shows how motion pictures may physically affect the spectator: it is not "she" who performs the act of interpretation but rather the repeated appearance of the image (oil bottles) that forces about the emergence of the "symbol." It is as if reading were not an act that takes place on the part of the spectator but rather a function of the image itself, which seems to have congealed into a real physical object. Suddenly the scene is no longer limited to fantasy, as one might expect in the movies, but rather becomes threateningly real: she is sick, as if the oil bottles had punched her in the stomach. And even if her nausea is caused by way of association (seeing the "male member" would make her sick), this association is not made explicit, for it remains unclear what "the sight" refers to: the male member or the oil bottles. The appearance of the Man of Jasmine reiterates this optical illusion: he has taken a seat both in front of and behind the protagonist, as if he were able to duplicate himself or to project other selves into space. Unlike in Freud, where the "ego ideal" has a stabilizing function, the subject here is viciously persecuted by this image, which is externalized and directly related to the work of art. In Lacanian terms, it could mean that the subject has entered the realm of the "symbolic" (which he connects to paranoia), yet the problem is that "she" is unable to separate the symbolic from the imaginary: she is unable to perceive that the oil bottles are merely "symbols" in her mind, not to be mistaken for real, physical objects.

Zürn often refers to visual technology in regard to the protagonist's hallucinations, and she does not always make it clear how we should read these instances, for example, in this statement: "She is unaware that she is suffering from hallucinations. In her present state, the most incredible, hitherto unseen things become reality, so that when these images appear to her in the night sky, they are *really* there" (Zürn 1994, 33). Although we are informed, by the narrator, that the images "she" sees cannot be real, we are told emphatically that the images she sees are *really* there, so there is doubt as to whose perspective we should take as the "real" reality: that of the omniscient narrator, who presumably shares our view of reality, or that of the protagonist, whom we know to be mad, yet in whose subjective point of view we must participate if we want to continue reading the text. As in a theatrical performance, the text creates its own reality by setting up a frame for us to suspend our disbelief: we must take the statement for what it says, and if it tells us that the images are really there, they *are* really there. Language, in these instances, becomes performative, and our situation also resembles that of spectators in a movie theater, where we are "tricked" into believing that the images on screen are real. The department Zürn worked for at the Ufa was called *Zeichentrick*—cartoon, literally: "sign trick"—and it seems that, like the subject of hallucinations, we do not suspend our disbelief voluntarily, as the shifts between perspectives happen almost imperceptibly.

The seemingly supernatural "reality" of the movies is related to mirroring, as film scholar Christian Metz explains, but the medium of film "differs from the primordial mirror in one essential point: although . . . everything may come to be projected, there is one thing and one thing only that is never reflected in it: the spectator's own body" (1982, 45). Here is where Zürn's text truly departs from the mechanics of the cinema. In this hallucination that is compared to both a "photograph" and a "film," the scene witnessed by the protagonist includes herself:

> Suddenly a curious white aerodrome appears in the night sky before her opened window like a giant photograph. But no! The scene is in motion. It's like a film projected on the sky. . . . Suddenly she sees *him* in the foreground . . . embracing her own self. . . . Completely astonished, she observes the two of them as they board the plane, then watches as it ascends into the air and disappears into the sky. The sky is black once more, there is nothing to be seen. (Zürn 1994, 33)

In what is one of several airport scenes in *The Man of Jasmine,* the "white man" has come to embrace her and take her away. "She" who watches herself is split into actor and spectator, but here the action is not recorded; it takes place for the first time, as if she were looking through the camera at herself. Now "she" is able to duplicate herself as well and thereby produce her own film, which unites her with "him"; and yet her real, physical body remains apart from this action, on the bed of her hotel room (as in the initial dream of passing through the mirror). The plot of this "home movie" is simple: "he" transports her into a space beyond representation and the sky swallows them like an abyss, leaving nothing but darkness. Perhaps this is the fantasy of a happy ending to the little girl's desire to return to her mother's womb "to see nothing more," yet we know that that is impossible. Again, the reader encounters the impossible space (of death), where representation promises but fails to rescue the subject—as in the drama of Narcissus, whose desire to merge with the image ultimately leads to his demise.

The Return of the Flesh

"She," too, knows, on some level, that her condition is madness. Eventually, she wishes: "Ah, if only he had never come, if only The Man of Jasmine . . . had remained nothing but an oneiric picture" (Zürn 1994, 109). At the same time, she experiences a childlike sense of wonder: "Ceaseless amazement at the fact that a vision has become reality!" (30). Letting herself be guided by the Man of Jasmine, "she" is seduced by the hallucinations he sends her and eventually worships him: "He—who knows everything—who can do everything!" This illusion that he has superhuman powers is transferred onto her own self and is indicative of the megalomania Freud attributes to narcissism. Unlike Nora in *Nightwood,* with whom we at least are asked to maintain doubt as to the actual reality of the "object" (Robin), Zürn's "she" is shown to struggle with her paranoia by returning to the kind of "primary narcissism" Freud saw as an "ego protection device." Under the guidance of the Man of Jasmine, whom we know not to exist in reality (yet whom we may hold accountable, at least from her perspective), she develops delusions of grandeur that make her lose complete touch with reality.

Ironically, compared to the obsessive production of anagrams, these hallucinations are connected to positive feelings of a more complete physical self, which helps her counteract the negative feelings of disintegration she otherwise experiences. In fact, there are times at which she "incorporates" language into her body, rather than feeling as if it were separate from and directed against her. For example, when fellow asylum inmates ask her why she is there, "she" responds: "I heard a famous poet reciting a poem in my belly" (Zürn 1994, 70). And, at a police station, "she" feels compelled to perform an action in response to a sentence by Michaux: "I plant the breadfruit tree" which takes on shape inside her body: "The sentence is like a snake inside her, and she cannot resist it, she looks round in search of earth" (105) to plant the tree. In these instances, language and the body seem organically connected, and "she" takes pleasure in what seem to be real performances. Only the reader knows that, during these times particularly, she is most profoundly deluded. "She," on the other hand, comes to attribute healing powers to her hallucinations and thus presents us with a most troubling aspect of narcissism, as the remainder of this chapter is about to demonstrate.

Compared to the obsessive productivity that manifests itself through the anagrams, the protagonist's hallucinatory experiences seem gratuitous, yet they also take away the pressure of being an author (of anagrams) as they yield control to the Man of Jasmine. It is he whom she imagines to direct her from behind the scene, like a Svengali, to perform different visions of her own self. Like the anagrams, the hallucinations are a form of *ekphrasis*, yet they are not marked as forms of artistic production but rather as descriptions of seemingly immediate "happenings." Thus they constitute poetic moments of experience, in which "she" luxuriates because she is free from production, as well as from the "straightjacket" of the realist narrative (which revolves around arrests and hospitalizations). As in *Nightwood,* images are juxtaposed against a frame narrative, yet here they are not able to undermine this frame but rather, unfortunately, function in support of it. The Man of

Jasmine has the same function for Zürn's protagonist as Robin has for Nora; yet there can be no doubt here that the "other" is unreal.

Considering that, as Freud has argued (and as I outlined in chapter 2), love is synonymous with the ego ideal and that, as Lacan has concluded, "the human ego is founded on the basis of the imaginary relation" (1975, 115), the attraction "she" feels toward madness is profound. As the text tells us: "She would be happy to go mad if someone told her that it is necessary to go *mad* in order to experience these hallucinations" (Zürn 1994, 38). The hallucination to which this statement refers describes a sensation of disembodiment:

> Large shapes—like wings—float up to her, opening and closing—few at first—until they slowly fill the room. . . . Whenever these grayish-black wings without birds fly up too close to her she raises her hand in sudden anxiety and fends them off. They retreat for a moment into the background of the dark room, then approach once again, and slowly she gets used to this strange presence until she notices that these wings are insubstantial and can fly straight through her upright body, as if she herself had become bodiless. This both entrances and appalls her. Looking at them carefully, these creatures have in fact nothing terrifying about them. . . . They radiate an enormous dignity, an uncanny seriousness, something very noble. (Zürn 1994, 38–39; translation modified)

Similar to Hardenberg's poetry, the loss of physical boundaries is represented as a transformative experience. However, unlike Hardenberg's speaker, "she" does not delight in expanding her body to merge with the space but in the sensation of her own disembodiment. The phrase "as if she herself had become bodiless" implies that it is possible for her to feel herself without a physical body at all, whereas Hardenberg's speaker seems to perceive herself only through or in relation to her body. While Hardenberg also, at times, disconnects the "I" from a space in which it appears to "float," Zürn's "she" takes herself out of the space entirely; and while Hardenberg's voice creates its own landscape, Zürn's protagonist is placed in the dark by a narrator who continues to tell the tale, even if "she" is physically absent.

The experience of "the lunatic" has been described by Michaux as a form of disembodiment:

> For centuries . . . the lunatic has complained. He says he is beside his body. That his body is elsewhere . . . that he no longer weighs anything . . . that he is transparent . . . that he is empty, that he has been changed

into a doll, that he has no more organs . . . that he is artificial, that he is fake, that another occupies his body. (Michaux 1963, 134)

However, unlike Michaux's "lunatic," Zürn's protagonist does not complain: renouncing all physical resistance, "she" is free to experience the pleasure of yielding to the creatures her own imagination generates. Like a virus of her illness, they invade her body, yet "she" comes to appreciate the absence of her physical self. Since the connections between representation (anagrams, writing, drawing) and the body are often negative in Zürn, where "she" represents her body as fragmented in her manuscripts or mutilates herself in the attempt to inscribe symbols into her own flesh, such is not the case with the hallucinations. Here she may see herself perform on stage in an imaginary theater, in which her body is capable of performing beauty; and she is no longer passive but active: "she begins watching her own self. . . . She feels she has been invited to fulfil the old, hopeless wish of her childhood: to be a dancer. . . . She knows: *he* is somewhere in the darkness and will direct her like a dance master directing his pupil" (Zürn 1994, 95). What follows is a series of dances and performances in which "she" transforms herself into flowers and animals. The implications in terms of gender should be clear: the female subject can imagine herself performing only under the direction of a male counterpart.

Interestingly, in the case of Hardenberg, the subjective experience of the dancer is "expressed" in the form of a syntax that is fragmented or illogical; whereas in Zürn, the subjective experience of mental disintegration, which manifests itself not through a difference in style (it remains matter-of-fact) but in the form of a split between real and hallucinated bodies. As Weber explains, "the narcissistic conception of the body as a matrix for the ego: self-contained, unified, integrated" is tied to a "loss of consciousness . . . when it goes, so does consciousness—which must always be consciousness of an object, which is to say, consciousness of *an object that is one*" (2000, 15). In this sense, Zürn's dancing scenes are not about dispersion but about reconstructing the body as a "unified object." This object, however, is virtual, as is the following strange scene, in which the performance culminates:

What she is now "being ordered" to do is not a dance but the relatively short action which constitutes suicide: she is the scorpion which kills itself. She sees . . . her feet and legs grow together to form a dangerously long sting like a sharp pointed dagger, then curl slowly upwards in an elegant curve until its point hangs just above the center of her solar plexus. She lowers her eyes to this, her most precious possession, which reveals itself beneath her now transparent skin with all the beauty of its tiny and minuscule branchings which start to glisten like silver under her breath, and which resembles a paradisiacal, illuminated landscape which loses itself in its twisting paths, constantly awakening the desire to wander about within it and make completely new discoveries. . . . What cruelty, what devilry to compel her to stab this glory with her own sting. (Zürn 1994, 98)

In this sadomasochistic scene, "she" seems to return to the paradise from which she had been expulsed in the beginning, when she awoke from the dream and found a return to her mother's womb impossible. However, her own womb—which she must enter by way of self-destruction—is not dark but "glistening," a whole new world that opens up in front of her, and is ready to be explored. Earlier in the narrative, the narrator had described the solar plexus as "the one part of her body which reacted when she encountered those things that were of importance to her . . . music . . . books . . . art objects, indeed all those things which were necessary for establishing her inner kingdom" (Zürn 1994, 78). The "(pro)creation" suggested by the joining of two parts of herself (the "dagger" entering the solar plexus), which allows her to *see herself*, is thwarted, however, by the fact that the scorpion commits suicide. Instead of the image of what "she" might see, the text contains three dots marking the moment of death that is the loss of consciousness, the absence of any images. Hence, what has promised to become a utopian space does not, in fact, seem to exist, at least not in a form that would be accessible to the subject (once again, "she" is barred from returning to the womb). Body and subject remain separate, but the subject survives another day.

On the morning after, "she" wakes up thrilled by her own performance, shouting out of the window: "Someone has gone mad with joy at the superhuman abilities she has discovered this night!" (Zürn 1994, 100). Infused with the sense of immortality Freud attributes to the ego ideal (here: the Man of Jasmine), she is so euphoric that she does not realize that she is "superhuman" only in her imagination; after all, these hallucinations turn out to be essential to her survival, for they provide the only sense of hope in an increasingly sad scenario, where her real, physical body is systematically destroyed. The "long night of hallucinations," in which she watched herself perform, is preceded by this pitiful scene:

> She is rolled across the tarmac in a wheel chair to the plane for Paris. . . . A long time, filled with injections and medicines, passes until she can walk again. . . . She resembles a robot walking along. When she tries to read she sees the lines converge at an angle. . . . When she moves her hand she is startled by the motion, as if it were not her own hand and did not belong to her body. (Zürn 1994, 92)

It is the true face of her illness: an alienation from her own body that is so complete that she experiences herself only as no longer human ("like a robot"). It is the effect of medications she has been given in order to stop her from hallucinating; and it only precipitates more hallucinations, as she is now unable to physically perform the very activities that endow her with a sense of self, that is, reading, writing, and drawing. Caught within the limitations of her own physical body as in yet another straightjacket, "she" must depend on hallucinations to avoid a depression that all but obliterates her ability to tend to her body in its most basic form, such as washing herself or combing her hair. Any kind of narcissism "she" might have had—and here narcissism would seem vital—is lost in this condition, where her body seems to have lost all value: "And what if she were to roll about in her excrement like that woman in the other bed?" The only way in which "she" is able to stimulate her body is through masturbation, and this only leads to her being more ashamed of herself. A repetitive and rather mechanical activity, masturbation resembles the structure of this narrative, in which "she" is caught.[23]

To perform a better self within her hallucinations, the Man of Jasmine is needed. Unlike Hardenberg's autonomous expressionist dancer, Zürn's "she" is like Rilke's ballet dancer, an instrument in need of direction. The Man of Jasmine functions as a master of ceremonies who guarantees that the show will go on. Thus "she" is never really free of him, who keeps the split between her real body and its image in place. As in the myth of Narcissus, "she" is really cut off from the "other" that is her own reflection: she watches herself "perform," yet she does not realize that everything else about her is deteriorating.

As in *Nightwood,* gradual "decay" is part of this narrative as well, but there is nothing organic about this situation, which repeats itself ad nauseam: another move into a hotel; another hospitalization; another return to the "friend"; and the same cycle starts all over again. Her body is transported among various spaces—the cities of Berlin and Paris, various hotels, vacation places, and institutions—yet her inner life takes place in the "virtual" space of her imagination. The people she encounters, friends, doctors, strangers, remain sketchy, overpowered by the only figure "she" can relate to: the Man of Jasmine.

Whereas in *Nightwood*, sentences seem to "twist and turn" and language draws attention to its "brilliance"; and whereas in Hardenberg, "the body" stretches beyond the limits of language to open up the possibility of encountering an "other"; there is nothing "narcissistic" about Zürn's language, nor does there seem to be any real faith in the redemptive power of language (in this aspect, she is no longer "modernist"). Painful to read, *The Man of Jasmine* seems more "realist" than experimental, yet it experiments with the very nature of representation itself, as it illustrates the subject's dependence on the self-observing gaze. Without this gaze, Zürn seems to say, we would be "nothing." When "she" is arrested and finds herself alone in a prison cell,

> she performs for the first time, just for herself, a long mime-show whose meaning and details she is later unable to recall. But while she occupies herself with her game in this gracious and imaginative way, she thinks briefly that there ought to be someone to record this mime for posterity in a little film—but there is no one. (Zürn 1994, 106)

The way the last sentence concludes suggests that "she" herself is included in this "no one." Truly, there seems to be "no one" left when the technology is gone. Threatened with disappearance due to the absence of a recording device, "she" seems lost and so are we: If she cannot "recall" what she has done, what is it that marks the reality of her existence?

At the very end of the book, "she" considers that it may be "all a question of remembering" (Zürn 1994, 126) and that this question may be what keeps her going. Then she asks the question with which *The Man of Jasmine* concludes: "Would that save her?" (*Wäre das eine Rettung?*).[24] It is a question posed to the reader, who is now in a position to recognize the danger of Narcissus's madness, the inability to separate fact from fiction, reality from fantasy, and, at the same time, acknowledge that this delusion may also sustain the subject (at least for the time being, we don't know how long Narcissus spends gazing at his reflection—it could be a lifetime).

The problem Zürn's text seems to illustrate is that art cannot replace "reality"—whatever that may be—yet that one may be tempted to assume that it could. Virtual realities and artificially altered bodies may have their place, yet the disappearance of the human subject is painful. If identity is "constructed," as much of recent academic discourse has suggested, Zürn's *Man of Jasmine* dramatizes the implications of such a proposition: in her "writing on the body," the nail file is lowered into the skin like the scorpion's dagger as if to arrest the flow of signification and fulfill the desire to merge with the sign. As a result, there is no room left for further interpretation. Everything is reduced to a single digit. What remains is a gothic tale of the body's unreality: "The six is marked in blood on her hand. She had felt no pain" (Zürn 1994, 40). Like the "bodies" in her drawings, which seem to consist of only writing, writing in Zürn is, somehow, always prior. The subject is "nothing" without a text—and text is all that is left.

Epilogue: Reconsidering "Subjectivity"

This book began with reference to the sexologists of the late nineteenth century and ended with the portrayal of psychiatric institutions in the late 1960s. What these two points in time have in common is an emphasis on the body as a biological organism, assumed to be shaped by genetics and changeable through scientific advances, such as DNA research and increasingly sophisticated psychiatric drugs. Psychoanalysis, in this context, seems out-of-date: its emphasis is on language and self-reflection; and it assumes the human subject to be shaped by the influences of society, including family structures, instead of "nature." Freud, as I have shown, was unclear as to what role biology should play in his thinking: on the one hand, he conceived of the "ego ideal" as an imaginary, culturally constructed image of one's self; on the other hand, he attributed its emergence to the repression of a biologically determined state of nature, "primary narcissism." To link these apparently contradictory positions, he argued that our relationships with others ("objects") are also narcissistic so that it becomes difficult to tell where we recognize the other as "other" and where it is a mere reflection of ourselves.

This condition, where subject-object boundaries are shifting and it becomes difficult to differentiate between fantasy and reality, seems relevant to a culture that makes it more and more difficult to distinguish between virtual reality, as generated by new media such as the Internet, and the reality of our own, mortal bodies. Like Narcissus, we may delude ourselves about the "reality" of artificially produced images and at the same time take pleasure in being protected from the depressing events that take place in the real world, against which we seem to be powerless.

Narcissism is about the pleasures of fantasy, and it is connected to literature and art. Narcissus seems emblematic of the decentered subject of modernity, who struggles with the disappearance of his or her humanity in an increasingly technological world; and of the "post-human" subject of postmodernity, who inhabits a virtual world of images that flood the screens and monitors by which we seem inevitably surrounded. He wants to merge with this "other" world by wanting to embrace his lover in the pool; and he wants to escape from the schizoid condition of being split by his own self-observing gaze. At the same time, he exists in a moment of suspense, where there is an oscillation between two points that may seem static (ahistorical) but lasts for an indefinite period of time so that, consequently, an erotic tension is generated by which he sustains himself.

This tension, as I have shown in my discussion of Hardenberg's poetry, provides the opening between self and other, for it undoes subject-object boundaries. It reveals the indeterminacy of the "object" with which we must reckon, knowing it may be impossible to ever know who the "other" really is. As my discussion of *Nightwood* intended to illustrate, the recognition that one knows little of "the other," apart from what one believes to know about one's self, may be a crucial insight, for it grants others the freedom to be different, to remain unassimilable. Both Hardenberg and Barnes, belonging to the same generation of modernists, seem to emphasize the possibilities of narcissism by depicting art as a form of pleasure that differs from reality.

When, in the quotation at the beginning of this book, Thomas Mann writes about Narcissus's "deep, beguiled, unresisting smile," he calls it "a very slightly distorted smile" because reflections—whether produced by water or celluloid—are by definition distorted. The "other," regardless of how much one attempts to see it as "the same," is never quite like one's self, and its reality may forever escape representation. As Zürn's text shows, "the body" is constructed by the subject who wishes to represent herself, yet her "flesh" can not be assimilated into the text—it serves as a reminder that art is *not* reality. Like Narcissus's madness, which leads to disintegration and death, the image is not capable of sustaining the subject indefinitely. *The Man of Jasmine* no longer offers a refuge in fantasy because now art has *become* reality. As if anticipating the emergence of computers and new media, Zürn used the medium of film to represent that confusion between reality and fiction which is also symptomatic of early twenty-first-century culture. It is as if, somehow, we have to live with the uncertainty of not knowing how real our bodies are, for they appear subject to the delusion that there is no difference between them and the images of fantasy. Anesthetized by the flood of images, we are like Freud's "primary narcissistic" child, who believes in magic, the power to animate the inanimate, and who overestimates the power of his own wishes.

In Freud, this condition yields to the superego, which monitors the subject to keep his or her narcissism in check in the name of reason, the opposite of madness, where the "other" becomes more important than the self. However, as it turns out, the "other" that is the lonely reflection in the pool appears to be the same as those "others" whose ideals and rules the subject internalizes to repress his or her original narcissism. Thus Freud's argument closes in on itself like Zürn's narrative, to perform the "truth" it purports to represent.

This tautology is unlike the literary texts I have discussed, for they do not make a claim toward "objective" truth. Rather, they suggest a "truth" that is performative, as it situates itself in the moment of tension between self/other, inside/outside, reality/fantasy, where we can never really know which is which. We are reminded, by the same token, that what we are engaged in reading is a work of art, *not* a representation of reality. All three experimental women writers attempt to represent "subjectivity" by way of invoking narcissism, which acts as a paradigm for representation: In Hardenberg, the body is explored as a landscape by a voice that appears to be synonymous with the "body" of the text itself; in Barnes, an absent lover is represented through visual and verbal reflections, thereby opening up a new perspective on a seemingly closed, discursive framework; and in Zürn, an imaginary figure acts as a projective surface for the subject's own desire, which is to represent herself through writing.

What they have in common, in contrast to Freud, is that they dwell on the uncertainty of "not knowing." They raise the question: Who is this "I" that sees itself? Through narcissism, we are presented with the illusion that it may be possible to momentarily suspend the historical narratives by which we seem determined. The subject gazes at her own reflection and she perceives what looks like an objective rendering of herself, an apparent extension of her body to which she sees herself, somehow, connected. Through this confusion, the knowledge that the "image" is *not* oneself can never fully disappear.

Notes

Chapter 1

1. Among psychoanalysts, the debate over narcissism is known as the "Kernberg-Kohut debate." While Kohut is the main proponent of a positive narcissism within the context of "self psychology" (see his 1971 *The Analysis of the Self*), his theories have been questioned from within the discipline. My sense is that some of his views promote a rather simplistic vision of mental "health" as a condition that is, supposedly, free from neuroses.

2. The standard reference is Vinge 1967.

3. The most popular work on masturbation during this period was Rohleder 1898.

4. Although many of the documents are in German and remain to be translated, the collection by Lucy Bland and Laura Doan, *Sexology Uncensored: The Documents of Sexual Science* (Bland and Doan 1998a), provides a good overview of the discipline of sexology—it contains documents by Havelock Ellis, Richard von Krafft-Ebing, and Magnus Hirschfeld. It is accompanied by a volume of recent critical essays, *Sexology in Culture: Labelling Bodies and Desires* (Bland and Doan 1998b).

5. For example, under the heading of "contrary sexual sensations," Krafft-Ebing (1886/1997) lists four distinct stages: (1) "psychic hermaphrodism"; (2) "homosexuality"; (3) "effeminatio"; and (4) "androgyny." Particularly the last two stages are said to be connected to physical "deviances" as well, for example, men develop "wider hips" and women become "flat-chested." Although I was not able to discern the causality between sexual behavior and atypical physical appearance—that is, which was believed to come first—it is obvious that Krafft-Ebing and his contemporaries wished to show that such a connection existed, as they tried to prove it by means of empirical observation, that is, measuring the body's shape, genitalia, facial hair, and so on, as well as by observing related behavior, such as a person's gait. Clearly, this pseudoscience is related to the dangerous racial pseudoscience, eugenics, which drew similar analogies between physiognomy and human character and was widely practiced during the late nineteenth century.

6. Freud became convinced of this fundamental bisexuality through his friendship with the general practitioner Wilhelm Fliess, whose theories are recorded in a famous exchange of letters between the two. Another popular theory of bisexuality was that of Otto Weininger in *Geschlecht und Character* (*Sex and Character*) (1903/1980).

7. To combat homophobia on both the legal and the scientific level, Hirschfeld founded the Wissenschaftlich-Humanitäres Komitee in Berlin in 1896; and he edited two journals, the *Zeitschrift für Sexualwissenschaft* and the *Jahrbuch für sex-*

uelle Zwischenstufen, in which articles by both sexologists and psychoanalysts (including Freud) were published. Sadly, the Institut für Sexualwissenschaft, including its voluminous library, was burned down by the National Socialists (its ruins are now covered by the Berlin Kongresshalle).

8. Hirschfeld's concept of "intermediary sexual stages" bears some similarity to the current concept of "queerness": both are designed to deconstruct the system of binary oppositions that holds the homo/hetero distinction in place. Eve Sedgwick lists, for example, "secrecy/disclosure, knowledge/ignorance, private/public, masculine/feminine, majority/minority, innocence/initiation, natural/artificial" (1990, 11), to name just a few.

9. Paragraph 175 in Germany, which was instituted in 1868 (and was not abolished until well after World War II!), enabled the Nazis to incarcerate more than 200,000 homosexuals in concentration camps (see, for example, the 1999 documentary entitled *Paragraph 175,* by Rob Epstein and Jeffrey Friedman). Unlike what one might expect based on sexological and psychoanalytic discourses about homosexuality, these prisoners were not classified as "mentally ill" (nor as "degenerate" in racial terms) but as "criminals." According to a 1944 report (printed in Brecht et al. 1985): "The delinquent . . . may be either—and this is at least very rare—a homosexual by nature, or someone who, originally with normal sexual tendencies, was led astray . . . from the medical point of view there is no reason to treat homosexuals differently from other offenders" (171). Perhaps not surprisingly, this view is consistent with that of religious fundamentalists and other conservatives today, who see same-sex desire as a "moral aberration."

10. A complete list of Sadger's publication appears in May-Tolzmann 1991, which is seminal to any research on how "narcissism" began.

11. In a footnote to his second edition of *Three Essays,* in 1910, Freud argues that the "compulsive longing for men" by homosexuals has been "determined by their ceaseless flight from women" (1910/1962, 11).

12. A good example of this approach is Bruhm's *Reflecting Narcissus* (2001), on narcissism in narratives about male same-sex desire. My project is similar, except that it deals with female authors and experimental writing.

13. Näcke was a forensic psychiatrist with an interest in "craniology," the nineteenth-century pseudoscience of determining criminal behavior by way of measuring the shape and size of the human skull (its most famous practitioner was Cesare Lombroso in Italy).

14. As the source of this quote, Ellis cites page 824 of Moll's *Untersuchungen über die Libido Sexualis* (1898).

15. This reference is to the Hungarian analyst Sandor Radò, a student of Karl Abraham's, who practiced psychoanalysis in Berlin.

16. According to Lilli Gast, there was a "debate over femininity" (*Weiblichkeits-Debatte*) among psychoanalysts during the twenties and thirties, where the concept of "penis envy" was disproved by some of the female psychoanalysts of the

second generation, such as Karen Horney and Melanie Klein. As they have shown through their own observations, little girls are positively aware of the uniqueness of their own genitalia, that is, they are not under the mistaken impression that, somehow, they are "lacking" a penis.

17. Object relations theory, which is largely based on the writings of British psychoanalyst Melanie Klein (see, e.g., Klein 1986), is practiced mostly in the United Kingdom and, to a lesser extent, in the United States (where Heinz Hartmann's "ego psychology," for reasons which to discuss would exceed the scope of this introduction, has had a similar amount of impact). The principles of object relations theory appear to be in sharp opposition to those of French psychoanalysis, notably the theories of Jaques Lacan, but also of Laplanche and Pontalis. This difference may be due to the way in which psychoanalysis was received critically in France, whereas in the English-speaking countries, it became institutionalized, as Dean and Lane (2001) have also noted, to become part of the medical establishment.

18. This does not mean that psychoanalysis is not guilty of biological determinism even if (or perhaps because) it seems to have distanced itself from questions of gender and sexuality. As is well known, Freud himself stated that "anatomy is destiny" (the sentence appears twice in Freud's writings: first in "Beiträge zur Psychologie des Liebeslebens" in 1912, then again in *Der Untergang des Ödipuskomplexes* in 1924). For more on Freud's relation to biology, see Sulloway 1982.

19. The notion that texts are "performative," that is, that they create rather than just represent reality, has been explored by Judith Butler (see, e.g., Butler 1990, 1993), especially in relation to texts about gender. Although most of the texts I analyze here are fictitious, they can enter a dialogue with theoretical writings if one considers that *all* language is performative.

20. Note that the term "libido" was coined by Krafft-Ebing (1899) and then taken up by Freud. As for the history of the term "narcissism," see chapter 2.

21. A similar line of thought was pursued by Otto Rank in *Das Trauma der Geburt* (1923), which caused a great deal of controversy, as it shifted the emphasis away from the Oedipus complex and onto the moment of birth. However, whereas Rank limited his theory to the individual, Ferenczi took it further: to him, intrauterine existence was merely the extension of life in the sea, as shared by all creatures.

22. *Thalassa* was not published until 1924, but Ferenzci had conceived of it, according to his own words, nine years earlier. His 1913 essay "Stages in the Development of the Sense of Reality" can be seen as a precursor to *Thalassa.* For more on the connection between *Thalassa* and Ferenczi's other writings—mainly, his contributions to child psychology—see Balint 1973.

23. In another stunning passage, Ferenzci draws an analogy between the penis and the tooth, based on "the uniformity . . . with which the symbolic identity of penis and tooth recurs, both in dreams and in neurotic symptoms. According

to our conception the tooth is therefore really a primal penis (*Urpenis*)" (1924/1968, 22).

24. See S. Levine 1994.

25. See Edschmid 1918 and Hatvani 1917. The translations are mine.

26. For more on Salomé, see Martin 1991. For a discussion of the relationship between Freud and Salomé in terms of its influence on Freud's conception of narcissism, see Gast 1992. Gast also refers to the anecdote of the "narcissistic cat" which was described by Salomé in her *Freud-Journal* in 1913: "While Freud maintained his office on the ground floor, the cat had climbed in through the open window. . . . In the beginning the cat aroused mixed feelings in him [but then] his heart melted and he ordered milk for it. . . . However, despite Freud's increasing affection and admiration, the cat paid him not a bit of attention" (Gast 1992, 89). As Salomé's description continues, the cat remains "cold" toward Freud and in the end dies from its so-called egotism, having refused all of Freud's efforts to feed it. As Gast points out, both Freud and Nietzsche frequently compared women to cats. Chapter 2 will show how this version of an attractive but inaccessible "femininity" (which precedes Freud's later views of female sexuality as based on the Oedipus complex) relates to Freud's concept of "primary narcissism."

27. Ulrichs borrowed the term "third sex" from Plato's *Symposium* and, according to James Steakley, it appeared in the *Kama-Sutra* as well. Ulrichs also coined the term "Uranism" to identify homosexuality and, subsequently, homosexuals began to call themselves "Uranians" or *Urninge,* a term that continued to be in use well into the twentieth century. Ulrichs's collected works, originally published from 1864 through 1897, were reedited in German by Hubert Kennedy and published by Verlag Rosa Winkel in 1994; and in 2000, an exhibit and lecture series at the Frankfurt Institut für Sexualwissenschaft (Volkmar Sigusch) celebrated Ulrichs as the "the first gay man in history." It is unfortunate that Ulrichs's writings have not yet been translated into English. For further information on the "third sex" within the context of nineteenth-century sexology, consult Hekma 1993.

28. Homosexuals were declared either "criminal" or "mentally ill": for example, the American Psychiatric Association did not eliminate homosexuality from its *Diagnostic and Statistic Manual of Mental Disorders* until 1973—and then only after repeated pressure from gay-rights activists.

29. This includes *Nightwood*'s first chapter about the figure of the Austrian Jew Felix Volkbein, which tends to be treated as separate from the rest of the novel, as critics tend to be embarrassed by its anti-Semitic connotations.

30. The notion of the "ego ideal," whose origin is also described in chapter 3 of *The Ego and the Id,* is essential to Lacanian theory and will be discussed in detail in the following chapter.

31. Surrealism's well-known emphasis on dreams and images, as well as its use of techniques such as "automatic writing," brings it in close proximity to psychoanalysis. André Breton, the main proponent of surrealism, had been interested in

psychiatry and hypnosis as a medical student and had visited Freud in Vienna in 1921. The surrealists eventually rejected psychoanalysis, but many of their findings resembled those of the psychoanalysts. For example, Henri Ellenberger, in *The Discovery of the Unconscious,* notes that Breton was under the impression that he had discovered a certain type of dream that emerges during the hypnagogic state, yet "was unaware that [it] had been thoroughly investigated by Herbert Silberer" (1970, 835)—whereas Freud was quick to add Silberer's research to his *Interpretation of Dreams.* That there exists an essential link between surrealism and psychoanalysis has recently been argued by David Lomas in regard to hysteria: "Despite Freud's professed incomprehension [of surrealism], an examination of the theme of hysteria reveals the extent to which surrealism and psychoanalysis are linked" (2001, 75).

32. For discussion on the question of "autobiography" in Zürn, see Rupprecht 2000, my introduction to my English translation of Zürn's 1969 novella *Dark Spring,* which ends with the suicide of its protagonist and is followed by the real-life suicide of its author only one year later.

33. Bellmer's dolls have been interpreted as a critique of fascism, yet they are also "embodiments of female . . . victimization" (Taylor 2000, 5). While Hal Foster notes that "we should not be too quick to pathologise Bellmer . . . these scenes are representations, not realities" (2001, 207), Susan Suleiman asks: "How are we to distinguish Bellmer's sadism from Nazi sadism, both of them directed against the 'feminine'?" (1998, 135).

34. Bellmer's view is expressed in a letter to his psychoanalyst, Gaston Ferdière, who treated him for alcoholism and who also treated Unica Zürn. See Bellmer and Zürn 1994.

35. The antipsychiatry movement was received particularly well in France, which helps explain the differences between Anglo-American and Lacanian psychoanalysis, with the latter being generally more skeptical of institutionalized psychiatric practices.

36. Sheperdson (2000) asks this question in relation to Kristeva's version of narcissism in *Histoires d'amour* (1983), which he critiques for failing to adequately address the issue of temporality in the myth of Narcissus.

Chapter 2

1. For a discussion of this shift from "ideal ego" (*Idealich*) to ego ideal (*Ichideal*), see Lacan 1975, chap. 11.

2. The comment that Ferenczi can be seen as the first object relations theorist was made by Hilary Beattie in a personal conversation with me in 2003.

3. Freud uses the term "paraphrenia," which was originally "schizophrenia." However, according to Laplanche and Pontalis, (1973, 140), "paraphrenia" was eventually termed "schizophrenia" again.

4. According to May-Tolzmann (1991), it was Sadger's research on the relationship between homosexual men and their mothers that paved the way for Freud's new classification into two types.

5. *Anlehnung* refers to the way in which drives "lean on" objects, not to the way in which persons lean on one another.

Chapter 3

1. As outlined in the previous chapters, Lacanian theory holds that "the unconscious is structured like a language," and that "the real" is not immediately accessible; whereas object relations theory holds that the relationship between the individual's physical body and his or her environment is immediate (the prototype of this being the Kleinian object, the mother's breast).

2. This opposition collapses near the end of Freud's essay, as I showed in the previous chapter, when Freud discusses his discovery of the "dream-censor," citing research by Herbert Silberer.

3. On the friendship between Rilke and Hardenberg, see Vollmer 1993.

4. My translation. This quotation is part of the following passage, which in the original reads: "Während meiner Besuche 1991 in London lernte ich schließlich die 98-jährige Dichterin als eine Person kennen, die . . . den Eindruck vermittelte, sehr lange auf die Wiederentdeckung ihrer Dichtungen . . . gewartet zu haben. Hardenberg formulierte ihren Wunsch nach Unsterblichkeit, bzw. nach dem Überschreiten der Grenzen des eigenen Körpers und der eigenen Identität bereits 1918."

5. The concept of a "lyrical I" is also in Adorno 1971, 249, where he distinguishes between the private and the social subject with reference to utopia.

6. Take, for example, the titles of the sections in the popular 1920 anthology of expressionist poetry *Menschheitsdämmerung* (*Dawn of Humanity*): "Sturz und Schrei" ("Fall and Scream"), "Erweckung des Herzens" ("Awakening of the Heart"), "Aufruf und Empörung" ("Outrage and Uprising"), and "Liebe den Menschen" ("Love Mankind"). Although they refer to highly emotional states, they were not intended to represent individual experiences but rather the condition of humankind in general.

7. As described by Anz (1980).

8. My translation. The full sentence reads: "Mit der Thematisierung von Außenseiterfiguren . . . gibt die Autorin Hinweise auf ihre eigene problematische Identität als Jüdin, Dichterin und Frau in einer männlich dominierten literarischen Bewegung."

9. My translation. The original passage reads: "Die verhaltene Sprache der Expressionistinnen begleitet die wortgewaltigen Aufstände der expressionistischen

Autoren. Die schreibenden Frauen korrigieren das Bild einer literarischen Epoche. In dem schmalen Werk Henriette Hardenbergs lernen wir einen 'anderen Expressionismus' kennen" (Raabe 1988, 8).

10. A good example of this bourgeois, biologically essentialist feminism is the work of Lou Andreas-Salomé, which I mentioned in chapter 1 (1921). Salomé believed, for example, that women were better at being creative artists because of their innate ability to give birth.

11. Take, for example, the expressionist and later futurist Carl Einstein, who opposed the sentimental stance of romantic art by a demand for a more "masculine," more "intellectual" approach to art, whereby one would be able to confront the power of modernity. Sentimentality, in turn, is associated with impotence: "feelings are usually displayed as a matter of having to cover up one's impotence" ("Gefühl hat immer statt, wenn es gilt, Impotenz zu verbergen"; Anz and Stark 1982, 656).

12. The (ongoing) political discussion over expressionism and primitivism began with a debate between Georg Lukasc and Ernst Bloch in 1934, when Lukasc charged expressionism with having been a "precursor to fascism" because of its emphasis on the mythical, irrational. In hindsight, it seems that the expressionists were not motivated by the kind of "escapism" Lukasc attributed to them but rather by a naïve belief in the power of art to change the world (see the historical documents on expressionism in Anz and Stark 1982). More ironic is the fact that the Nazis considered expressionist art to be "degenerate," that is, subversive of their ideology. One of the recent attempts to deal with the issue of primitivism in expressionism is by David Pan, *Primitive Renaissance* (2001), which focuses on Nietzsche, Freud, Kandinsky, and Carl Einstein, claiming that "because the structures of reason are incapable of organizing individual experience, the return of mythic forces . . . is not a regression but rather the return of a repressed dimension in human experience to its rightful place" (13). I myself find that not only are the structures of reason quite capable of organizing all kinds of experiences but also, following Foucault's *Madness and Civilization* (1965), the barbarism associated with primitivism in the Western world can be understood only in conjunction with the Enlightenment's emphasis on reason, not in opposition to it—there is no "rightful place" to which human experience could be restored.

13. My translation. The phrase appears in conjunction with the notion of a transformation and "naturalization" of self in the following sentence from Vollmer's essay on Hardenberg and Rilke: "Überhaupt können wir in diesem Prozeß einer 'Naturisierung' des Ich, getrieben von der Sehnsucht nach menschlicher Allverbundenheit, einen Grundzug der Dichtungen Henriette Hardenbergs erkennen." (Vollmer 1993, 76).

14. All translations of Hardenberg are mine.

15. This translation is by Babette Deutsch and was published in Ashton 1960, 214.

16. This translation is by MacIntyre (1964), 111.

17. This type of nonmimetic representation is typical for expressionism: although still often figurative (compared to its later version, abstract expressionism), the aim was to represent hitherto unseen, subjective states of mind, not reality as commonly perceived—an example of such representation would be the horses by Franz Marc, whose shape resembles that of real horses but whose color is blue. A thorough discussion of expressionist esthetics is Worringer 1913. For a useful introduction, see Selz 1974.

18. The original passage reads as follows:

> Wir selber schreiten . . . in unseren inneren Spiegel hinein. Wir verschwinden in der kleinen gemalten Tür des fabelhaften Palastes und werden nicht mehr gesehen, weder in dieser noch in jener Welt; der allbewegende, allverbergende Augenblick ist angelangt und aufgebrochen, die Zeit steht still im Innenraum absoluter Enthüllung, Gegenwart . . . in Explosion fliegt auf das Draußen . . . indes drinnen, in der gotischen Stube der Selbstbegegnung, diese ganze weite und scheinbar so sehr reale Welt dereinst nur selber wie ein Bild unschädlicher Erinnerung an den Wänden hängt. (Bloch 1918, 79)

19. I am indebted to Tamara Evans for this observation.

Chapter 4

1. For a good discussion of the connection between *Nightwood,* surrealism, and the Marquis de Sade, see Chisholm 1997.

2. Perhaps due to this formal structure of "narcissism," *Nightwood* has a tendency to reflect right back whatever a given critic might wish to read into it, including the need to construct the kind of airtight, literal reading that can easily be turned into its opposite. Looking at the reception history, there seem to be a number of diametrically opposed viewpoints based on the same evidence, attesting, perhaps, to Barnes's having created a text that ultimately defies interpretation. Like Narcissus's reflection, *Nightwood* holds up the mirror to its critics more than it reveals, so that an endless series of oscillations might ensue.

3. Robin's last name, "Vote," probably refers to the suffragette movement in which Barnes had been active; "Nora" might refer to the heroine of Henrik Ibsen's feminist play; whereas "Flood" may suggest Nora's being swept away by her feelings for Robin.

4. The only other critic who, before Allen, mentioned narcissism in *Nightwood* was Alan Singer, and he did so only in passing, and with negative connotations: "Desire . . . is tragically experienced by Barnes's characters as a crushingly narcissistic isolation" (1984, 70).

5. Altman sees him as "a mirror image (or a parody) of Radcliffe Hall's Stephen Gordon" (1993, 165) in *The Well of Loneliness,* a novel that has become paradigmatic for the stereotypical image of the melodramatically suffering lesbian, whose plea for sympathy is based on the sense of having been cursed by nature.

6. Obviously, the fact that Matthew does not have a permanent relationship makes it more difficult to apply the paradigm of narcissism to him—which only confirms my reading that narcissism yields to more possibilities than the concept with which he identifies, the "third sex."

7. The issue of shifting paradigms should be evident from the fact that what began as a politically necessary effort to prove that homosexuality was "inborn" (see Ulrichs 1994) could later be perverted into representing "the third sex" as *freakish.* Consequently, it seems that, since Hirschfeld and other gay-rights activists were forced to prove that they were genetically and intellectually superior (not inferior), they eventually would be stuck with biologically based paradigms of homosexuality. Working as or together with sexologists, they published elaborate studies to prove that there was indeed physical evidence for the genetic basis of homosexuality—see, for example, Roemer 1906, which contains graphs that show that homosexuals have less "brain disease" but higher rates of suicide than heterosexuals (due to persecution). Such studies, as I mentioned in chapter 1, were based on the method of empiricism, involving visual descriptions of the body (e.g., the lesbian woman as "flat-chested"); and they included scurrile genetic theories of "bisexuality," such as Konrad Küster's assertion, published by Hirschfeld in *Zeitschrift für Sexualwissenschaft,* that the male, because he has nipples, has the potential to breastfeed; whereas the clitoris is really an "atrophied penis" (Küster 1908, 543; my translation). As James Steakley notes, Hirschfeld "grew increasingly dissatisfied with the third-sex terminology and would soon drop it entirely, for he was coming to regard it as both scientifically inaccurate and tactically counterproductive to minoritize homosexuals in a world populated entirely, as he ultimately saw it, by sexual intermediates" (1997, 137). However, what I found troubling when actually reading some of Hirschfeld's writings (e.g., 1899–1923, 1908) is that he employs the same terminology as the Nazis, with concepts such as *Rassenhygiene* (racial hygiene), *Volksgesundheit* (public health), and *Züchtungspolitik* (laws for procreation) designed to promote an ideal of a healthy "Aryan" body. Barnes takes the opposite approach: by making it clear that human beings are essentially weak, vulnerable, and "perverse," she resists taking the moral high ground.

8. See the psychoanalyst Joan Riviere's 1929 essay "Womanliness as Masquerade" (1929/1986), on whose insights Judith Butler bases her theory of gender as "performative." Also see the turn-of-the-century concept of the "New Woman" that led to texts such as Ernst von Wolzogen's 1900 novel *Das dritte Geschlecht* (*The Third Sex*), where he refers not so much to same-sex desire as to the image of women as "masculine" (e.g., when they want to join the workforce). This image in turn led to a hostile rejection of the third sex on the part of heterosexual

"feminists" like Marie Anderson, who wrote in a 1903 diatribe that "women who are completely flat-chested . . . are often completely heterosexual" ("Weiber mit völlig flachem Busen sind . . . sehr oft durchaus heterosexuell"; 1904, 50) so as to prove that homosexuals must be criminals because "a third sex does absolutely not exist" ("ein drittes Geschlecht gibt es überhaupt nicht"; 54).

9. The literary expatriate scene on the Paris Left Bank, which is known through Gertrude Stein, includes, for example, Janet Flanner, who wrote for the *New Yorker,* and Sylvia Beach, who cofounded the bookstore Shakespeare & Co. See Benstock 1986 as well as the 1996 documentary film *Paris Was a Woman* (which seems largely based on Benstock's book). Also see Löffelholz 1992 and Busch 1989.

10. On circus imagery and the "carnivalesque" in *Nightwood,* see Marcus 1991 and Winkiel 1997.

11. As Tyrus Miller points out, "Barnes' modernist predecessors had long before begun to turn the screw of irony in order to evade identification of the author's perspective with the literary conventions employed, the events represented, and the limited perspectives of the characters in the work" (1999, 148).

12. In addition to Herring's, which is most thoroughly researched, there are an earlier one by Andrew Field (1985); two German ones by Katharina Kaever (1985) and Kyra Stromberg (1989); and the memoir by Hank O'Neal (1990), who spent time with Barnes during her final years.

13. Obviously, the two are connected, yet Barnes did not see it that way: for example, she refused to grant permission to quote *Nightwood* to Kenneth Burke (1968), whose essay includes discussion of homosexuality and race—as a result, the essay is now printed with blank spaces in lieu of quotes.

14. The building still exists (near Greenwich Avenue and Tenth Street) and is known as the home of a number of artists and writers, such as Theodore Dreiser and Jane Bowles. The poet E. E. Cummings was Barnes's neighbor across the way.

15. In *Ryder,* the figure of Doctor Matthew O'Connor appears for the first time. The book can be read in support of Margaret Sanger's birth control movement, since it highlights the negative effects of childbearing on women's lives. See Stevenson (1993).

16. Howes (2000) provides a useful, detailed essay on the Felix chapter. Howes takes the polarized debate over the representation of Felix to another level by illuminating Barnes's painstakingly researched references to Austrian and European history and culture. His interpretation that the novel is "at one level . . . a confrontation of an American attitude with a European one" (269) opens up new possibilities for looking at this chapter.

17. The reference to Matthew's performing abortions is evident from his conversation with Felix in the latter part of the novel, when Felix notes that "you are seen nearly every day in a certain convent, where you bow and pray and get free meals and attend cases which are, well, illegal" (Barnes 1995, 97). I assume

the "convent" refers to a brothel (based on the Shakespearean double entendre of the "nunnery" in *Hamlet;* see Partridge 1998) and that the "illegal cases" are abortions.

18. The concept of the "angel" is related to that of the "third sex," since it implies being of both genders but also sexless, suggesting a concept of androgyny more connected to forms of asexual, religious mysticism; see, for example, Balzac's *Séraphîta* (1835), where the angel is beyond corporeality, allowing him or her to shift shapes into either gender. The reference to angels appears throughout *Nightwood* (in opposition to its counterpart, the "beast"; see Arthur O. Lovejoy's *Great Chain of Being* [2001]). It may also be connected to the vernacular term for one who performs abortions, the "angelmaker."

19. *Nightwood*'s German translator, the writer Wolfgang Hildesheimer, observes in his afterword to the German translation, *Nachtgewächs,* that "the identity of the characters is blurred into subjectivity because they are all using the same linguistic register" ("das Sprachregister wird auf die Handvoll Sprecher verteilt; damit wird die Identität der Personen subjektiv verwischt"; 1998, 193). However, my sense is that Nora's register differs from that of Matthew and the narrator, since it seems more affect-laden.

20. Nancy Levine compares Robin to a "cinema vamp," a femme fatale like Greta Garbo or Marlene Dietrich who "possesses the ability, usually described as masculine, to divorce her sexual behavior from her capacity to think and feel. . . . She comes most alive at night, and, like the legendary blood-sucking vampire, the ancestor of the cinema vamp, she fears the morning light" (1989, 278). Mario Praz (1933) traces this image to late nineteenth-century Décadence, but the vamp is also related to twentieth-century technology, as Andreas Huyssen has shown: "The fears and perceptual anxieties emanating from ever more powerful machines are recast and reconstructed in terms of the male fear of female sexuality, reflecting, in the Freudian account, the male's castration anxiety" (1986, 70). Robin certainly "castrates" those who look at her.

21. I am indebted to Vincent Crapanzano for this observation (1996 conversation).

22. This appearance resembles the image of Hermaphrodite, as in a replica of a fourth-century B.C. statue at the Staatliche Museen Berlin, reproduced by Marie Delcourt, who observes that "at first sight the body would seem to be that of an adolescent boy, if the breasts were not delicately molded" (1961, 59). My own viewing of the statue in Berlin confirms this impression. Delcourt also quotes a more detailed 1926 description by Paul Richer from *Le Nu dans l'art*: *L'art grec*: "On each side [of the subumbilical region] are the well-formed flanks of a boy, but it ends in a young woman's pubis, below which are attached male organs, broken, but indicating only a slight development. . . . The lumbar region is intermediate between man's and woman's. Finally, the high, prominent buttocks could as well be those of a girl whose

sexual development is still incomplete as of a young boy" (Delcourt 1961, 59). According to Sara Friedrichsmeyer, an androgyne is "a combination of masculine and feminine," but, she explains, "biological hermaphrodism in all ages has been extremely rare—the concept of an androgynous entity has originated in the imagination" (1983, 7). Friedrichsmeyer, within the context of German romanticism, describes the androgyne in terms of a "longing for totality and its ensuing harmony . . . a penchant for the completion accompanying the union of male and female" (1983, 9), which she finds problematic, since this "union" is based, by definition, on distinguishing between the sexes. A similar critique has been made of Virginia Woolf's "Room of One's Own" and *Orlando* (1928), since the combining of the two sexes always entails that they are first separate. Still, I find that the appearance of androgyny is indicative of the performativity of gender, which contains its own undoing, as it becomes impossible to tell which is which.

23. Many of Matthew's statements resemble the epigrams of Oscar Wilde, whose purpose is to amuse, not emotionally affect, the reader.

24. Catherine Hollis notes in regard to this passage that Thelma Wood "etched her designs in silver . . . the 'stitches' left on the grass by the absence of the corpse resemble the pin-prick designs done in silver-point" (2000, 242).

25. See Partridge 1990. Shakespeare's line is: "Cupid is a knavish lad. Thus to make proper females mad" (142).

Chapter 5

1. Originally written in German, *Der Mann im Jasmin: Eindrücke einer Geisteskrankheit* was first published in France in 1970 as *L'Homme Jasmin,* translated by Ruth Henry. The German publication did not take place until 1977, in a paperback edition by Ullstein Verlag, which contains minor alterations. The English translation by Malcolm Green, which I am using, is based on this edition; I have indicated discrepancies between it and the version published in 1989, in volume 5 of *Gesamtausgabe* (1988–99). Edited and annotated extensively by Erich Brinkmann and Günter Bose, it is the definitive, collected edition of Zürn's texts as well as the source of information about her life, including documents such as personal communications, hospital files, and so forth.

2. Bürger (1974) argues that once art has lost its social function, it enters a stage of self-criticism ("Stadium der Selbstkritik"; 22), which contains its undoing.

3. The connection to *Art Brut* has been made by several critics, especially in regard to Zürn's drawings. The term *Art Brut* refers to Jean Dubuffet's collection of outsider art, by people who have had no formal training and include the mentally ill, because, as Dubuffet himself wrote: "Madness helps, assuredly, severing links as it does, effacing memories, and is often an excellent teacher. . . . The strongest

works, those freest of any received influence of 'learned' art, often come from its crucible" (1986, 3).

4. Zürn was hospitalized for schizophrenia, but the diagnosis was later retracted. The present-day diagnosis, according to *DSM-IV* (1998), as noted by Brinkmann, would be "bipolar affective disorder." Zürn's identification with Artaud is evident from statements such as: "This is how she realizes what someone like Antonin Artaud must have suffered through" (Zürn 1988–99, 4:290; my translation).

5. My translation of: "la résolution future de ces deux états, en apparence si contradictoires, que sont le rêve et la réalité, en une sorte de réalité absolue, de surréalité" (Breton 1924, 23).

6. The reference to Zürn as "a Nadja who has learned to speak" comes from a 1977 German radio interview whose moderator, Lothar Baier, is quoted by Schneider (1979, 75): "In vielem gleicht Unica Zürn einer Nadja, die aber ihr Schweigen gebrochen und ausgeprochen hat, was aus ihr gemacht worden ist" ("In many ways, Zürn is like a Nadja who has, however, broken her silence and talked about what happened to her"). As Katharine Conley has observed, "Zürn idealizes her Jasmine Man the way Nadja idealized Breton" (1996, 108); and as Sigrid Weigel, in *Frauenliteratur ohne Tradition?* (1987, 256), has observed, *The Man of Jasmine* reverses the genders of medieval, early modern, and romantic love poetry, in which the (male) poet worships his (female) lover from afar (e.g., Petrarch and Laura).

7. The journal, at La Fond in La Rochelle, was called *MÉTÉORE;* it was discontinued after the first issue, which does not contain Zürn's contribution (see the letter by Zürn to Alexander Koval of September 18, 1964, in Zürn 1988–99, 4:357). The text dedicated to Lacan is entitled "MISTAKE" (Zürn 1988–99, 4:415) and, as Brinkmann notes, was written in 1964, with the dedication added in 1970 (Zürn 1988–99, 4:435). For communications between Zürn and Ferdière, see Bellmer and Zürn 1994.

8. According to Susan Suleiman, "the women were generally younger . . . their version of Surrealist practice included a component of response to, as well as adaptation of, male Surrealist iconographies and mythologies" (1990, 27).

9. The quotation is from Joris's translation of Bellmer's preface to Zürn's 1954 volume of anagrams, *Hexentexte.*

10. The statement is from Zürn's letter to Mia Lederer of August, 20, 1960 (Zürn 1988–99, 4:648). For information on Die Badewanne, see Lenk 1991. On the art scene in postwar Berlin, see Gillen and Schmidt 1985. The "Zone 5" of their book title was an art exhibit whose title indicates the apolitical attitude of Berlin artists at that time. Zürn's newspaper stories (of which she produced more than 120) are representative of a 1950s popular aesthetics: light, easily digestible entertainment; they have a fairy-tale quality and are mostly about small, everyday occurrences, revealing nothing of the drama to come.

11. A list of these medications and their dosages appears in the hospital file: Paraldehyd, Megaphen, Atosil, Protorit, Valamin, Penicilin, and Effortil (Zürn 1988–99, 4:307). Zürn attempted to commit suicide twice, first by cutting her wrist, then by trying to hang herself.

12. For information about Bellmer, see his correspondence with Ferdière, who treated him for alcoholism, and to whom he also wrote about Zürn (Bellmer and Zürn 1994). For his attitude about Zürn's hospitalizations, see the letters contained in Zürn 1988–99, vol. 4; in his letters to Herta Hausmann he expresses his need for "a woman at his side."

13. For Zürn's drawings, see Zürn 1998.

14. For an insightful discussion of *Das Haus der Krankheiten,* see Hilmes 2002.

15. The classic example is the 1928 surrealist film *Un Chien Andalou* by Luis Buñuel, in which the eyeball is slit with a razor blade.

16. As Brinkmann notes, Zürn's likely familiarity with Freud may have come from Bellmer, who, for example, in a 1946 letter to Robert Valançay, asked to be sent a copy of Freud's *Vorlesungen zur Einführung in die Psychoanalyse* (Zürn 1988–99, 4:42). Freud's interpretation of the fear of losing one's eyes as castration anxiety is in his essay "Das Unheimliche" (1919).

17. According to Renate Kühn, the history of the anagram goes back to sixteenth-century France, when it replaced the sonnet in popularity; it then deteriorated into a game in the seventeenth century, when it was no longer considered a serious literary genre; in the nineteenth century, it had deteriorated to the level of a puzzle, which one played simply for fun. Kühn points out that the surrealists, who were critical of traditional conceptions of "high art," were particularly interested in adopting genres or techniques that would be considered culturally inferior, which is why they "revived" the anagram (1989, 160).

18. For an argument relating Zürn's madness to the feverish production and claustrophobic nature of the anagrams in *The Man of Jasmine,* see Hilmes 1994. Also see the dissertation on Zürn's anagrams by Ute Baumgärtel (2000).

19. My translation. Originally: "IHR HAETTET EURE AUGEN AUSGERISSEN: Euer Tag heisst: hart / Eure Augen: sein / Eure Haut ist Gesang—euer Rat: seh' ein / Euer Haus ist getarnt. Eure Siege nah. / Eure Tat: ein sarg-geeintes Ruhehaus."

20. The dream could be interpreted as a search for identity, which remains, however, illegible: "This mirror becomes an open door through which she steps to reach a long avenue lined with poplars leading in a straight line to a small house. The front door of the house is open. She enters and finds herself before a staircase which she climbs. She does not encounter anyone. She stops in front of a table. On the table is a small white card. As she picks up the card to read the name on it, she awakens" (Zürn 1994, 25).

21. For an application of Lacan's concept of the "mirror stage" to the opening sequence of *The Man of Jasmine,* see Morrien 1996.

22. Bellmer also produced illustrations for Heinrich von Kleist's 1810 essay "Über das Marionettentheater."

23. I am indebted to Hilary Beattie for her comment about the mechanical, repetitive nature of masturbation, which is no longer connected to fantasy but rather a mere physical stimulus (2003 conversation). In *Dark Spring,* masturbation is a dominant theme that would merit further discussion.

24. My translation. This last question was omitted from the Ullstein version and is thus not contained in Green's translation.

Works Cited

Abraham, Julie L. 1991. "'Woman, Remember You': Djuna Barnes and History." In Broe 1991, 252–69.

Abraham, Karl. 1908/1953. "Die psychosexuellen Differenzen der Hysterie und der Dementia Praecox," *Centralblatt für Nervenheilkunde und Psychiatrie* 19:521–33. Translated by Douglas Bryan and Alix Strachey as "The Psycho-Sexual Differences between Hysteria and Dementia Praecox," in *Selected Papers of Karl Abraham*. New York: Basic. Page references are to the 1953 edition.

———. 1924/1965. *Versuch einer Entwicklungsgeschichte der Libido aufgrund der Psychoanalyse seelischer Störungen*. Translated by Douglas Bryan and Alix Strachey as "A Short Study of the Development of the Libido, Viewed in the Light of Mental Disorders," in *Selected Papers of Karl Abraham*. London: Hogarth. Page references are to the 1965 edition.

Adorno, Theodor Wiesengrund. 1971. *Ästhetische Theorie*. Edited by Gretel Adorno and Rolf Tiedemann. Vol. 7 of *Gesammelte Schriften*. Frankfurt am Main: Suhrkamp.

Allen, Carolyn. 1993. "The Erotics of Nora's Narrative in Djuna Barnes' *Nightwood*." *Signs* 19:177–200. Reprinted in *Following Djuna: Women Lovers and the Erotics of Loss*. Bloomington: Indiana University Press, 1996. Page references are to the 1993 edition.

Altman, Meryl. 1993. "A Book of Repulsive Jews? Rereading *Nightwood*." *Review of Contemporary Fiction*, Fall, 160–71.

Anderson, Marie. 1904. *Wider das dritte Geschlecht: Ein Wort zur Aufklärung über die konträre Sexualempfindung und die Abschaffung des Paragraphen 175 des Reichsstrafsgesetzbuchs*. Berlin: Bermühler.

Andreas-Salomé, Lou. 1921. "Narzißmus als Doppelrichtung." *Imago: Zeitschrift für Anwendung der Psychoanalyse auf die Geisteswissenschaften*, edited by Sigmund Freud, 361–86. Leipzig: Internationaler Psychoanalytischer Verlag.

———. 1964. *The Freud Journal*. Translated by Stanley A. Leavy. London: Quartet.

Anz, Thomas. 1980. Afterword to *Phantasien über den Wahnsinn*, edited by Thomas Anz, 148–73. Stuttgart: Hanser.

Anz, Thomas, and Michael Stark, eds. 1982. *Expressionismus: Manifeste und Dokumente zur deutschen Literatur 1910–1920*. Stuttgart: Metzler.

Anzieu, Didier. 1980. "Skin Ego." In Lebovici and Wildlöcher 1980, 17–32. Originally published in 1970.

Artaud, Antonin. 1978. *Lettres de Rodez*. In *Oeuvres Complètes*, vols. 9–11. Paris: Gallimard. Originally published in 1942.

Ashton, E. B., ed. 1960. *Primal Vision: Selected Writings of Gottfried Benn*. New York: New Directions.

Balint, Michael. 1973. "Sándor Ferenczi." In *Collected Papers*. New York: Liveright. Originally published in 1949 in the *International Journal of Psychoanalysis*.

Balzac, Honoré de. 1835. *Séraphîta*. Paris: Editions L'Harmattan, 1995.

Barnes, Djuna. 1958. *The Antiphon*. London: Faber and Faber.

———. 1990. *Ryder*. With illustrations by the author. Reprint, Normal, IL: Dalkey Archive Press. Originally published in 1928.

———. 1995. *Nightwood: The Original Version and Related Drafts*. Edited by Cheryl J. Plumb. Normal, IL: Dalkey Archive Press. Originally published in 1936. Page references are to the 1995 edition.

Baumgärtel, Ute. 2000. "'. . . dein Ich ist ein Gramm Dichtang': Die Anagramme Unica Zürns." PhD diss., Humboldt-Universität.

Bellmer, Hans. 1934. *Die Puppe*. Karlsruhe: Th. Eckstein. Reprint, Frankfurt am Main: Ullstein, 1983. Translated by Robert Valançay as *La Poupée*. Paris: G.L.M., 1936.

———. 1949. *Les Jeux de la Poupée*. Illustrated with texts by Paul Eluard. Paris: Editions Premières.

———. 1954. Preface to *Hexentexte,* by Unica Zürn, 85–86. Berlin: Galerie Springer. Translated by Pierre Joris, 1992, in "Introducing Unica Zürn," edited by Renée Riese Hubert.

Bellmer, Hans, and Unica Zürn. 1994. *Lettres au Docteur Ferdière*. Edited by Alain Chevrier. Paris: Nouvelles Éditions Séguier.

Benn, Gottfried. 1912. "Schöne Jugend." *Morgue*. In *Gesamelte Werke,* vol. 3, edited by Dieter Wellershoff. Wiesbaden: Limes, 1958–61.

———, ed. 1962. *Lyrik des expressionistischen Jahrzehnts*. Munich: dtv. Originally published in 1955.

Benstock, Shari. 1986. "Djuna Barnes: Rue St.-Romain." In *Women of the Left Bank: Paris 1900–1940*. Austin: University of Texas Press.

Benveniste, Emile. 1971. "The Nature of Pronouns." In *Problems in General Linguistics*, translated by M. E. Meek, 217–30. Coral Gables, FL: University of Miami Press. Originally published as *Problèmes de linguistique generale*. Paris: Gallimard, 1966. Page references are to the 1971 edition.

Bersani, Leo. 1990. "Erotic Assumptions: Narcissism and Sublimation in Freud." In *The Culture of Redemption*. Cambridge, MA: Harvard University Press.

Bjorklund, Beth. 1990. Review of *Dichtungen*, by Henriette Hardenberg. *World Literature Today* 64 (Winter): 103–4.

Bland, Lucy, and Laura Doan, eds. 1998a. *Sexology in Culture: Labelling Bodies and Desires*. Cambridge: Polity.

———. 1998b. *Sexology Uncensored: The Documents of Sexual Science*. Cambridge: Polity.

Bleuler, Eugen. 1911. *Dementia praecox oder die Gruppe der Schizophrenien*. Leipzig and Vienna.

Bloch, Ernst. 1918. *Der Geist der Utopie*. Leipzig: Verlag von Duncker & Humblot.

Borderie, Roger, and Michel Camus. 1977. "Unica Zürn." In *La Femme Surrealiste*. Edited by Roger Borderie and Michel Camus. Special Issue of *Obliques*, vol. 14–15, pp. 253–62. Paris: Editions Borderie.

Brecht, Karen, Volker Friedrich, Ludger H. Hermanns, Isidor J. Kaminer, and Dierk H. Juelich, eds. 1985. *Here Life Goes on in a Most Peculiar Way: Psychoanalysis before and after 1933*. London: Goethe Institute.

Breton, André. 1924. *Le manifeste du surréalisme*. Paris: Gallimard.

———. 1928. *Nadja*. Paris: NRF. Translated by Richard Howard. New York: Grove, 1960.

Broe, Mary Lynn, ed. 1991. *Silence and Power: A Reevaluation of Djuna Barnes*. Carbondale: Southern Illinois University Press.

Bruhm, Steven. 2001. *Reflecting Narcissus: A Queer Aesthetic*. Minneapolis: University of Minnesota Press.

Buckley, Peter, ed. 1986. *Essential Papers on Object Relations*. New York: New York University Press.

Bürger, Peter. *Theorie der Avant-garde*. Frankfurt am Main: Suhrkamp, 1974.

Burke, Kenneth. 1968. "Version, Con-, Per-, and In- (Thoughts on Djuna Barnes' novel *Nightwood*)." In *Language as Symbolic Action*. Berkeley and Los Angeles: University of California Press.

Busch, Alexandra. 1989. *Ladies of Fashion: Djuna Barnes, Natalie Barney und das Paris der 20er Jahre*. Bielefeld: Haux.

Butler, Judith. 1990. *Gender Trouble: Feminism and the Subversion of Identity*. New York: Routledge.

———. 1993. Introduction to *Bodies That Matter: On the Discursive Limits of Sex*. New York: Routledge. Reprinted in *Women, Autobiography, Theory: A Reader*, edited by Sidonie Smith and Julia Watson, 367–79. Madison: University of Wisconsin Press, 1998.

Carlston, Erin. 1998. "'The Learned Corruption of Language': *Nightwood*'s Failed Flirtation with Fascism." In *Thinking Fascism: Sapphic Modernism and Fascist Modernity*. Stanford, CA: Stanford University Press.

Carrington, Leonora. 1946. *En bas*. Paris: Fontaine.

Caws, Mary Ann. 1989. "Ladies Shot and Painted: Female Embodiment in Surrealist Art." In *The Art of Interference: Stressed Readings in Verbal and Visual Texts*. Cambridge: Polity.

Chasseguet-Smirgel, Janine. 1989. "The Paradox of the Freudian Method: From the Abolishment of Otherness to the Universal Law." In *Sexuality and Mind: The Role of the Father and Mother in the Psyche*. London: Maresfield.

Chisholm, Dianne. 1997. "Obscene Modernism: *Eros Noir* and the Profane Illumination of Djuna Barnes." *American Literature* 96, no.1 (March): 167–206.

Conley, Katharine. 1996. *Automatic Woman: The Representation of Woman in Surrealism*. Lincoln: University of Nebraska Press.

Dalton, Anne. 1993. "Escaping from Eden: Djuna Barnes' Revision of Psychoanalytic Theory and Her Treatment of Father-Daughter Incest in *Ryder*." *Women's Studies* 22:163–79.

Dean, Tim, and Christopher Lane. 2001. "Homosexuality and Psychoanalysis: An Introduction." In *Homosexuality and Psychoanalysis*, edited by Tim Dean and Christopher Lane, 3–42. Chicago: University of Chicago Press.

de Lauretis, Teresa. 1994. *The Practice of Love: Lesbian Sexuality and Perverse Desire*. Bloomington: Indiana University Press.

Delcourt, Marie. 1961. *Hermaphrodite: Myths and Rites of the Bisexual Figure in Classical Antiquity*. London: Studio.

DeSalvo, Louise. 1991. "'To Make Her Mutton at Sixteen': Rape, Incest, and Child Abuse in *The Antiphon*." In Broe 1991, 300–339.

Dubuffet, Jean. 1986. *Collection de L'Art Brut. Lausanne*. An exhibition catalog.

Edschmid, Kasimir. 1918. "Expressionismus in der Dichtung." *Die neue Rundschau* 29, no. 1: 359–74. Reprinted in Anz and Stark 1982, 42–55.

Eifler, Margret. 1991. "Unica Zürn: Surreale Lebensbeschreibung." In *Autoren damals und heute*, edited by Gerhard Knapp, 775–92. Amsterdam and Atlanta: Rodopi.

Eliot, T. S. 1936/1961. Introduction to *Nightwood*, by Djuna Barnes. Reprint, New York: New Directions.

Ellenberger, Henri. 1970. *The Discovery of the Unconscious*. New York: Basic Books.

Ellis, Havelock. 1897a. "The Conception of Narcissism." In *Studies in the Psychology of Sex*. Vol. 7, *Eonism and Other Supplemental Studies*. Reprint, Philadelphia: Davis, 1928.

———. 1897b. "The Study of Sexual Inversion." In *Studies in the Psychology of Sex*. Vol. 2, *Sexual Inversion*. Reprint, Philadelphia: Davis, 1928.

Eschenbach, Wolfram von. 1300. *Parzival*.

Fairbairn, W. R. D. 1986. "A Revised Psychopathology of the Psychoses and Psychoneuroses." In Buckley 1986, 71–101.

Felman, Shoshana. 1975. "Women and Madness: The Critical Phallacy." *Diacritics* 4: 2–10. Reprinted in *What Does a Woman Want?* Baltimore: Johns Hopkins University Press, 1993. Page references are to the 1975 edition.

Ferenczi, Sándor. 1913. "Stages in the Development of the Sense of Reality," *Internationale Zeitschrift für ärztliche Psychoanalyse*. Reprinted in *Sex in Psycho-Analysis: Contributions to Psycho-Analysis*, edited by Sándor Ferenczi and Otto Rank, translated by Ernest Jones. Boston: Gorham, 1916. Reprint, New York: Dover, 1956.

———. 1924/1968. *Versuch einer Genitaltheorie*. Translated by Henry Alden Bunker as *Thalassa: A Theory of Genitality*. New York: Norton. Page references are to the 1968 translated edition.

Field, Andrew. 1985. *Djuna: The Formidable Miss Barnes*. Austin: University of Texas Press.

Foster, Hal. 1993. *Compulsive Beauty*. Cambridge, MA: MIT Press.

———. 2001. "Violation and Veiling in Surrealist Photography: Woman as Fetish, as Shattered Object, as Phallus." In Mundy 2001, 203–26.

Foucault, Michel. 1978. *The History of Sexuality*. Vol. 1, *An Introduction*. Translated by Robert Hurley. New York: Random House. Originally published as *Histoire de la sexualité*. Vol. 1, *La volonté de savoir*. Paris: Gallimard, 1976. Page references are to the 1978 edition.

———. 1965. *Madness and Civilization: A History of Insanity in the Age of Reason*. Translated by Richard Howard. New York: Random House. Originally published as *Histoire de la Folie*. Paris: Librairie Plon, 1961. Page references are to the 1965 edition.

Frank, Joseph. 1963. "Djuna Barnes' *Nightwood*." In *The Widening Gyre: Crisis and Mastery in Modern Literature*. Bloomington: Indiana University Press.

Frederiksen, Elke. 1981. *Die Frauenfrage in Deutschland 1865–1915: Texte und Dokumente*. Stuttgart: Reclam.

Freud, Sigmund. 1900. *Die Traumdeutung*. In Freud 1999, vols. 2–3.

———. 1910. *Leonardo da Vinci*. In Freud 1999, vol. 8.

———. 1911. "Über einen autobiographisch beschriebenen Fall von Paranoia." In Freud 1999, vol. 8.

———. 1912. "Beiträge zur Psychologie des Liebeslebens." In Freud 1999, vol. 8.

———. 1914/1986. "On Narcissism: An Introduction." Translated by James Strachey. In *Standard Edition of the Complete Psychological Works of Sigmund Freud*, edited by James Strachey; reprinted in Morrison 1986, 17–43.

———. 1914/1999. "Zur Einführung des Narzißmus." In Freud 1999, vol. 10.

———. 1916–17. "Die Libidotheorie und der Narzißmus." In Freud 1999, vol. 11, *Vorlesungen zur Einführung in die Psychoanalyse*.

———. 1917. "Trauer und Melancholie." In Freud 1999, vol. 10.

———. 1919. "Das Unheimliche." 1919. In Freud 1999, vol. 7.

———. 1923. *Das Ich und das Es*. In Freud 1999, vol. 8.

———. 1924. "Der Untergang des Ödipuskomplexes." In Freud 1999, vol. 8.

———. 1905/1999. *Drei Abhandlungen zur Sexualtheorie*. In Freud 1999, vol. 5.

———. 1905/1962. *Three Essays on the Theory of Sexuality*. Translated by James Strachey. New York: Basic Books.

———. 1999. *Gesammelte Werke*. 18 vols. Frankfurt am Main: Fischer Taschenbuch Verlag, 1999.

Friedrichsmeyer, Sara. 1983. *The Androgyne in Early German Romanticism: Friedrich Schlegel, Novalis and the Metaphysics of Love*. Stanford German Studies 18. New York: Peter Lang.

Fuchs, Miriam. 1993. "Djuna Barnes and T. S. Eliot: Authority, Resistance, and Acquiescence." *Tulsa Studies in Women's Literature* 12, no. 2 (Fall): 289–313.

Gast, Lilli. 1992. "Die Entsexualisierung des Narzißmus am Beispiel der Modifikationen Ferenczis. Die Sehnsucht nach dem Paradies." In *Libido und Narzissmus: Vom Verlust des Sexuellen im psychoanalytischen Diskurs*. Tübingen: Diskord.

Gauthier, Xavière. 1971. *Surrealisme et sexualité*. Paris: Gallimard.

Gerstenberger, Donna. 1989. "The Radical Narrative of Djuna Barnes' *Nightwood*." In *Breaking the Sequence: Women's Experimental Fiction*, edited by Ellen Friedman and Miriam Fuchs, 129–39. Princeton, NJ: Princeton University Press.

Gide, André. 1892. *Le Traité du Narcisse (Théorie du symbole)*, edited by Réjean Robidoux. Ottawa: Éditions de l'Université d'Ottawa, 1978.

Gillen, Eckhart, and Diether Schmidt, eds. 1989. *Zone 5: Kunst in der Viersektorenstadt*. Berlin: Nische.

Gordon, Donald E. 1987. *Expressionism: Art and Idea*. New Haven, CT: Yale University Press. See Plate 8: Erich Heckel, *Glassy Day*, 1913. Oil on canvas, Bayerische Staatsgemäldesammlungen, Staatsgalerie Moderner Kunst, Munich.

Grosz, Elizabeth. 1994. *Volatile Bodies: Toward a Corporeal Feminism*. Bloomington: Indiana University Press.

Hardenberg, Henriette. 1988. *Dichtungen*. Edited by Hartmut Vollmer. Zurich: Arche.

———. 1994. *Südliches Herz: Nachgelassene Dichtungen*. Edited by Hartmut Vollmer. Zurich: Arche.

Hàrnik, Jenö. 1924. "The Various Developments Undergone by Narcissism in Men and Women." *International Journal of Psychoanalysis* 5:66–83.

Hatvani, Paul. 1917. "Versuch über den Expressionismus." *Die Aktion* 7:146–50. Reprinted in Anz and Stark 1982, 38–43.

Hekma, Gert. 1993. "'A Female Soul in a Male Body': Sexual Inversion as Gender Inversion in Nineteenth-Century Sexology." In *Third Sex, Third Gender: Beyond Sexual Dimorphism in Culture and History*, edited by Gilbert Herdt, 213–40. New York: Zone.

Henry, Ruth. 1977. "Begegnung mit Unica Zürn." Afterword to *Der Mann im Jasmin/Dunkler Frühling*, by Unica Zürn, 204–16. Frankfurt am Main: Ullstein. Translated by Judd D. Hubert as "My Encounter with Unica." In "Introducing Unica Zürn," edited by Renée Riese Hubert, 67–71, *Sulfur* 29:67–104, 1992.

———. 1977. "Le printemps noir d'Unica." *La Femme Surrealiste*. Special Issue of *Obliques* 14–15:255–60.

Herring, Phillip. 1995. *Djuna: The Life and Work of Djuna Barnes*. New York: Viking.

Hildesheimer, Wolfgang. 1958. Afterword to *Nachtgewächs*. Pfullingen: Neske. Reprint, Frankfurt am Main: Suhrkamp, 1998. Page references are to the 1998 edition.

Hilmes, Carola. 1994. "Buchstabenrätsel: Unica Zürn und die Kunst der Anagramme." *Spielzüge des Zufalls: Zur Anatomie eines Symptoms,* edited by Carola Hilmes and Dietrich Mathy, 149–62. Bielefeld: Aisthesis.

———. 2002. "Zeigen und erzählen: Texte, Bilder und wie sie zusammengehören; Überlegungen zu den Arbeiten von Unica Zürn." *Arcadia: Zeitschrift für Vergleichende Literaturwissenschaft,* Spring.

Hirschfeld, Magnus, ed. 1899–1923. *Jahrbuch für sexuelle Zwischenstufen: Unter besonderer Berücksichtigung der Homosexualität.* 23 vols. Leipzig: Spohr.

———. 1908. *Zeitschrift für Sexualwissenschaft.* Leipzig: Wigand.

Hoffmann, E. T. A. 1960. "Der Sandmann." *Fantasie und Nachtstücke.* Munich: Winkler.

Hollis, Catherine. 2000. "No Marriage in Heaven: Editorial Resurrection in Djuna Barnes' *Nightwood.*" In *TEXT: An Interdisciplinary Annual of Textual Studies,* vol. 13, pp. 233–49. Ann Arbor: University of Michigan Press.

Howes, Geoffrey C. 2000. "The Idea of Austria in Djuna Barnes' *Nightwood.*" In *Austria in Literature,* edited by Donald G. Daviau, 256–75. Riverside, CA: Ariadne.

Hubert, Renée Riese. 1992. "Introducing Unica Zürn," in *Sulfur* 29:67–104.

———. 1994. "Self-Recognition and Anatomical Junctures: Unica Zürn and Hans Bellmer." In *Magnifying Mirrors: Women, Surrealism and Partnership.* Lincoln: Nebraska University Press.

Huyssen, Andreas. 1986. "The Vamp and the Machine: Fritz Lang's *Metropolis.*" In *After the Great Divide: Modernism, Mass Culture, Postmodernism.* Bloomington: Indiana University Press.

Kaever, Katharina. 1985. *Die Nachtwachen der Djuna Barnes.* Bremen: Bettina Wassermann.

Kaivola, Karen. 1993. "The 'Beast Turning Human': Constructions of the 'Primitive' in *Nightwood.*" *Review of Contemporary Fiction,* Fall, 172–86.

Kernberg, Otto. 1986. "Factors in the Psychoanalytic Treatment of Narcissistic Personalities." In Morrison 1986, 213–44.

Klein, Melanie. 1986. "A Contribution to the Psychogenesis of Manic-Depressive States." In Buckley 1986, 40–70.

Kofman, Sarah. 1980/1987. "The Narcissistic Woman: Freud and Girard." *Diacritics* 9 (Fall): 36–45. Reprinted in *French Feminist Thought: A Reader,* edited by Toril Moi, 210–26. New York and London: Basil Blackwell, 1987. Originally published in *L'Enigme de la femme: La femme dans les textes de Freud,* 60–80. Paris: Galilée, 1980. Page references are to the 1987 edition.

Kohut, Heinz. 1971. *The Analysis of the Self.* New York: International University Press.

———. 1986. "Forms and Transformations of Narcissism" In Morrison 1986, 61–88.

Kraepelin, Emil. 1889. *Psychiatrie: Ein Lehrbuch für Studierende und Ärzte*. Leipzig: Barth.

Krafft-Ebing, Richard von. 1899. Preface to *Die konträre Sexualempfindung*, 3d ed., by Albert Moll. Berlin: Fischers Medicinische Buchhandlung.

———. 1886/1997. *Psychopathia sexualis*. Stuttgart. Reprint, Munich: Matthes and Seitz.

Kristeva, Julia. 1983. *Histoires d'amour*. Paris: Éditions Denöel, 1983. Translated by Leon Roudiez as *Tales of Love*. New York: Columbia University Press, 1987.

Krug, Marina. 1994. *Imaginationen im Gedichtzyklus "Neigungen" von Henriette Hardenberg*. Freiburg: Hochschulverlag.

Kühn, Renate. 1989. "Writing without Apollo I: Versuch über das Anagramm." *Schreibheft: Zeitschrift für Literatur* 35:159–69.

Küster, Konrad. 1908. "Erworben oder angeboren?" *Zeitschrift für Sexualwissenschaft* 9:539–45.

Lacan, Jaques. 1975. "On narcissism/The two narcissisms/Ego-ideal and ideal ego." *The Seminar of Jaques Lacan, Book I: Freud's Papers on Technique 1953–1954*. Edited by Jaques-Alain Miller. Translated by John Forrester. New York: Norton. Originally published as "Sur le narcissisme/Les deux narcissismes/Idéal du moi e moi idéal." *Le séminaire de Jaques Lacan, Livre I: Les écrits techniques de Freud*. Paris: Éditions du Seuil, 1973. Page references are to the 1975 edition.

———. 1977. "The Mirror Stage as Formative of the Function of the I." In *Écrits: A Selection*, translated by Alan Sheridan. New York: Norton. Originally published as "Le stade du miroir comme formateur de la fonction du Je." Zurich, 1949. Page references are to the 1977 edition.

———. 1981. "Of the Gaze as 'objet petit a.'" In *The Four Fundamental Concepts of Psychoanalysis*, translated by Alan Sheridan. New York: Norton. Originally published as "Du regard comme objet petit a." In *Le séminaire de Jaques Lacan*, vol. 11, *Les quatre concepts fondamentaux de la psychanalyse*, edited by Jaques-Alain Miller, 65–112. Paris: Éditions du Seuil, 1973. Page references are to the 1981 edition.

Laing, R. D. 1965. *The Divided Self: An Existential Study in Sanity and Madness*. New York: Penguin.

Lanham, Richard. 1991. *A Handlist of Rhetorical Terms*. 2d ed. Berkeley and Los Angeles: University of California Press.

Laplanche, Jean. 1976. "The Ego and Narcissism." In *Life and Death in Psychoanalysis*, translated by Jeffrey Mehlman, 66–84. Baltimore: Johns Hopkins University Press, 1990.

Laplanche, Jean, and Jean-Bertrand Pontalis. 1973. *The Language of Psychoanalysis*. Translated by Donald Nicholson-Smith. New York: Norton.

Lebovici, Serge, and Daniel Wildlöcher, eds. 1980. *Psychoanalysis in France*. New York: International University Press.

Lejeune, Philippe. 1982. "The Autobiographical Contract." In *French Literary Theory Today,* edited by Tzvetan Todorov, 192–222. Cambridge: Cambridge University Press.

Lenk, Elisabeth, ed. 1991. *Die Badewanne.* Berlin: Hentrich.

Levine, Nancy. 1989. "'I've always suffered from sirens': The Cinema Vamp and Djuna Barnes' *Nightwood.*" *Women's Studies* 16, no. 3–4: 271–81.

Levine, Nancy, and Marian Urquilla, eds. 1993. *Review of Contemporary Fiction: Djuna Barnes Centennial Issue* 13. Normal, IL: Dalkey Archive Press, 1993.

Levine, Steven. 1994. *Monet, Narcissus and Self-Reflection: The Modernist Myth of the Self.* Chicago: Chicago University Press.

Lichtenstein, Thérèse. 2001. *Behind Closed Doors: The Art of Hans Bellmer.* Berkeley and Los Angeles: University of California Press.

Löffelholz, Mary. 1992. "Expatriates and Experimentalists: Gertrude Stein and Djuna Barnes." In *Experimental Lives: Women and Literature 1900–1945.* New York: Twayne.

Lomas, David. 2001. "Surrealism, Psychoanalysis and Hysteria." In Mundy 2001, 55–78.

Lovejoy, Arthur O. 1936. *Great Chain of Being.* Cambridge, MA: Harvard University Press, 2001.

Lukasc, Georg. 1965. "Grösse und Verfall des Expressionismus." In *Expressionismus: Der Kampf um eine literarische Bewegung,* edited by Paul Raabe. Munich, 1965. Originally published in 1934.

Macey, David. 1988. *Lacan in Contexts.* London: Verso.

MacIntyre, C. F. 1964. *Sonnets to Orpheus.* Berkeley and Los Angeles: University of California Press.

Mann, Thomas. 1994. *Death in Venice.* Translated by Clayton Koelb. New York: Norton Critical Edition, 1994. Originally published in 1912.

Marcus, Jane. 1991. "Laughing at Leviticus: *Nightwood* as Woman's Circus Epic." In Broe 1991, 221–51.

Marcuse, Herbert. 1966. "The Images of Orpheus and Narcissus." In *Eros and Civilization: A Philosophical Inquiry into Freud.* Boston: Beacon Press, 1955.

Martin, Biddy. 1991. *Woman and Modernity: The (Life)Styles of Lou Andreas-Salomé.* Ithaca, NY: Cornell University Press.

May-Tolzmann, Ulrike. 1991. "Zu den Anfängen des Narzißmus: Ellis—Näcke—Sadger—Freud." *Luzifer-Amor: Zeitschrift zur Geschichte der Psychoanalyse* 4, no. 8:50–88.

Meissner, William. 1986. "Narcissistic Personalities and Borderline Conditions: A Differential Diagnosis." In Morrison 1986, 403–37.

Melville, Herman. 1851. *Moby Dick.* Reprint, New York: Bantam, 1967.

Metz, Christian. 1982. *The Imaginary Signifier: Psychoanalysis and the Cinema.* Translated by Ben Brewster. Bloomington: Indiana University Press. Originally published as *Le Signifiant Imaginaire*. Paris, 1977. Page references are to the 1982 edition.

Michaux, Henri. 1963. *Light through Darkness*. Translated by Haakon Chevalier. New York: Orion. Originally published as *Connaissance par le gouffre*. Paris: Gallimard, 1961. Page references are to the 1963 edition.

———. 2000. *Untitled Passages*. New York and London: Drawing Center and Merrell Publishers. An exhibition catalog.

Michel, Frann. 1993. "'I just loved Thelma': Djuna Barnes and the Construction of Bisexuality." *Review of Contemporary Fiction*, Fall, 53–61.

Miller, Tyrus. 1999. "Beyond Rescue: Djuna Barnes." In *Late Modernism: Politics, Fiction, and the Arts between the World Wars*. Berkeley and Los Angeles: University of California Press.

Morrien, Rita. 1996. "Unica Zürn." In *Weibliches Textbegehren bei Ingeborg Bachmann, Marlen Haushofer und Unica Zürn*. Würzburg: Königshausen und Neumann.

Morrison, Andrew, ed. 1986. *Essential Papers on Narcissism*. New York: New York University Press.

Mundy, Jennifer, ed. 2001. *Surrealism: Desire Unbound*. London: Tate.

Näcke, Paul. 1894. *Verbrechen und Wahnsinn beim Weibe: Mit Ausblicken auf die Criminalanthropologie überhaupt*. Vienna and Leipzig: Braumüller.

———. 1899. "Kritisches zum Kapitel der normalen und pathologischen Sexualität." *Archiv für Psychiatrie und Nervenkrankheiten* 32, no. 13:356–86.

O'Neal, Hank. 1990. *"Life is painful, nasty and short . . . in my case, it has only been painful and nasty."* New York: Paragon House.

Ovid. 1967. "Echo and Narcissus" from *Metamorphoses*, book 3, translated by Frank Justus Miller. In Vinge 1967, 7–11.

Pan, David. 2001. *Primitive Renaissance: Rethinking German Expressionism*. Lincoln: University of Nebraska Press.

Partridge, Eric. 1990. *Shakespeare's Bawdy*. Reprint, New York: Routledge. Originally published in 1947. Page references are to the 1990 edition.

Pellegrini, Ann. 1997. *Performance Anxieties: Staging Psychoanalysis, Staging Race*. New York: Routledge.

Petermann, Theodor. 1908. "Dämonen- und Phantomenliebe." *Zeitschrift für Sexualwissenschaft* 5:289–98.

Pinthus, Kurt, ed. 1920. *Menschheitsdämmerung: Ein Dokument des Expressionismus*. Reprint, Berlin: Rowohlt, 1959. Translated by Robert C. Conard, Ralph Ley, and Joanna M. Ratych as *Dawn of Humanity*. Columbia, SC: Camden, 1994.

Praz, Mario. 1933. "La Belle Dame Sans Merci." In *The Romantic Agony*. Reprint, Cleveland: Meridian, 1967.

Pulver, Sidney. 1986. "Narcissism: The Term and the Concept." In Morrison 1986, 91–111.

Raabe, Paul. 1988. Preface to *Dichtungen,* by Henriette Hardenberg, edited by Hartmut Vollmer. Zurich: Arche.

Rabain, Jean-François. 1998. "Quelques roses pour Unica Zürn." In *La Femme S'Entête: La Part du Féminin dans le Surréalisme,* edited by Georgiana Colvile and Katharine Conley. Paris: Lachenal and Ritter.

Rank, Otto. 1914. "Der Doppelgänger." In *Imago: Zeitschrift für Anwendung der Psychoanalyse auf die Geisteswissenschaften,* vol. 3, edited by Sigmund Freud, 97–164. Leipzig: Internationaler Psychoanalytischer Verlag.

———. 1923. *Das Trauma der Geburt.* Leipzig: Internationaler Psychoanalytischer Verlag.

Reich, Annie. 1986. "Narcissistic Object Choice in Women." In Buckley 1986, 297–317.

Rilke, Rainer Maria. 1958. "Die Sonette an Orpheus." In *Sämtliche Werke,* vol. 1, pp. 769–70. Stuttgart: Insel.

Riviere, Joan. 1929/1986. "Womanliness as Masquerade." *International Journal of Psychoanalysis* 10. Reprinted in *Formations of Fantasy,* edited by Victor Burgin, James Donald, and Cora Kaplan, 35–44. London: Methuen.

Roemer, L. S. A. M. von. 1906. *Die Uranische Familie: Untersuchungen über die Aszendenz der Uranier.* Vol. 1 of series *Beiträge zur Erkenntnis des Uranismus.* Leipzig and Amsterdam: Maas and Van Suchtelen.

Rohleder, Hermann. 1898. *Die Masturbation: Eine Monographie für Ärzte, Pädagogen und gebildete Eltern.* Leipzig: Wigand.

Rosolato, Guy. 1980. "The Narcissistic Axis of Depression." In Lebovici and Wildlöcher 1980, 269–301.

Rupprecht, Caroline. 2000. Introduction to *Dark Spring,* by Unica Zürn, translated by Caroline Rupprecht. Cambridge, MA: Exact Change.

Rustin, Michael. 1995. "Lacan, Klein and Politics: The Positive and the Negative in Psychoanalytic Thought." In *Psychoanalysis in Contexts: Paths between Theory and Modern Culture,* edited by Anthony Elliott and Stephen Frosh, 223–45. New York: Routledge.

Schneider, Franziska. 1979. "Unica Zürn: Zu Ihrem Leben und Werk." Master's thesis, University of Zurich.

Schrenck-Notzing, A. von. 1892. *Die Suggestions-Therapie bei krankhaften Erscheinungen des Geschlechtssinnes. Mit besonderer Berücksichtigung der Conträren Sexualempfindung.* Stuttgart: Enke.

Scholl, Sabine. 1990. *Unica Zürn: Fehler, Fallen, Kunst; Zur Wahrnehmung und Re/Produktion bei Unica Zürn.* Frankfurt am Main: Hain.

Sedgwick, Eve Kosofsky. 1990. *Epistemology of the Closet.* Berkeley and Los Angeles: University of California Press.

Segal, Hanna, and David Bell. 1991. "The Theory of Narcissism in the Work of Freud and Klein." In *Freud's "On Narcissism: An Introduction,"* edited by Joseph

Sandler, Ethel Spector Person, and Peter Fonagy, 172. New Haven, CT: Yale University Press.

Selz, Peter. 1974. "Art Criticism and Esthetic Thought." In *German Expressionist Painting*. Berkeley and Los Angeles: University of California Press.

Shakespeare, William. *Hamlet*. New York: Cambridge University Press, 1985.

———. *A Midsummer Night's Dream*. New York: Cambridge University Press, 1984.

Sheperdson, Charles. 2000. "Telling Tales of Love: Philosophy, Literature, and Psychoanalysis." *Diacritics* 30, no. 1 (Spring): 89–105.

Singer, Alan. 1984. "The Horse Who Knew Too Much: Metaphor and the Narrative of Discontinuity in *Nightwood*." In *A Metaphorics of Fiction*. Tallahassee: Florida University Press, 1983. Reprinted in *Contemporary Literature* 25:66–87.

Smith, Victoria L. 1999. "A Story Beside(s) Itself: The Language of Loss in Djuna Barnes's *Nightwood*." *Publications of the Modern Language Association* 114, no. 2 (March): 194–206.

Sokel, Walter. 1959. *The Writer in Extremis: Expressionism in Twentieth-Century German Literature*. Stanford, CA: Stanford University Press.

Stark, Michael. 1982. "Probleme der modernen Lyrik." In Anz and Stark 1982, 630–34.

Starobinski, Jean. 1980. *Wörter unter den Wörtern: Die Anagramme von Ferdinand de Saussure*. Edited and translated by Henriette Beese. Frankfurt am Main: Ullstein.

Steakley, James. 1997. "Per scientiam ad justifiam: Magnus Hirschfeld and the Sexual Politics of Innate Homosexuality." In *Science and Homosexualities:* 133–54, edited by Vernon Rosario. New York: Routledge.

Stevenson, Sheryl. 1993. "*Ryder* as Contraception: Barnes v. the Reproduction of Mothering." In *Review of Contemporary Fiction* (Fall): 97–106.

Stromberg, Kyra. 1989. *Djuna Barnes: Leben und Werk einer Extravaganten*. Berlin: Wagenbach.

Suleiman, Susan Rubin. 1990. *Subversive Intent: Gender, Politics, and the Avant-Garde*. Cambridge, MA: Harvard University Press, 1990.

———. 1998. "Dialogue and Double Allegiance: Some Contemporary Women Artists and the Historical Avant-Garde." In *Mirror Images: Women, Surrealism, and Self-Representation,* edited by Whitney Chadwick, 128–54. Cambridge, MA: MIT Press.

Sulloway, Frank J. 1982. "Freud and Biology: The Hidden Legacy." In *The Problematic Science: Psychology in Nineteenth Century Thought,* edited by William R. Woodward and Mitchell G. Ash, 199–227. New York: Praeger.

Swarbrick, Katharine. 2000. "Avant-Garde Productions and Psychoanalytic Theory: The Story of an Encounter." In *European Avant-Garde: New Perspectives,* edited by Dietrich Scheunemann, 229–44. Amsterdam and Atlanta: Rodopi.

Taylor, Sue. 2000. *Hans Bellmer: The Anatomy of Anxiety*. Cambridge, MA: MIT Press.

Ulrichs, Karl Heinrich. 1994. *Forschungen über das Räthsel der mannmännlichen Liebe*. 4 vols. Edited by Hubert Kennedy. Berlin: Verlag rosa Winkel. Originally published 1864–97. Page references are to the 1994 edition.

Ursprung, Philip. 1999. "'Catholic Tastes': Hurting and Healing the Body in Viennese Actionism in the 1960s." In *Performing the Body/Performing the Text*, edited by Amelia Jones and Andrew Stephenson, 138–52. New York: Routledge.

Valéry, Paul. 1944. *Cantate du Narcisse*. Paris: Gallimard.

Vinge, Louise. 1967. *The Narcissus Theme in Western European Literature up to the Early Nineteenth Century*. Lund: Gleerups.

Volckmann, Silvia. 1982. "Die Lust am Verrücktsein: Eros und Wahnsinn im Surrealismus." In *Literarische Utopie-Entwürfe*, edited by Hiltrud Gnüg, 250–65. Frankfurt am Main: Suhrkamp.

Vollmer, Hartmut. 1988. "'Wir werden herrlich aus Wunsch nach Freiheit': Einige Gedanken zu Leben und Werk Henriette Hardenbergs." In *Dichtungen*, by Henriette Hardenberg, edited by Hartmut Vollmer, 111–40. Zurich: Arche.

———. 1993. "'Wie ein glückliches Bild innen unter sicheren Lidern': Rainer Maria Rilke und Henriette Hardenberg." *Euphorion: Zeitschrift für Literaturgeschichte* 87, no.1: 69–89.

———. 1994. Afterword to *Südliches Herz: Nachgelassene Dichtungen*, edited by Hartmut Vollmer. 185–210. Zurich: Arche.

Warner, Michael. 1990. "Homo-Narcissism: Or, Heterosexuality." In *Engendering Men: The Question of Male Feminist Criticism*, edited by Joseph A. Boone and Michael Cadden, 190–206. New York: Routledge.

Weber, Samuel. 2000. "Uncanny Thinking." In *The Legend of Freud*. Expanded ed. Stanford, CA: Stanford University Press.

Webster's Ninth Collegiate Dictionary. Springfield, MA: Merriam-Webster, 1987.

Weigel, Sigrid. 1987a. "Hans Bellmer, Unica Zürn: Junggesellenmaschinen und die Magie des Imaginären." In *Weiblichkeit und Avantgarde*, edited by Sigrid Weigel and Inge Stephan, 187–230. Berlin: Argument. Reprinted in *Topographien der Geschlechter: Kulturgeschichtliche Studien zur Literatur*. Hamburg: Reinbek, 1990. Page references are to the 1987 edition.

———. 1987b. "'Wäre ich ein Mann, hätte ich aus diesem Zustand vielleicht ein Werk geschaffen': Unica Zürn." In *Frauenliteratur ohne Tradition?—Neun Autorinnenportraits*, edited by Sigrid Weigel, Inge Stephan, and Regula Venske, 243–77. Frankfurt am Main: Fischer.

Weininger, Otto. 1903/1970. *Geschlecht und Charakter*, edited by Jörn Luther and Jürgen Paasch. Reprint, Cologne: Krash.

Westphal, Carl. 1870. "Über die konträre Sexualempfindung." In *Archiv für Psychiatrie und Nervenkrankheiten*, vol. 2. Berlin.

Wilde, Oscar. 1891. *The Picture of Dorian Gray*. Reprint, New York: Norton, 1988.
Winkiel, Laura. 1997. "Circuses and Spectacles: Public Culture in *Nightwood*." *Journal of Modern Literature* 21, no. 1 (Fall): 7–28.
Winnicott, D. W. 1953. "Transitional Objects and Transitional Phenomena." *International Journal of Psychoanalysis* 34:433–56. Reprinted in Buckley 1986, 255–71.
———. 1971. *Playing and Reality*. London: Tavistock.
Wittig, Monique. 1983. "The Point of View: Universal or Particular?" *Feminist Issues* 2, no. 3: 63–69.
Wolzogen, Ernst von. 1900. *Das dritte Geschlecht*. Berlin: Eckstein.
Woolf, Virginia. 1928. *Orlando: A Biography*. Reprint, San Diego and New York: Harcourt, 1980.
Worringer, Wilhelm. 1911. *Abstraktion und Einfühlung*. Munich: Piper, 1959.
Zürn, Unica. 1954. *Hexentexte*. Berlin: Galerie Springer.
———. 1969. *Dunkler Frühling*. Hamburg: Merlin. Reprinted in Zürn 1988–99, vol. 4. Translated by Ruth Henry as *Sombre Printemps*. Paris: Ecriture, 1997. Translated by Caroline Rupprecht as *Dark Spring*. Cambridge: Exact Change, 2000.
———. 1970. *L'Homme Jasmin*. Translated by Ruth Henry. Paris: Gallimard.
———. 1977. *Der Mann im Jasmin: Eindrücke einer Geisteskrankheit*. Frankfurt am Main: Ullstein. Reprinted in Zürn 1988–99, vol. 4.
———. 1986. *Das Haus der Krankheiten: Geschichten und Bilder einer Gelbsucht*. Berlin: Lilith. Reprinted in Zürn 1988–99. Translated by Malcolm Green as *The House of Illnesses: Stories and Pictures from a Case of Jaundice*. London: Atlas, 1993.
———. 1988–99. *Gesamtausgabe*. 5 vols. Edited by Erich Brinkmann and Günter Bose. Berlin: Brinkmann and Bose.
———. 1994. *The Man of Jasmine: Impressions from a Mental Illness*. Translated by Malcolm Green. London: Atlas.
———. 1998. *Bilder 1953–1970*. Edited by Erich Brinkmann, Ralf Helmes, Wolfgang Knapp, Inge Morgenroth, and Klaus Theuerkauf. Berlin: Brinkmann und Bose, Neue Gesellschaft für Bildende Kunst.

Index

About the Author

Caroline Rupprecht is an assistant professor of comparative literature at Queens College, City University of New York. She is the translator of Unica Zürn's *Dark Spring* and an internationally published author of articles on avant-garde literature and gender studies.

Avant-Garde & Modernism Studies